M000268649

GLOBAL TRADE AND CULTURAL AUTHENTICATION

GLOBAL TRADE AND CULTURAL AUTHENTICATION

The Kalabari of the Niger Delta

Edited by
JOANNE B. EICHER

INDIANA UNIVERSITY PRESS

This book is a publication of

Indiana University Press
Office of Scholarly Publishing
Herman B Wells Library 350
1320 East 10th Street
Bloomington, Indiana 47405 USA

iupress.org

Manufactured in the United States of America

First printing 2022

Cataloging information is available from the Library of Congress.

ISBN 978-0-253-06259-8 (hardback)
ISBN 978-0-253-06260-4 (paperback)
ISBN 978-0-253-06261-1 (ebook)

Frontispiece, Erekosima family, 1966: Tonye Victor,
Victoria Adaba, and Chief Isaac Dagogo.

Trade and exchange across cultural lines have played a crucial role in human history, being perhaps the most important external stimuli to change, leaving aside the unmeasurable and less-benign influence of military conquest. External stimulation, in turn, has been the most important single source of change and development in art, science, and technology. Perhaps this goes without saying, since no human group could invent by itself more than a small part of its cultural and technical heritage (Curtin 1984, 1).

Contents

Preface

Joanne B. Eicher

THIS BOOK FOCUSES on the global trade and the Kalabari material world of Nigerians who live on mangrove swamp islands of the Niger River, where it meets the Atlantic. Kalabari involvement in global trade resulted in their creativity in modifying seemingly "borrowed" artifacts. This book uses the concept of cultural authentication to analyze how these modified artifacts became singularly identified as Kalabari.

The Kalabari kingdom, which has existed since the seventeenth century, underwent British colonization and incorporation into the British Commonwealth and became part of Nigeria on Nigeria's 1960 independence. The Kalabari are still recognized as a prominent linguistic group and sociocultural entity. They initially traded salt and fish for goods; later, they traded slaves, first with other Nigerians and West Africans, then with the world beyond. Their trade provided imported materials, which they embraced as part of daily life. Their material world became global. Our collegial research on the Kalabari world will interest Africanists, anthropologists, art historians, textile scholars, and textile enthusiasts as well as bead scholars and aficionados and anyone interested in multicultural gender studies. In addition, Kalabari in Nigeria and abroad will find it appealing, because we focus on their heritage and commitment to proudly being Kalabari.

My introduction to the Kalabari people began after Tonye Victor Erekosima (1940–2008) joined the staff of the Economic Development Institute (EDI) in 1964 on the University of Nigeria (UNN) Enugu campus, recruited from the University of California, Los Angeles (UCLA) after completing his MA degree. We met because from 1963 to 1966, I was an EDI research associate on faculty leave from Michigan State University (MSU), where I served as assistant professor in the department of Textiles, Clothing and Related Arts. Erekosima invited my former husband, Carl Eicher (1930–2014), and me in July 1966 to visit his home and meet his parents in Buguma, a Kalabari island in the Niger River delta, before our August return to Michigan. We accepted his invitation for a July weekend. We discovered the weekend was important with a midyear, homecoming celebration of the Buguma Baptist Church. Driving from our Enugu campus home to Port Harcourt, we left from the Port Harcourt wharf for Buguma, traveling in a large, engine-powered dugout, a variation of its historic man-powered versions.

We accepted the invitation as a social visit to Buguma, coupled with wanting to learn about a Nigerian area we had not yet seen during our three years. Carl, recruited as one of the EDI economists, conducted research on Nigeria's developing economy. With a Harvard degree in development economics and John Kenneth Galbraith (1908–2006) as his adviser, he joined MSU in 1961 as an assistant professor in Agricultural Economics. At MSU he focused on Africa while two colleagues focused on South America and Asia. Michigan State had entered into an agreement with the University of London to cooperate in developing the University of Nigeria with two campuses at that time—the primary one in Nsukka and a second in Enugu, then Nigeria's Eastern Region capital city.

In preparing for Nigeria, I planned to expand my focus on the cultural significance of dress, receiving a modest research grant for Nigerian dress from MSU's African Studies Center. After arrival in 1963, I observed many Nigerians wearing handcrafted textiles. I decided to collect examples and gather written documentation and oral history. Returning to MSU, I initiated an African Dress course and encouraged my graduate students to choose related research topics.

Serendipity, accidental good fortune, plays a larger role in research than often acknowledged. Before visiting Buguma, I had no knowledge about the Kalabari people or their textile or dress practices. My weekend in Buguma brought surprises. Erekosima's parents welcomed us to their home, Seaview, on a tributary riverbank near the Buguma wharf. Their two-story metal-and-frame house echoed the design of others owned by the seven early trading families, of which the Erekosimas were one, a fact we learned. They drew us quickly into family life, sharing knowledge about Buguma and the Kalabari, with Erekosima showing us around the island.

Erekosima's father, Isaac Dagogo Erekosima (1912–1996), also known as Papa I. D. or "Daddy," as his family called him (and as I was expected to do later during my fieldwork), a paramount chief for twenty years, descended directly from Kalabari Chief Ikiri JohnBull (1810–1893). Earlier he served as the first African principal of the prestigious Nigerian boys' secondary school, Government College Umuahia, an institution designed after English "public" schools like Eton, Harrow, and Winchester. He attended it, as did his son, Tonye. Although selected to go to Cambridge, England, for a bachelor's degree, Papa I. D. demurred, refusing to take a physical exam, which was contrary to his devout beliefs of Faith Tabernacle, his church. He had given up his chieftaincy before we met, becoming a businessman in Port Harcourt, his primary residence. The Erekosimas were multilingual, speaking fluent English, Kalabari, and Igbo.

Tonye Erekosima's mother, Victoria Ada Princewill (c. 1916–1980), was called "Mommy" by her family (and me, later). Her kinship background stemmed from the first king (*Amanyanabo*), Abbi Amachree I (died c. 1800, said to be one hundred years old), and his descendant, her father, King (Amanyanabo) Charlie Kieni "Cane" Amachree, who ruled from 1900 to 1917. Erekosima arranged that we visit the reigning Amanyanabo, His Royal Highness Obaye Abbiye-Suku Amachree X, Commander of the Order of Nigeria, and his council of chiefs.[1] The Amanyanabo received us and agreed to be photographed (see fig. 13.2) with his council of chiefs. The men wore different ensembles—an aspect of research I later pursued. Throughout the weekend, I also observed women's dress.

I saw both men and women wearing Indian madras, the US name for the plaid or checked fabric. I inquired about it and was told, "It's 'our cloth,' Madam," which puzzled me. Later I learned that sometimes threads were cut in the madras and removed, producing small, subtle designs by subtraction. As we left Buguma, the Erekosimas promised to send me a wrapper set, two pieces of cut-thread indigo-and-white gingham, which arrived after our US return. I called it "Buguma cloth" and included a photo of Erekosima's mother wearing a cut-thread wrapper set in *Nigerian Handcrafted Textiles* (Eicher 1976).

Returning home, I showed my approximately five-hundred-piece textile collection, ranging from indigo-dyed Yoruba *adire*, handwoven Igbo *Akwete*, and northern Nigerian examples, to family, friends, and colleagues.[2] Prominent textile scholar Helen Louise Allen (1902–1968), founder of the Helen Louise Allen Textile Collection at the University of Wisconsin, Madison, came to see my treasures. Especially intrigued by my Kalabari wrapper set, she exclaimed she knew of only one similar textile, white Norwegian Hardanger, with embroidery stitches around small, cut openings, but none like the Kalabari cut-thread cloth with no stitching.

Discovering the textile was unusual, I decided to conduct research. I contacted Erekosima, who was working toward a PhD at Catholic University of

America. I suggested the plaid and checked madras might relate historically to Scottish missionary presence in Nigeria over time, possibly a Scottish tartan influence. I suggested we write a paper for the 1979 African Studies Association meetings. He vehemently disagreed about any Scottish connection and drafted a paper (essentially a retort), convincingly arguing that these textiles exhibited a Kalabari aesthetic. He developed his concept of cultural authentication by analyzing the Kalabari practice of cutting designs into imported madras. I read his draft, insisting that he alone author and present the paper. Simultaneously, and by chance, an invitation came for me to present a paper in Kaduna, northern Nigeria, at a 1980 Textile Institute conference (an international association headquartered in Manchester, England, founded in 1910). Having been recruited to the University of Minnesota as a department head in 1977, I requested funds from my dean, Keith McFarland, to extend travel to Port Harcourt and Buguma to visit Erekosima's parents. He agreed; I launched my first dedicated research trip on Kalabari textiles and dress.

FIELDWORK

Thus, my intentional research in Buguma began in 1980. Little did I know that it would be the first of eight research trips to document Kalabari culture and dress. After arriving to find and interview women who cut cloth, which I found they call *pelete bite* (meaning "cut-thread cloth"), one woman said, "Madam, if you like our cloth, you should see our funerals."[3] Another path of research serendipitously opened for collaboration with Erekosima. After 1980 I traveled annually from 1981 to 1984, then 1987, 1988, and 1991, which included two major events: the 1984 Buguma Centenary and the 1991 masquerade parade, *Owuarusun*. In observing Kalabari material artifacts, I understood that their isolated island location, nestled among the mangrove swamps in the Lower Niger delta, necessitated trade. The Kalabari were embedded in a global network.

Erekosima and I originally focused on cut-thread cloth, followed by men's and women's dress and funeral celebrations, all involving textiles and global trade. Later, I observed diaspora cultural events in the United States, such as a 1999 birth celebration in Oakland, California; two Kalabari reunions; and Erekosima's 2008 funeral in Maryland. I continued communication with his family. These research efforts all involved focus on cultural authentication related to global trade goods over centuries.

DEVELOPMENT OF THE RESEARCH PROGRAM

Erekosima and I partnered as "outsider" and "insider" researchers, he an equal with academic credentials, not an indigenous "informant." We discussed advantages of the outsider and insider approach, known as etic and emic in anthropology; I raised questions about Kalabari life that he and other Kalabari took for granted, a typical anthropological situation. He, adept in English, answered questions, interpreted Kalabari, and collaborated in analysis and writing. After his UCLA paper and my 1980 research, we coauthored "Kalabari Cut-Thread and Pulled-Thread Cloth" (1981; chap. 2 in this volume). By then involved in his PhD in Educational Technology at Catholic University of America, he contemplated research on physics students' learning processes. I urged him to choose a Kalabari topic. He agreed, conducted Buguma fieldwork, and produced "Analysis of a Learning Resource for Political Integration Applicable to Nigerian Secondary School Social Studies: The Case of Kalabari Men's Traditional Dress" (1989). Both he and my Kalabari graduate student advisee, Manuella Petgrave (Manuella Daba BobManuel-Meyer Petgrave), provided insider knowledge of Kalabari aesthetics.

After my 1980 fieldwork, I encouraged my Minnesota graduate advisees to consider Kalabari research opportunities and continued collaborating with Erekosima. He called Buguma his home, although he had grown up in Owerri and Umuahia, Nigerian cities, postings of his father. Of the thirty-two islands comprising the Kalabari community, the Kalabari claim Buguma, a main island (our primary fieldwork site), as their cultural capital, with nearby Abonnema (another research site) as the commercial capital. Erekosima's family traveled often to Buguma, following the Nigerian pattern for visiting "home," a pattern including expected retirement there, no matter how far or how long one had lived away.

Erekosima, my graduate students, and I began a long-term project sans master funding, doggedly embarking on topics and creatively seeking funds. I initiated research on Indian madras and the special Kalabari glassblown bead (one family's emblem) by going to India during my 1987–1988 sabbatical and to Venice in 1996–1997, where the bead was said to be from. With Erekosima's and my work providing a springboard, students added concrete and detailed data from research in the UK, India, and Italy, all elaborating on the cultural authentication and global trade themes. Ten graduate-degree projects resulted. M. Catherine Daly, Elisha Renne, Petgrave, and Hazel Lutz carried out single projects. Sandra Evenson, Susan Torntore, and Susan Michelman for both MAs and PhDs conducted Kalabari research. Their focused research, totaling more than two thousand pages, provides data to elaborate on our work that we could not have undertaken. In addition, two of my research assistants also published articles: Otto Charles Thieme (1942–1996) on pelete bite (1982) and Barbara Sumberg on Indian velvets (1995), both included in this volume. Carl

Leidholm, an MSU economist and EDI faculty in Enugu in the 1960s, agreed to collaborate with Erekosima and me for an article, also included here, that analyzes the economics of making pelete bite.

The longitudinal and team research efforts arose from the circumstance of serendipity, handled differently than starting with a master plan. Fieldwork approaches and methods diverged from the standard expectation of year-long immersion with learning the language and extended residence. As a department head, that was not feasible for me. However, collaboration with Erekosima overcame these deficiencies. The students also used shorter-term commitments, benefiting from prior data collection, collegial cooperation, and a shared respondent base. My 1980–1991 fieldwork allowed continuous contact to check and add data with Erekosima, his family, and other key Kalabari respondents.

Preceding us, other scholars contributed immeasurably to the wellspring of writing on delta culture from which we drew, such as colonial officers and historians: G. I. Jones (1963), P. Amaury Talbot (1926, 1932, 1967), and Kenneth O. Dike (1956). I visited libraries at the University of Nigeria, Nsukka, and University of Port Harcourt, accessing student theses. The Nigerian historian E. J. Alagoa (1965, 1966, 1967, 1970a, 1970b, 1972) focused widely on delta history. The British anthropologist Robin Horton (1932–2019) began research in Buguma, remaining to reside there, firmly embedded in Kalabari life while teaching at the University of Port Harcourt. He centered publications on Kalabari religion and cultural practices including masquerades (1960a, 1960b, 1962, 1965, 1969, 1970, 1971). Victor Madume also wrote on Kalabari masquerades (1976), and Bliss Iyalla wrote on Kalabari *iria* practices and dress (1968). After the 1984 Buguma Centenary, two volumes sponsored by the Buguma Internal Affairs Society resulted: Erekosima, Kio Lawson, and Obeleye MacJaja, eds., *Buguma Centenary: A Hundred Years of Buguma History in Kalabari Culture*, and *Buguma 1984 Centenary Symposia on Kalabari* (both 1991). Other Kalabari writers on Kalabari life include Danate Tariah (1982), Chief Alaye Fubara Manuel (1977, n.d.), Tubonimi J. Isokariari (1983) on Madam Orupumbo, and Charles Jenewari (1973). Enefaa JohnBull penned biographies of two prominent Buguma trading families: Ikiri JohnBull (2004) and Omekwe Horsfall (2005). In 2012 Sir (Chief) O. K. Isokariari published his autobiography, *My Mission*.

This volume originated from my three-year Nigerian residence with a congenial weekend visit to the Niger delta, which resulted in over fifty-three years of focused research on Kalabari dress and textiles. Kalabari global trade brought faraway material goods into their lived experiences. Our chapters focus on Kalabari creativity in using global trade goods, both in Kalabariland and the diaspora, goods that they authenticated and cherished as Kalabari.

The thorough research of other scholars' voices expanded Erekosima's and my efforts, thus providing a more comprehensive perspective of Kalabari culture, dress, and textiles. Our collaborative research illustrates that one focus can generate several strong and compelling analyses with varied voices and research approaches, highlighting senior and emerging scholars' relationships. In addition, the combined efforts provide research depth on global trade based on interviews and records from England, Italy, and India that focused on the involvement of Kalabari who requested specific (1) types of colors of madras, (2) madras patterns for cutting pelete bite, (3) colors and shapes of coral, and (4) designs for embroidered velvets. Presenting the original research from all efforts contributes a dimension that can be lost when some are summarized and recapitulated. The original accounts provide rich detail and documentation about how Kalabari adapted artifacts from global resources. Both Erekosima and Petgrave supply their firsthand knowledge from lived experience. Erekosima's chapter includes descriptions and rarely seen drawings of how Kalabari men tie their wrappers, and Petgrave's records how Kalabari use madras throughout life. She found Urie Bronfenbrenner's ecological systems theory applicable across all stages of the Kalabari life course. These diverse perspectives and fieldwork approaches stem from anthropology, history, art history, textile, dress, and fashion studies. Understanding the adaptation of global artifacts in the Kalabari material world provides singular insight into one African group's ongoing quotidian and ritual life.

In my publications and presentations relating to global cultural diversity, I included examples of the Kalabari people's cultural practices, and these have been added to the bibliography.

Acknowledgments

I GRATEFULLY ACKNOWLEDGE many individuals and institutions in Nigeria, the US, the UK, and India who provided hospitality, help, and funding. For my serendipitous 1980 return to Nigeria, deep appreciation to my textile scientist colleague Dr. Peter Brown. Attending the 1979 International Textile Institute conference in India, he met Nigerian scholars Drs. S. C. O. Ugbolue and P. O. Adegbile, cochairs for an upcoming 1980 Textile Institute Symposium in Kaduna, northern Nigeria, and suggested they invite me to present a paper. On receiving the invitation, I asked my dean, the late Dr. Keith McFarland, if I could extend my trip south to Buguma to research my 1966 cloth gift. He agreed and provided funds.

From 1980 on, many Kalabari people backed my research in many ways, including funds and in-kind support. Tonye Erekosima asked his parents, Chief and Mrs. I. D. Erekosima, to host me, taking me in as a family member. His sister, the late Stella Kintebe, and cousin, Bekinwari Higgwe Elebe, provided hospitality in Port Harcourt, along with Mrs. N. B. Whyte in Abonnema, where I attended my first Kalabari funeral. On later trips, Donald Diboyesuku graciously provided me private quarters in Buguma. Throughout all visits, Erekosima family members smoothed my fieldwork and interviews, especially Chief I. D.'s sister, "Opumama," (Madame Elizabeth Princewill), along with the late Chief Immanuel, Michael, Lawrence, Edwin, Promise, Siya, Dorcas, Deborah, Seleye, Tomboye, Ekperre, and Jenbretoa, a steady research assistant.

Neighbors of the Erekosimas, the Cliscent Horsfalls, cordially helped in many ways, along with Oporibo Horsfall, my fieldwork assistant. The Honourable O. E. Dakaru was gracious with his time and with lending me his amazing headpiece, his *ajibulu*, for a Goldstein Gallery exhibit. Mrs. Nume Taiwo West, a friend and fount of information, related the story of the fragile Jackreece bead. Erekosima introduced me to Sir (Chief) O. K. Isokariari, who supported my continuing research with funding. As the 1984 Buguma Centennial Chair, he spearheaded a grant from both the Buguma Internal Affairs Society and Buguma Centenary Committee to attend the Centenary. On my 1980 return, I fortuitously met Amonia Akoko, a *pelete bite* artist and spirit medium, and we developed a friendship that spanned my trips. She willingly answered questions and invited me to her Abalama home to attend her spirit medium séance. Other pelete bite artists agreed to photographs, also sharing details about their work. Danate Tariah offered his useful BA thesis on Kalabari material culture. Manuella Petgrave, from Abonnema, came to UMN as a graduate student, enhancing my understanding of Kalabari life, and transcribed my taped interviews. Heartfelt thanks to unnamed Kalabari who, when I encountered them casually, courteously answered my questions. And many thanks to all who let me photograph them.

Particularly important is my admiration for Kalabari knowledge about their Kalabari history and family genealogy, learned orally and memorized. Thus, several interpretations exist. This volume represents versions told to me that I recorded in field notes, buttressed by available references. I take full responsibility for errors and any misrepresentations.

Beyond Nigeria, others deserve appreciation and thanks. At the University of Oxford, the late Dr. Helen Callaway facilitated my invitation to be Visiting Fellow at the Center for Cross-Cultural Research on Women (CCCRW) for my 1987–88 sabbatical, where I met colleagues Dr. Shirley Ardener and Dr. Lidia Dina Sciama, all becoming fast friends. Dr. Ardener invited me to participate in two 1989 workshops: (1) "Dress and Gender," culminating in my coediting *Dress and Gender* (1992) with Dr. Ruth Barnes; and (2) "Dress and Ethnicity," also culminating in an edited book with that title (1995). In 1996, Dr. Sciama and Centro Donna, Municipality of Venice, invited me to present the Kalabari bead paper at the University of Venice. Sciama and I consequently coedited *Beads and Beadmakers: Gender, Material Culture and Meaning* (1998). Returning to Venice in 1997, I researched the possible Venetian origin of the Jackreece bead, graciously hosted and helped again by Dr. Sciama and Dr. Francesca Trevillato. Sciama and I interviewed Murano beadmakers and Venetian bead boutique owners. The National Geographic Society funding supported my 1991 Buguma research on the Owuarusun masquerade festival, where Carolyn Eicher and Bryan Burkhart respectively conducted photography and videography.

I owe thanks for my consequent research in India to Arun Kumar and P. S. A. Sundaram, whom I met in Oxford at Queen Elizabeth House, where they were on leave from the Indian Civil Service. Sundaram provided introductions and contacts for Delhi, with the S. S. Gupta family providing me hospitality. I thank Kumar and his wife, Neelam, for graciously hosting me on later trips to Delhi. Diana Eicher and I traveled in 1990 to Manchester, England, to interview manufacturers producing Indian madras. Later, I met renowned Indian textile scholar Jasleen Dhamija, who became enthusiastic about the transformation of Indian madras into pelete bite by Kalabari women. She assisted our textile research in India, promoted a 1994 seminar in Madras on the textile called madras, and graciously became my escort and hostess on later trips with many introductions to textile scholars and experts.

Sources from the University of Minnesota (UMN) supplied critical funding: the Minnesota Experiment Station (1979); the Midwestern Universities Consortium on International Activities (1980); the Graduate School Grants-in-Aid (1980, 1993, 1997); the Graduate School Summer Research Grant (1981); the University Convocation and the Arts (1982); the Office of International Programs (1984); the Bush Sabbatical Grant (1987–88), the College of Human Ecology (1989); the Office of International Education (1991); the Institute of International Studies and Programs (1994, 1996); and research stipends attached to my Regents Professorship (1995–2005). Appreciation for funds to organize this book with color photographs extends to the University of Minnesota Retirees Association (2018, 2021), who also funded establishing an online site for my African textile collection (2015–16).

At both Michigan State and the University of Minnesota, I had superb staff support: Jean Grof, Connie Strand, Barbara Conklin, Mary Andrews, Kathy Guiney, and Arlene Jones Swenson. They supplied stalwart administrative and secretarial help stretching over my fieldwork trips. Graduate assistants provided enthusiasm and assistance: Meriem Chida, Hazel Lutz, Susan Michelman, Manuella Petgrave, Patrick Redmond, Elisha Renne, Barbara Sumberg, the late Otto Thieme, and Susan Torntore. After my retirement, many thanks to Megan Wannarka and Kate Leibfried, who became personal assistants. Kate provided unfailing support for compiling this book to its completion.

For the preparation and completion of this volume, I thank Helen Bradley Foster and Karen Tranberg Hansen, who carefully read and edited my drafts. Susan Torntore helped locate images for the final draft. Kate Daly, congenial companion to the 2018 KNA event, provided collegiality as we participated in the weekend's program and got news about our Kalabari friends. I thank Sir (Chief) O.K. Isokariari's sons, Obelema, and Osemate, and daughter, Boma Isokariari Jack, for providing contact with their father, who sent me his valuable autobiography. Professor Anto Saka, from Baltimore, has continued invaluable assistance in pursuing information, as has Telemate Jackreece on the Jackreece bead. I also want to cite the help throughout my research from Dr. Erekosima's wife, Dinah; his sons Dagogo and Onimi; his brother Telema and sister-in-law Ibiso; his cousin Rose Barango; and her daughter Otonye Barango.

This book reflects my academic life coinciding with my personal life as a mother. I had many women steadfastly providing childcare and household management throughout Cynthia, Carolyn, and Diana's years in East Lansing and St. Paul: Barb Benson, Delores Colangelo, Ophelia Drake, Sadie Gray, Mrs. Charles Hatt, Vera Nofzinger, Mitzi Soegondo, Carolyn Orr and Sherry, Ruth Reetz, Terry Wilson, Raija Makkonen Manning, and "Grandma and Grandpa" Wilson. In Nigeria, Carolyn and Edward Hammaskjold cared for Cynthia and Carolyn while Carl and I traveled. All of them supported me as a mother and professional. More recently, the most helpful Suzan Natterstad has been my mainstay.

My daughters, Cynthia, Carolyn, and Diana, my pride and joy, constantly cheerlead. Thanks also to Cynthia's family, Blake, Spencer, and Isabella Johnson; Carolyn's, Andy, Wiley, and Sabina Zink; and Diana's, Keith Seiji and Violet Michiko Eicher. They've endured my trips away for fieldwork, professional conferences, and a time-consuming job. I appreciate their love, support, and patience. My late brother, George C. Bubolz Jr., enjoyed teasing me that I was a rolling stone; his wife, Marianne, is like a sister. I want to mention that my close friends, Karin Parekh, Dr. Kathleen Campbell, and the two Jans, Drs. Hogan and McCulloch, are always here for me.

My appreciation goes to the Indiana University Press staff, starting with Gary Dunham, Director, and Dee Mortensen, Editorial Director, who urged emphasis on global trade which captures the theme of Kalabari material culture. Ashanti Thomas, Acquisitions Editor, courteously answered questions and helped me upload the manuscript. Pam Rude, Senior Artist and Book Designer, carefully reviewed my images. Marketing Manager Stephen Matthew Williams's guidance on the book cover is appreciated, as is the fastidious work of Darja Malcolm-Clarke, Project Editor and Manager. Thank you also to Jillian Harvey, copyeditor, and Tony Brewer, Compositor. I am delighted with the design work of Indiana University Press and commitment to publishing *Global Trade*.

NOTES

1. I have not met the current Amanyanabo, King Amachree XI, Professor Theophilus Princewill, Commander of the Order of the Federal Republic, who assumed the honored position in 2002. He is a former professor of medical

microbiology at the University of Port Harcourt and University of Science and Technology in Port Harcourt.

2. I created a digital archive of my collection in 2017 with a grant from the University of Minnesota Retirees Association. It can be found through searching for Eicher Textile Collection at the University of Minnesota Libraries UMedia.

3. Pronounced /peh-leh-tay bih-tay/.

I

Cultural Authentication and Textiles

Chapter 1, in this section of nine chapters, places the Kalabari in the geographic and historical setting that encouraged their global trade, providing the base for the concept of cultural authentication elaborated in chapter 2, which relates to the Kalabari use of Indian imported madras to fashion the cut-thread cloth *pelete bite*. Although similar to bricolage, cultural authentication more importantly stresses agency involved through creative transformation. Chapters 3–5 expand on the making of pelete bite, its significance, and its economic importance during the 1980s. Chapters 6–9 present the research on madras and embroidered velvets throughout the Kalabari life course that underpin the role of textiles in everyday and ritual dress. Two Kalabari scholars, Erekosima and Petgrave, contribute insiders' knowledge about the significance of pelete bite and madras.

Dress, Textiles, and the Kalabari Material World

Joanne B. Eicher and Tonye Victor Erekosima

IN THE TWENTY-FIRST CENTURY, everyday life in the world is intrinsically connected. On the seven continents, internet and cell phone technology provides easy and effortless communication across oceans and geographic borders. In the 1800s in Africa, when explorers Henry Morton Stanley and David Livingstone traveled and described their experiences, global involvement of Africans seemed impossible, even unlikely. Our focus on the material world of the dress of the Kalabari people of Nigeria, however, provides documentation that the Kalabari engaged with a world beyond their islands for millennia, not just decades. We additionally focus on their aesthetics: the Kalabari view of their imported dress and textile items and the importance in their cultural practices of everyday and ceremonial occasions. Such indigenous aesthetics, an emic view, are less often addressed than the etic view when only outsiders conduct research.

The Kalabari islands, among the mangrove swamps of the Niger River at the Atlantic Ocean's edge, were geographically well positioned for international commerce, as seen in figure 1.1.

The Kalabari became deeply embedded in world trade. As we examined the cultural significance of Kalabari dress, our data led us again and again to document their strong global trading history with integration of foreign materials and dress into their daily lives. We zero in on Kalabari involvement in global trade. We provide a different picture of Africa, with a special focus on taste and aesthetics of dress, far from the one implied by the stereotype of "Dark Africa."

3

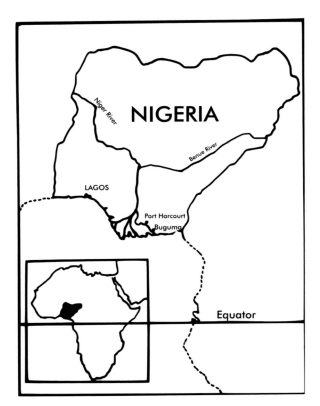

Fig. 1.1. Map of Africa with inset of Nigeria and Kalabari area.

Perhaps surprisingly, the Kalabari neither wove nor dyed textiles themselves but were middlemen in mercantile trade for several centuries in the Niger delta on the Atlantic coast. Although they often mention *okuru*, a raffia cloth, as being locally woven and worn in early days, no data about it exists. But their use of considerable quantities of imported cloth and other goods from European, Indian, and West African sources indicates global involvement before the term *globalization* became fashionable. They adapted their acquisitions for everyday and ritual use to effect requisite symbolic communication. The consumption patterns of their society were expressed through forms of taste and social structure, in the historical setting of the nineteenth century. The emerging Kalabari demand for imported goods, particularly cloth, used in daily and ceremonial life related to the setting and structure of their society. The Kalabari were consumers in a world economy, illustrating that trade pattern complexity can easily match manufacturing and marketing complexity.

KALABARILAND

Who are the Kalabari of Nigeria? Their population is perhaps 1 million of 198 million, according to the United Nations estimate for Nigeria in 2018. The larger Ijo language group to which they belong is the fourth largest in Nigeria, after Hausa, Yoruba, and Igbo. Like most Nigerians, Kalabari speak English, because with Universal Primary Education in Nigeria, children learn English in school. In addition, indigenous languages (approximately 250 in Nigeria) are commonly spoken, meaning most Kalabari are bi- or multilingual.

Specifically identified as the Kalabari Ijo of the Niger delta of Nigeria, they live a riverine life in the lower Niger delta area, four degrees above the equator, where the Niger River flows into the Atlantic. They experience two seasons yearly, dry and rainy; temperatures range from 75 to 85 degrees Fahrenheit. The Ijo people, including the Kalabari, possibly immigrated into the delta sometime between 800 and 1000 CE, settling the land prior to Europeans' arrival by sea in the fifteenth century. Thus, the Kalabari occupied a strategic position in the Niger delta trade and, consequently, global trade for several hundred years (Dike 1956; Jones 1963; Horton 1969b; Alagoa 1972). When Portuguese ships arrived in the Niger delta in the late 1400s, the Kalabari had existing trade routes and networks, bartering with Nigerians as far north as Aboh and Onitsha and as far west as Lagos. They exchanged salt and dried fish for canoes and foodstuffs such as yam, cocoyam, and plantain, none of which grew in the Kalabari saltwater environment (Alagoa 1970a). The foodstuffs provisioned their crews and those enslaved; from the mid-nineteenth century, they exchanged palm oil from the hinterlands of Nigeria for beads, iron bars, and vast quantities of cloth from Europe, India, and West Africa. Historical records indicate well-established trading stations at New Calabar (the original island of the Kalabari people) by 1588. In 1676, the Dutch travel writer Olfert Dapper described New Calabar on the New Calabar River as one of the three chief ports on the Nigerian coast (Talbot 1926). In 1823, Captain John Adams (1823) reported detailed lists of textiles preferred by Kalabari traders.

In the eighteenth and nineteenth centuries, the Kalabari strengthened their societal structure based on lineages; these were known as *wari* in Kalabari and War-Canoe House in English, denoting a social, political, economic, and defense unit that supports a main chief. The Kalabari word *polo* refers to the geographic location of the wari rather than the social unit concept. The wari expanded its lineage by incorporating as family members those enslaved who had served the wari and become successful traders, displaying both loyalty and trading skills. These nonkin persons attained equal rights to those born into the family and could rise to inherit and administer all family property on behalf of their children once their father died (Jones 1963).

This structural change occurred in response to internal rivalries arising among the Atlantic coastal societies of the Niger delta and to inroads made by the seafaring European traders. Within Kalabari society, lineage rivalries extended to claiming "ownership" and naming specific textile patterns and other items of dress, including beads. Such names still highlight lineage prestige when worn or displayed.

When the Portuguese and other Europeans encountered them, the delta inhabitants acted as a conduit between the foreign traders and the Nigerian hinterland peoples, the latter known to have been sold as slaves. As trade changed from slaves to palm oil, the trading tributaries' name also changed from Bight of Biafra to Oil Rivers. Beginning with Portuguese exploration in the late 1400s, the trade included imported goods and much cloth coming from beyond Africa (Vogt 1975). Extensive trading with Portuguese, Dutch, and English traders came through the East India Companies to West Africa, accompanied by sporadic attempts at missionary work. The 1700s and 1800s were the heyday for the Kalabari as superb traders and middlemen with the Europeans.

In the late 1800s, the English became the prominent colonizers and took complete control of the land, which was named Nigeria in 1897 and became independent in 1960 (Jones 1963). The fortunes of the Kalabari shifted markedly after the British takeover. Instead of the king and chiefs overseeing their own political and economic affairs, they fell subject to British machinations. By 1960, with Nigerian independence, the Kalabari maintained pride in their ethnic heritage, but many rose to the challenge of seeing themselves as part of the larger political, economic, and geographical unit of the Nigerian polity.

During the twentieth century, types of work expanded; many Kalabari attended university and beyond, and like other Nigerians, some studied and worked abroad in Europe and the United States. In Nigeria, others found jobs living away from the delta in larger Nigerian cities: nearby Port Harcourt; Lagos; Kano; or the later capitol, Abuja. In the twenty-first century, the Kalabari engage in many occupations and professions: medicine, law, commerce, education, petty trading, and manual work. Whether working and residing abroad or in Nigeria, however, they attempt to return to their delta islands to celebrate major life events and, when possible, ultimately to retire.

Christianity predominates in the twenty-first century, existing alongside ideas and practices from the Kalabari traditional belief system, which many Kalabari still accept and integrate with Christianity. Kalabari customs influence their rich cultural life, including birth, marriage, and death rituals.

But involvement in modern, everyday life accounts for the way Kalabari men, women, and children often dress. Their wardrobes include a blend of non-Kalabari dress (suits, shirts, and trousers for men and dresses, skirts, and blouses for women) and Kalabari dress (wrappers and other ensembles, along with ritual and ceremonial garb). Schoolchildren wear uniforms. These non-Kalabari examples typify the terms *world dress, fashion* (Eicher and Sumberg 1995), and *contemporary dress*. During our research years, however, on the islands, we saw men and women primarily wearing Kalabari dress. In the twenty-first-century North American diaspora, Kalabari people continue to display their heritage with Kalabari dress during special events.

HISTORY AND STRUCTURE OF KALABARI SOCIETY

Understanding Kalabari history provides the context for our research. The Kalabari were strategically a part of a global network; their isolated island location necessitated trade. They were "[dependent] on the specialized fishing of their menfolk and on the exchange of their smoke-dried fish and salt with the people of the hinterland for bulk foodstuffs, tools, clothing, and domestic gear" (Jones 1963, 9). Primarily men, and occasionally women, fished. Early transport to and from the main city of Port Harcourt was by large dugout canoes; later, it was by motorboats, although small boats and canoes provided transportation among the islands. On the islands, common transport was by foot and later by motorcycles. With two-thirds of the area only navigable by water until the late 1980s, cars could not travel from the mainland to the islands. Then bridges were built, allowing the occasional auto. More cars are common in the twenty-first century, but water transportation is most frequently used.

The eastern delta Kalabari, after apparently leaving the gerontocratic freshwater farming community in the central delta and ending up in a saltwater zone dependent on trading, had to make other changes in social life (Alagoa 1971), such as developing the wari or "trading house" system (Horton 1969b). Talent, not age, became the main leadership factor, and enterprise, not inheritance, determined the pattern of wealth.

As these migrants settled into the island locale and community of New Calabar (known by the Kalabari as *Elem-Ama*), through the period up to the sixteenth century, antagonisms receded between the main Endeme group from the central delta and other distinct settler groups (which oral history designates as up to seven). Consequently, cannibalism, which had kept them segregated, disappeared. A united society emerged, alternatively called Kengema and Owame in addition to Kalabari (Horton 1969b). A common language evolved, a confederacy pattern of leadership arose, and local trade routes were developed

(Erekosima 1989). Pacheco Pereira, the Portuguese adventurer, recorded that at the end of the fifteenth century, he encountered Kalabari traders who used canoes that were "the largest in the Ethiopias of Guinea" (Jenewari 1976, 13), a reference to the black territories of the West African coast. They exchanged their marine goods of fish and salt for food products from the farming communities to the north (Pereira 1937). Pereira added that these traders transported goods down the Rio Real estuary, "from a hundred leagues more up this river in canoes that could hold 80 men and carried yams in large quantitates as well as slaves, cows, goats and sheep." He also noted trade in cloths, beads, animal skins, and palm oil.

SUBSEQUENT EUROPEAN MERCANTILE IMPACT

After the Portuguese explorers of the fifteenth and sixteenth centuries established contact with the Kalabari, the Dutch and English followed in the seventeenth and eighteenth centuries (Blake 1942; Davis 1954). Dutch influence waned as British trading interests grew, and the main commodity shifted sharply to slaves. The need to supply the American and West Indian colonies with African labor from the early 1700s produced a massive pressure on the Niger delta communities, recasting their social orders once again. Rivalries were fanned by local competition and manipulation by foreign intrigues, employing European guns, alcohol, credit, and consumer baubles. The rivalry sent the region into a spin of continual warfare and turmoil through the next two centuries or more (Alagoa 1972; Dike 1962; Jones 1963).

Each society needed an ample supply of slaves to sell along with an abundance of able-bodied men to row the boats to hinterland markets to obtain slaves. Males needed to be sufficiently strong or armed to ward off rivals who might attack them en route to the slave markets. In addition, a large contingent was needed at home to defend the town settlements and to work the outlying farm plantations, market outposts, and fishing grounds in order to ensure a steady food supply to the huddled town dwellers.

The Kalabari were responding to two challenges: one being the internal rivalries arising among the Atlantic coastal societies of the Niger delta; the other being part of the inroads made by the Europeans arriving by ship to engage in trade. As missionaries arrived alongside European traders, the Kalabari apparently saw the practical benefit of embracing Christianity. They recognized the importance of the introduction of modern schools but rejected foreign ideology or beliefs. They gave the Christians only a ten-year trial period, from 1875 to 1885, to prove the religion's value (Ejituwu 1971). Dike writes about a strict code related to evangelization: "The children were sent to mission schools for

one purpose only: that they might learn the business methods of the West ...
they want them to be taught how to gauge palm oil and other mercantile business as soon as possible" (Dike 1965, 161). The chiefs thus claimed they did not
want their children to have religious teachings, for they taught them enough
of that at home.

On the political front, the chiefs, in fulfilling their designated role, mani-
fested the same self-assertiveness. G. I. Jones illustrates this by the letter Kalabari chiefs wrote in 1882 giving an ultimatum "that ran counter to the British
government's principles and policy but one that was accepted and supported
by the European traders and even by the Consul." They wanted monopoly of
the up-country trade and overseas trade to the European trading community,
requesting dues from the Europeans for the rights to the river trade (Jones
1963, 82). The British acceptance of such Kalabari intransigence over the terms
of trade had its roots in hard military realities, as Dike (1962, 30) outlined: "On
the whole, the political power of the African states reigned supreme over aliens
and natives, for the strong and despotic governments provided by the coastal
principalities suited the semi military society of the time."

However, the Kalabari were in the forefront of the struggle that took on the
complexion of not only military but also economic and ideological resistance.
Dike observed, "Of all the Delta states the Royal House of Amakiri, New Calabar, alone had never tolerated the credit system ... and her prosperous state in
the nineteenth and twentieth centuries was undoubtedly due to rejection of the
trust system all its works" (1962, 125–126). As for ideology, Dike also indicates
that the impact of three centuries of Western commercial enterprise "was more
evident on the material than on the ideological plane." The unwritten traditional religious and political beliefs dominated nineteenth-century African
daily life (Dike 1962, 161). The anthropologist Robin Horton corroborates this
for the Kalabari: "The hectic competition for power and wealth which followed
the economic revolution of Owame (or Kalabari) brought an element of os-
tentation into those religious practices which were carried out on a House-to-
House basis. ... In this intensely pushful, virile culture ... it may seem strange
that so much enthusiasm could be spared for religious activities [or aesthetic
considerations, we might add]" (Horton 1960a, 38).

In other words, the Kalabari commitment to their beliefs that stemmed from
the past continued to permeate daily life, which influenced their preferences
in dress and textiles, obvious throughout our research. Their entrepreneurial
drive and trading organization became so remarkable that P. Amaury Talbot,
a British colonial officer trained as an anthropologist, writing about them in
the early twentieth century, noted with phrasing and stereotypes of that time

that "they are a people of great interest and intelligence, hard-headed, keen witted, and born traders. Indeed, one of the principal agents here [a European] of worldwide experience stated that in his opinion, the Kalabari compete on equal terms with Jew or China-man [*sic*]" (Talbot 1932).

TYPES AND SOURCES OF CLOTH

The Kalabari used textiles from both internal West African and external European trade, with the latter seeming most prominent. Ocean trade brought printed woolen flannel from England and artisan-produced textiles from India (cotton plaid madras, striped silks, embroidered velvets, and heavy woven cotton) via the British East India Companies. John Vogt (1975, 142) claimed that Portugal was the "undisputed economic mistress of West Africa's coastal trade" from 1480 to 1540, citing Portugal's two most important trade items as copper and cloth. The textiles were "an impressive array of cloth varieties . . . at least 102 major types of fabricated textiles, not counting size or color variations" (ibid.). The majority of the cloth came from textile centers beyond Portugal but within its far-flung empire. Although Vogt's (1975, 143) brief article does not mention India, he diagrammed textile sources showing India as a source for Portugal's West African outlets. Sea captains, explorers, and traders wrote descriptions from the late fifteenth century about the delta of the River Niger with comments about textile types desired by its inhabitants.

The first European histories that refer to the Kalabari come from Portuguese sources documenting West African coastal journeys, indicating a hostile reception when landing in 1480 at the port known as Kula, still identified as a Kalabari settlement on the edge of the Atlantic coast. By the early 1500s, maps were drawn and settlements identified on the New Calabar River (called Rio Real by the Portuguese), an important source for slaves and a key location of Kalabari traders who controlled up-country trade—that is, the areas north of the Kalabari (Pereira 1937). Dutch and English merchants followed the Portuguese in coastal trade; when slave trading was abolished by the mid-nineteenth century, palm oil became the main Kalabari export. The coastal Kalabari did not permit up-country contact between the European traders and those who supplied slaves or palm oil (Dike 1962).

Both oral tradition and linguistic evidence that compares words similar to Portuguese strongly indicate Kalabari and Portuguese trade. Reinforcing oral histories, Kalabari have written histories that corroborate European documentation. Photographic and other visible documentation, such as the textiles kept in Kalabari family cloth trunks, also provide evidence of trade. Our early research on the textile trade did not disclose many written materials, but two

2019 books provide data about the Indian to West African textile trade: *The Anarchy* by William Dalrymple (2019) delineates the role of the East India Company and trade to West Africa, briefly referring to textiles, and *Indian Cotton Textiles in West Africa* by Kazuo Kobayashi (2019) highlights the Indian sources for export to West Africa, providing solid data about what he titles the "South/South" trade route. For the Niger delta, he cites Bonny, an island of the Ibani people (who are also Ijo), near the Kalabari. It also served as an entrepôt, confirming that Indian textiles were arriving in the delta.

Linguistic evidence reinforces the presence of early international trade. The Kalabari word for dress (*kappa*) is a direct derivative from the Portuguese term that similarly designates cloth (Jenewari 1976). The Kalabari word for cloth, however, is *bite*, indicating they had engaged in West African cloth trade before Portuguese contacts. An important handwoven cotton plaid or checked textile, known in the West as madras and gingham, was and continues to be imported to the Kalabari from the India subcontinent, suggesting that the Kalabari word *injiri* relates to the word *India* (Eicher 1988; Evenson 1991; Talbot 1932).[1] In India, the textile is referred to as RMHK, meaning Real Madras Handkerchief, the Indian export term relating to the size of each pattern repeat.

By 1823, Captain Adams noted that the Kalabari imported many commodities: cowrie shells, beads, iron bars, and cloth from several locations—West Africa, Europe, and India. His appendix documents the appeal of different textiles by specifically listing the textiles preferred by the natives for each port (Adams 1823). In the late 1800s and early 1900s, Talbot described Indian madras as the prized textile of the Kalabari: "*Injiri* (the local pronunciation of the word India) cloth, the trade name of which is 'real India' and which was first introduced to these regions by the Portuguese, was for many years the finest material obtainable and therefore became the dress of the Kalabari chiefs and is still worn on ceremonial occasions" (1932, 279).

The Kalabari place high value on injiri, apparently based on factors other than sheer opulence and expense because costlier cloths are and have been admired and chosen for ceremonial and special use: ones richer in texture, more elaborate, brighter, and more varied in design and more durable. Injiri, viewed as Americans might view their flag, when worn or displayed by Kalabari, however, signifies their identity and is viewed emblematically (Erekosima 1982).

Also in the past, wealthy families of the War-Canoe Houses purchased in bulk the cloth that became named after them. On ceremonial occasions, only family members of one War-Canoe House would be decked out with their particular cloth. For example, the King Abbi Group or subunit of the Royal House claims red and gray types of *ikaki*, while the Tariah family of the Birinomi

Group of Houses claims injiri with an elephant emblem. The John Bull family and the Ombo Group of Houses own a yellow madras and an indigo and white plaid cotton called *amasiri*. The Horsfall Family and the (Dodo) West Group of Houses have textiles called *egenebite*, *onunga*, and *accraa*, while the George Amachree House of the Karibo Group of Houses has "real India."

ARTISAN CLOTH VARIETIES AND USES

Handwoven Indian madras is worn and called *George* by the neighboring Igbo and their Ijo neighbors. Jasleen Dhamija, an Indian textile scholar, claims the cloth comes from Fort St. George, the port of Madras, thus responsible for the name (1989). Erekosima claims it is named after a major Kalabari lineage in Buguma (1989). Costlier cloths, some imported from India and used for special occasions to exhibit wealth and flamboyance, include hand-embroidered velvets and soft, striped silks. Heavy printed woolens from England are also treasured, and all have found their way into the Kalabari hierarchy of prized textiles.

Details about the trade, however, are sketchy; more information about why some of these cloths were first traded is lacking. For example, the posh embroidered velvets used in India for wall hangings and to decorate elephants seem singularly unsuitable to be worn as garments on the humid, tropical Kalabari islands. Yet the Kalabari have prized these heavy textiles for several generations as materials for men's gowns, women's wrappers, and funeral displays. An Indian civil servant in the handloom industry told Eicher that Indians have known about Kalabari preferences in textiles for many years. He stated that the handloom industry has been more fine-tuned to consumers abroad than in India (Eicher 1988a). Similarly, company personnel Eicher interviewed in Manchester, England, provided data confirming this statement (Eicher 1990).

Local trade within West Africa (Alagoa 1972) brought the Kalabari several types of handwoven textiles from many sources, from both the east–west and the north–south trade routes (Alagoa 1970a). This trade was well established before the first Europeans arrived at the close of the fifteenth century (Alagoa 1970a; Boahen 1971, 88; Davidson 1966, 89–92; Ryder 1965; Sundstrom 1974). The Yoruba and Igbo living in the area now known as Nigeria, as well as the Ewe peoples in Ghana and Togo, produced fabrics that appealed to the Kalabari (Aronson 1980a; Aronson 1980b; Aronson 1982; Aronson 1989; Eicher 1988).

Puzzling questions arise: What was the appeal of Indian madras and the other imported cloths? How long *have* they been traded into the Kalabari area? Why do they continue to have appeal? Answers to some of these questions come from understanding more about the setting and structure of Kalabari society as summarized above, concerning: (1) the emergence of the Kalabari as a distinct cultural group as indicated by their history and (2) change to a new social order in their society as a result of European mercantile impact in the nineteenth century. A third answer comes from reviewing Kalabari social differentiation of gender in the new social order.

THE SOCIAL DIFFERENTIATION OF GENDER

As a result of social challenges, a high militaristic and despotic order of social organization marked the eastern delta states of the nineteenth century (Dike 1962; Jones 1963). A definite hierarchy of authority structured the roles and relationships of the men within Kalabari society, and a clear-cut differentiation needed to be established between them and other societies, partly in order to generate collective pride and loyalty.

This organization for responding to the external challenges was indigenously generated and did not displace the previous cultural focus on kinship and community as foundations of social existence. The role of women as initiators or generators of the social order became equally highlighted. A complementary status pattern emerged where the creative order generally fell to women and the regulative function to men. Chapters following in section two present detailed descriptions and analyses of the two gender categories, both being hierarchical. Their forms of dress relate to each of the ranks that claims specific garb and styles distinguishing it from other ranks. Males command roles in the political order, beginning with young adulthood, ending with the epitome of chieftaincy and kingship. Females, in contrast, are ranked by early onset of marked bodily changes. Based on physical maturation and its social application as the paramount consideration, grooming a young girl toward motherhood is the prime goal.

The male and female gender hierarchies were the critical foundations of social organization in the Kalabari city-state of the nineteenth century. Meticulous care ensured that the demarcations between Kalabari and non-Kalabari, between men and women as social categories, and within each hierarchy were kept highly visible to all members of society, with the use of cloth in the dress of men and women conveying these distinctions and demarcations.

TASTE AND SOCIAL DIFFERENTIATION THROUGH CLOTH

The varieties of cloth available to the Kalabari through internal and external trade allowed the ranking within each gender hierarchy to be visually communicated. The men's hierarchy of dress related to the sociopolitical functions of males in the community and the women's hierarchy for the physical reproduction and socialization functions of females as elaborated in following chapters.

Men and women are used as categories, because the Kalabari words *oyibo* for males and *erebo* for females hold for all ages. Children are labeled with diminutives. For what in English is thought of as a girl, in Kalabari is little woman (*erebotubo*), literally "child woman," and for a boy is little man (*oyibotubo*), literally "child man."

The gender hierarchies relate to textiles worn and the histories of textile trade. Ships' logs recording voyages from Portugal, Holland, France, and England to India and Indonesia with itineraries to Africa document the ocean traffic in textiles, indicating that the demand for luxury textiles accounted for complicated trade networks overland that crisscrossed Asia and the Sahara Desert in Africa. These examples have established that taste for luxuries also existed in tropical Africa, with supply and demand springing up to satisfy Africans where affordable (Nielsen 1980).

Kalabari data on men's and women's dress in later chapters illustrate that they exercised taste in textiles available to them through their patterns of trade and by specific selection and use criteria. The fact that Africans had discriminating tastes for specific textiles, in particular luxury textiles and other dress items, however, was not well documented or recognized until we researched historical documents and conducted fieldwork. The historical data cited pinpoint Kalabari preferences as very specific about color and pattern, contradicting Nigel Barley's (1987a) view that Africa was only a dumping ground for unwanted, rejected, or out-of-date items, such as hats.

Seventeenth-century evidence from the Dutch physician Olfert Dapper (1686), who reported on others' travels through the area, indicates that the Kalabari had selective taste. He related that they were "very particular about grey copper armlets used for exchange purposes," often rejecting "two to three hundred out of one barrel," expecting them to be "oblong with rounded curve and very well made" (Talbot 1926, 241). Kobayashi's (2019) subtitle of *African Agency, Consumer Demand, and the Making of the Global Economy, 1750–1850* with that theme reinforces Talbot's point of selective taste in textiles.

Nineteenth-century documentation also came from Captain Adams, Reverend Waddell, Consul Hutchinson, and Count de Cardi. Adams's 1823 report of Kalabari cloth preferences was supported by later recorded observation in that century, highlighting their selectivity. Reverend Waddell, visiting New Calabar in 1850, described both dress and demeanor: "Barboy, on whom we called, an intelligent man, was dressed in a long blue velvet shirt with red facings, in which he looked majestic" (1863, 420).

Count de Cardi, who traveled from 1862 to 1896 in West Africa, wrote that "another chief of no mean capacity is Bob Manuel, of Abonema [*sic*], exceedingly neat, almost a dandy in appearance" (1899, 507). Consul Hutchinson said about New Calabar: "All the people met in the town have an air of sturdiness in their walk, not to be seen elsewhere except at Lagos and Akra" (1858, 101). De Cardi contrasted the Kalabari with other groups in the area, because the Kalabari covered their bodies and preferred Indian madras: "Owing to some peculiarities in their dress, the New Calabar chiefs are very different to the chiefs in other parts of the delta. They never appear outside their houses unless robed in long shirts (made of real India madras of bold check patterns, in which no other colour but red, blue and white is ever allowed to be used) reaching down to their heels; under this they wear a singlet and a flowing loin cloth of the same material as their shirts" (1899, 508).

These same colors were primarily those that continued into the time of our fieldwork in the twentieth century. The definite hierarchy of Kalabari men's ranks that reflect a creative, indigenous adaptation of imported textiles and accessories and symbolizes age and rank distinctions is described and expanded in later chapters. The top garment, worn over a bottom wrapper, is the critical factor of men's dress in the ranking system; male bodies, after childhood, must be always fully covered in public with both top and bottom garments. The top garments distinguish the rankings.

For women, increasing amounts of body coverage and richness of dress mark each stage of the female hierarchy as also delineated in later chapters. Various forms of cultural values that emphasize body rotundity are imparted as the female body undergoes physical changes. The stages of dress refer to the cloth that covers the lower half of the body and distinguish the rankings. The Kalabari prize women's rotundity and men's tubular or linear bodies.

CULTURAL AUTHENTICATION

The material plane that Dike mentioned as important for the Kalabari becomes easily visible in their choices of the imported textiles and items of dress from their years of trading. The way they used the textiles and put together their ensembles of dress were not mere imitations but processes related to a textile or combinations of dress items reflecting indigenization processes we call cultural authentication, as elaborated in chapter 2.

The process of cultural authentication begins with the introduction of a new item into a culture unfamiliar with it and becomes an item of meaningful transaction or legitimate cultural currency only after it goes through a process and acquires such authentication. The specific artifact is initially singled out from a plethora of possibilities; that is, it is *selected* for some specific benefit. Named or *characterized* symbolically by the receiving community members, it becomes *incorporated* into the social order. The object is *transformed* through modification and is no longer perceived simply as a borrowed artifact. Although initially borrowed, the modification changes the artifact significantly. Such an artifact has crossed cultural boundaries and becomes used in a different way than originally conceived, thereby becoming culturally authenticated.

The process of cultural authentication is found throughout Kalabari life, the first example we present being the Kalabari transformation of Indian madras, or injiri. It is found not only in the cut-thread technique, called *pelete bite*, but also in men's and women's dress ensembles and in rituals, such as funeral displays and masquerades. The concept of cultural authentication provides the overarching theme throughout the volumes, beginning with its delineation in chapter 2.

ORGANIZATION OF CHAPTERS

The chapters in the first section elaborate on cultural authentication and more completely describe the textiles imported and used. The second section details men's and women's dress. The third section examines the Kalabari rituals of funerals, masquerades, and a centenary celebration, all involving large financial commitments of families and individuals. The fourth section focuses on Kalabari diaspora events going into the twenty-first century.

Our volume emphasizes the place of cloth and dress in the Kalabari material world, resources obtained from global sources tied to Kalabari pleasure in using imported textiles throughout their lives, from birth through death. They use all types of textiles, none of which they grow, spin, dye, or weave. They expressed creativity in choosing and using imported textiles daily and ritually. They also imported other articles of dress, using a definition of dress not just as clothing but as a totality of body supplements (not only garments but also items such as jewelry and hats) and body modifications (Eicher and Roach-Higgins 1992). These many choices relate to understanding their indigenous aesthetics in dress.

Aesthetics reflect the tension between conformity and differentiation, or matter and form in cultural life. Aesthetic standards are explicitly evident within Kalabari society as specific, acceptable general rules of expressive or appreciative representation. These standards include subtleties of taste that pervade the process of aesthetics and allow idiosyncratic (individual) or segmental (subgroup) emphases and include a knowledge of stylistic forms appropriate to specific categories of people or events and knowledge of the transitory fashions of a specific time and place.

Kalabari aesthetics of dress exemplify African aesthetics in other realms. Practical utility merges with meaning and use. Kalabari dress is neither mere commodity nor pure art.[2] This merger is the context within which we view Kalabari dress. Hence, Kalabari aesthetics simultaneously encompass the pairing of sentiment and substance. African aesthetics resonate as the vantage point, or basic perspective form, from which objects and events of reality obtain interpretation or assignments of meaningfulness in the setting of cultural lifeways.

Using dress and textiles as a lens, we provide evidence of Kalabari as players in the global trade arena for centuries. Their interconnectedness demonstrates that Africa was never a "dark continent" but was critically involved in a global trade showing Kalabari ingenuity and creativity in their aesthetic choices.

The chapters draw on the work of our team of researchers devoted to various dress and textile topics either focusing on Kalabari material culture directly through fieldwork in (1) the Niger delta or (2) the countries supplying Indian madras and velvet and Italian coral. Chapters also provide voices of several scholars with their own research perspectives and goals, which include two indigenous Kalabari, Tonye Victor Erekosima and Manuella Daba BobManuel-Meyer Petgrave. They provide insiders' cultural background and knowledge of Kalabari values and aesthetics, enhanced by their analytical tools gained from graduate education.

The insights and analyses from our research team with textile and dress expertise supplemented Erekosima's and my research focus. Two contributors, Barbara Sumberg and Susan Torntore, have been museum curators for ethnic textile and dress collections. Elisha Renne, Torntore, and Sumberg are also weavers. M. Catherine Daly, Sandra Evenson, Hazel Lutz, and Susan Michelman are scholars with backgrounds in the arts and design of textiles and dress. Their knowledge and skills span sewing, tailoring, alterations, embroidery, spinning, knitting, and crocheting that resulted in their finding data often overlooked, ignored, or not understood by other social scientists conducting fieldwork about textiles and dress. My own background came from growing up with a mother who sewed extensively for herself, my brother, and me. She and I spent much time during my childhood and teenage years poring over pattern books and fabric, conferring on her designs for gowns I wore to formal dances that were popular in my high school and college years.[3] I also took an undergraduate textile course in college. Our team's combined expertise allowed documentation that will engage textile, dress, and fashion scholars, experts, collectors, and enthusiasts, like members of the UK-based Costume Society, the Costume Society of America, the Textile Society of America, and the International Association of Textiles and Apparel, and those focusing on the topic of "decolonizing fashion and dress." Thus, some chapters may be read as stand-alone by readers with interests primarily on pelete bite, madras, velvet, glass and coral beads, male and female dress practices, funerals, and rituals.

An important point emerges in the final chapter regarding the Kalabari diaspora; they represent one of many immigrant groups across the world that honor cultural heritage by keeping their dress practices alive as they move and live away from their homeland. In relating to cultural identity at home or abroad, Karen Tranberg Hansen uses her Zambia research as an African example, pointing out that the Zambian dress called *chitenge* demonstrated "the material role of fashion in the experience and expression of a proud cultural identity" (2017, 153). Hansen also argued in "Not African Enough?" that the dichotomies of African/Western and traditional/modern are "worn out" (2019, 2), because "rather than being in opposition to one another, European/Western-style conventions and local/traditional ways of dress play out together on women's dressed bodies, depending on context" (12). Similarly, the 2019 Transboundary Fashion Seminar "(Re)Thinking Fashion Globalization," held at Bunka Gakuen University, Tokyo, dealt with "fashion globalization" that "too often refers to European fashion trends . . . adopted by the rest of the world . . . generally ignor[ing] the large diversity of fashion systems around the globe."[4] At a 2018 diaspora event near Baltimore, Maryland, I observed the Kalabari tenaciously continuing their dress and textile traditions stemming from global trade. They have either transformed or recombined artifacts from "the rest of the world" in such manner that their use has become truly Kalabari, documenting the concept of cultural authentication. I should note that my publications have been on the concept of cultural dress and identity (Eicher 1973, 1992, 1995, 2000, 2008, 2014a), a focus that applies to any culture, not specifically to the Kalabari. An exception is "Subtle and Spectacular: Dressing in Kalabari Style" (Eicher 2015a), an emphasis only implied in this volume, however, with its concentration on cultural authentication and global trade.

JOANNE B. EICHER, PhD, is Regents Professor Emerita in the Department of Design, Housing, and Apparel at the University of Minnesota. She is coeditor of *The Anthropology of Dress and Fashion: A Reader*; coeditor of *The Visible Self: Global Perspectives on Dress, Culture, and Society*, 4th ed.; and editor in chief of the *Encyclopedia of World Dress and Fashion*.

TONYE VICTOR EREKOSIMA (1940–2008), PhD, native-born Kalabari, lived in the Igbo towns of Owerri and Umuahia, because his father was an educator and secondary-school principal, until Erekosima's university years in the United States. He was steeped in Kalabari cultural tradition, however, thanks to his family's routine travel to Buguma, his parents' birthplace, for holidays and significant events like funerals. Following his PhD, he served as Director, General Studies, Rivers State College of Education, and Director, Instructional Resources Center, University of Port Harcourt. He coedited *A Hundred Years of Buguma History in Kalabari Culture* (1984) and *Buguma 1984 Centenary Symposia on Kalabari* (1991).

NOTES

Expanded from Joanne B. Eicher and Tonye V. Erekosima, "Taste and 19th Century Patterns of Textile Use Among the Kalabari of Nigeria," Paper presented at Cloth, the World Economy, and the Artisan: Textile Manufacturing and Marketing in South Asia and Africa, 1780–1950, Hanover, NH: Dartmouth College, 1993.

1. Thank you to Hazel Lutz for providing information about another possible export town and about Kalabari calling the textile "injiri" by discovering that an early British-India trading port is named Inzaram, or Injaram, depending on which northern Indian language is being used; j and z often are interchangeable in northern Indian languages. A British-India 1784 road map (reproduced in Schwartzberg 1992, 59) transliterates the spelling into English as Ingram or Ingerum (the print is not clear), with a soft g. Located on the Godavery River, the eastern Indian port of Inzaram, and the larger trading cities of Masulipatnam and Madras, is the closest of all colonial trading ports to the area in which Telia Rumal and its descendant RMHK are woven. Kalabari injiri, like many textiles traded in the colonial era, possibly took its name from the port through which it traveled to reach West Africa. The dates of operation of colonial Inzaram, 1708–1829 (Maclean 1982, 372) indicate the period when the plaid cotton cloth from eastern India, in contrast to the earlier western British-Indian plaids (Evenson 1994), first reached the Niger delta.

2. A parallel example is given by Ingold, Riches, and Woodburn (1991), who claim that for the Kalahari Bushmen of southern Africa, the two perspectives of utility and art merge regarding the animals they both hunt for food and depict in their exquisite cave paintings.

3. See Eicher 2001b.

4. "(Re)Thinking Fashion Globalization," seminar description, Transboundary Fashion Seminar, Research Collective for Decolonizing Fashion, Bunka Gakuen University, Tokyo, February 15–16, 2019, https://rcdfashion.wordpress.com/2019/02/10/seminar-rethinking-fashion-globalization-tokyo-15-16-february-2019/.

2

Kalabari Cut-Thread and Pulled-Thread Cloth

Tonye Victor Erekosima and Joanne B. Eicher

THE KALABARI, spread out over several urban and rural settlements, including Abonnema, Bakana, Sangama, Teinma, Tombia, Soku, and Degema, make cut-thread designs called *pelete bite* from the imported madras cloth from India called *injiri*. We present the concept of cultural authentication by analyzing the highly esteemed cut-thread cloths Kalabari men and women wear as wrappers, generally during ceremonial occasions, but sometimes as fashionable attire. The variety of gingham and multicolored madras, often with subdued backgrounds of indigo, black, violet, brown, and sometimes red or orange, are chosen for cutting the designs.

Women artisans create two types of designs by painstaking processes.[1] The first design, called pelete bite (cut-thread cloth) involves lifting either warp or weft threads singly or in groups with a needle and snipping them off with a razor or penknife. The second design requires the artisan to lift only certain weft threads with the needle and then cut and pull them out. This process results in *fimate bite*, or "pulled-thread" cloth. Examples of cutting cloth by using razor or penknife are shown in figures 2.1 and 2.2.

Both pelete bite and fimate bite openwork patterns are superimposed on checked, striped, or plaid cloth.[2] Given the limits of the warp and weft structure of woven textiles, an amazing number of geometric patterns result, and figure 2.3 shows attempting a daring intimation of the curve.

The artisans produce two basic types of patterns: regularly repeated ones and asymmetrical designs exhibited in figure 2.4, which may include such motifs

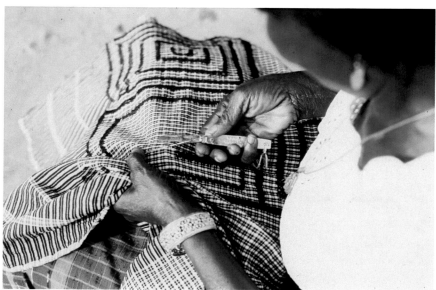

Top, Fig. 2.1. Amonia Akoko cutting cloth with razor, 1980.

Bottom, Fig. 2.2. Deborah JohnBull cutting cloth with penknife, 1980.

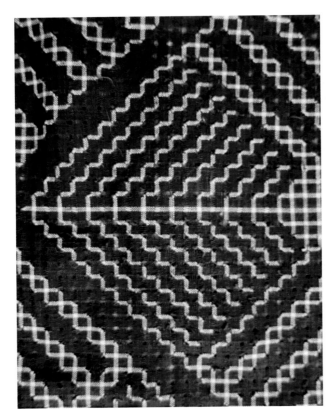

Fig. 2.3.
Pelete bite motif—
daring intimations of
the curve. Erekosima
gift to Joanne B.
Eicher, 1980.

Facing, Fig. 2.4.
Alphabet letters,
personalizing the
owner's wrapper
(H. Erekosima).
Buguma, 1980.

as letters of the alphabet. A refinement of abstraction and balance is achieved despite the simple techniques used to execute the designs. One example of their artistry seen in figure 2.5 is the wrapper worn by Victoria Adaba Erekosima, daughter of King (Amanyanabo) Charlie Kieni "Cane" Amachree. His reign lasted from 1900 to 1918, and he had initial importation rights over this cloth.[3]

Regarding early accounts of cloth, Kalabari lore claims that a raffia cloth called *okuru* was locally woven from fine, raffia-leaf strands and worn by Kalabari men and women as a loincloth. Women also often used it as a wrapper when harvesting marine delicacies from the riverbeds. No written documentation of a Kalabari origin exists, but Daly saw it used as an iriabo's undergarment (Daly 1982). Possibly it originated from elsewhere in Nigeria or from the Congo (Darish 1989, 74). Instead, a few photographs dating to the 1870s, still extant in some Kalabari households, show imported injiri, as shown by a few photographs

Fig. 2.5.
Detail of cut kieni cloth. White weft
threads removed, leaving indigo warp
threads. Photo: Kate Leibfried, 2015.

Fig. 2.6.
Victoria Adaba Erekosima,
daughter of King (Amanyanabo)
Charlie Kieni "Cane" Amachree,
wearing kieni wrapper. Buguma,
1980.

from this period. They picture women's bodies decorated with paint, a variety of coral beads, silk scarves, and other cloth, among them injiri, the base for making pelete bite and fimate bite.

We propose that pelete bite and fimate bite enhanced the importance of the special occasions at which they were worn; these occasions, in turn, provided the opportunity for the cloth to communicate and reinforce the community values represented. Some aspects of the value system that underlay the use of pelete bite and fimate bite must be considered to demonstrate the concept of cultural authentication. We suggest that the social etiquette of Kalabari women, the overall context of cultural resources (including artifacts and design inspiration), male-female role expectations, and kinship affiliation coalesce in pelete bite and fimate bite.

In social etiquette, the Kalabari woman projects a sense of style through a unique preoccupation with *iriabo ti* or "feminine elegance." This aesthetic quality is quite staid and refined, the converse of men's *asa-ti* or "dashing, sporty living." Women's disciplined manners, taste in speech, body control, and meticulous dress are reflected in the subtle patterns of pelete bite and fimate bite.

The material resources available to the Kalabari for creating such cloths involve a number of imported products, such as woven gingham and madras cloths, needles, penknives, and razor blades. There exists, in addition, a heritage of traditional designs for inspiration. One possible source for the design patterns was decorative shapes and forms that Kalabari women had been cutting and painting long before any foreign cloths became available. The hair and bodies of young maidens were the media for these traditional design patterns; their hair was shaved to form patterns on the scalp, and their bodies were beautified with designs painted with camwood and other dyes by older women. Animal motif symbols developed in relation to ritualized representation of the water spirits and a variety of geometrical forms depicting lizard or crocodile skins, turtle shells, and python markings appearing on palm frond screens for mounting ancestral or deistic icons (Horton 1965) are possible additional sources of design inspiration.

Male-female role expectations are also a significant factor in cutwork creation. Among the Kalabari, women are acknowledged as the creators and men the producers. The Kalabari regard the dances and masquerades as eminently in the domain of male personal and group achievement. For example, the water people carried away a beautiful woman named Ekineba to their watery home, and she watched them dance. Returning home, she taught their choreography to the Ekine Society, the exclusively male governing group, who produced the masquerade dances. In deference to the female realm of inspiration and creativity, thus, male dancers acknowledge Ekineba as goddess and patroness, believed to be the originator of aesthetic skills. Women guard the culture's creative impulse, and men translate its adaptive strength in pragmatic activities. The vitality of both creativity and production can be maintained only as long as various ceremonial occasions and representational forms are employed to reinforce awareness and commitment to these equally essential and complementary societal missions. Women are excluded from donning the *owu* masquerades because this is "a culture where such store is set by virtuosity in the masquerade, and where a man's prowess with a particular owu is one of his most important attributes" (Horton 1960a, 32). Nevertheless, women participate as spectators and "hostesses accompanying the gods." With shuffled steps and hand clapping, women turn out for the occasion in pelete bite, reaffirming their status as creators.

An additional aspect of social identification is that pelete bite and fimate bite symbolize lineage.[4] A special primarily yellow madras cloth called *epe injiri*, which is ordinarily worn with cut patterns, belongs to the Ombo family, one of the major Kalabari House groups (Jones 1963). An outsider who dons it during ceremonial occasions invites public stripping. Nevertheless, cloth that identifies family or house membership is not always exclusively used by that family or house. Often a wealthy merchant wears exclusively imported cloth of a specific pattern from overseas, which became named after him, as was the case with Kieni, *Anabraba*, and *Membere* (the latter two also family-named textiles). He or his family reserved the textile, either with or without cut patterns, only for ceremonial occasions. Anybody, however, could buy it and wear it on general occasions or could pay to get patterns cut on it.

The successful trade and enterprise of Kalabari men with the outside world is necessary to obtain the cloth that will be transformed into pelete bite and fimate bite. However, the acquisition of injiri, although a valuable input into the culture, does not sufficiently explain the concept of cultural authentication. Creativity of the women is mandatory. Therefore, we propose that cultural authentication requires not merely the acquisition and borrowing of artifacts but also their transformation (at differing levels of adaptation) to make them a part of the receiving culture.

Using the example of imported cloth as utilized by the Kalabari, we offer the following levels of cultural authentication: (1) *selection*, the borrowing and using of cloth as it exists; (2) *characterization*, the "naming" of a cloth to make it more easily "visible"; (3) *incorporation,* the exclusive owning of a specific cloth by a particular group, such as an ethnic group or Kalabari family or house; and (4) *transformation,* the creating of a modified cloth that has an additional design cut on it. Cloth at this level of creative adaptation is most valued and prized.[5]

An illustration of these levels involving the use of imported cloth by the Kalabari to satisfy the needs of social identification follows: (1) The individual chooses and wears a cloth of modern trade for self-enhancement and for making a statement about positive self-acceptance. To do so is to "dress up." The "dressed-up" person is valued at a level different from that of the same person attired for work and production. (2) The person wears a cloth with a "name," heightening the sense of positive self-presentation. This cloth may be more expensive than others, but it is not necessarily so, and the cloth's higher price may not reflect higher quality but only greater exclusiveness. (3) The person wears a restricted cloth for ceremonial occasions, which shows that he or she belongs to a specific lineage—for example, that of the royal family or an important house. (4) The person wears a cloth indicating that he or she belongs not just to a restricted group but also to a distinctive culture. When a Kalabari person wears pelete bite and fimate bite, with their cut-thread and pulled-thread designs, he or she exemplifies cultural authentication at this level.

This openwork may be said to represent preeminently for all Kalabari the women's creative imposition of a refined aesthetic symbolism—as a link to the sublime experience—on one material prize from the men's commercial exploits. The cloth serves to communicate the harmony of the Kalabari world by linking cultural ethos, women, men, and artifacts. Thus, the sophistication of the patterns the Kalabari women design, despite the simple techniques employed, derives from the traditional cultural values as a whole, not idiosyncratic fancy or the prestige of foreign example.

Kalabari commitment to such authentication has led to such cynical sayings as, "What the people have decided, the gods accept" (Horton 1960b, 274). This last sentiment was applied to justify Kalabari adoption of the motor-driven boat to speed far away the "year-old bundle-of-sins-and-troubles" that they had extracted from the town through traditional New Year cleansing rites. And it could apply, just as easily, to any other artifact of foreign make—such as the textile import that is the base of the prestige Kalabari cloth—and ritualize it into a transformed object that belongs in their own world. This process of ritualization is carried out largely by the activity of women.

The extended significance of this analysis of an imported and reworked cloth in Kalabari culture is the suggestion that cultural authentication exists with other peoples and their cultural artifacts. As example, we present a brief note on African aesthetics. We propose that the degree of involvement in aesthetics varies for any artifact of African culture, whether indigenous or foreign. Adoption of artifacts may be appraised at the four levels indicated above: selection, characterization, incorporation, and transformation. Other artifacts can be used as examples, as in the case of the Yoruba *adire eleko* from western Nigeria. The artist uses imported printed cloth as a base and transforms it by overlaying a starch resist stencil design.

The progression of levels meshes sentiment and symbolism as well as social roles and artifacts. The depth of aesthetic response to objects in the environment increases as sentiment, symbolism, social roles, and artifacts become more integrated with the special uses of the objects.

We propose that the concept of cultural authentication may be useful for analyzing still other examples of borrowing and transformation in technology, aesthetics, institutions, values, and practices. The implication is that modernization can occur by acknowledging and encouraging the creative process of cultural authentication, for not only the Kalabari and other African people but other groups across the world.

TONYE VICTOR EREKOSIMA (1940–2008), PhD, native-born Kalabari, lived in the Igbo towns of Owerri and Umuahia, because his father was an educator and secondary-school principal, until Erekosima's university years in the United States. He was steeped in Kalabari cultural tradition, however, thanks to his family's routine travel to Buguma, his parents' birthplace, for holidays and significant events like funerals. Following his PhD, he served as Director, General Studies, Rivers State College of Education, and Director, Instructional Resources Center, University of Port Harcourt. He coedited *A Hundred Years of Buguma History in Kalabari Culture* (1984) and *Buguma 1984 Centenary Symposia on Kalabari* (1991).

JOANNE B. EICHER, PhD, is Regents Professor Emerita in the Department of Design, Housing, and Apparel at the University of Minnesota. She is coeditor of *The Anthropology of Dress and Fashion: A Reader*; coeditor of *The Visible Self: Global Perspectives on Dress, Culture, and Society*, 4th ed.; and editor in chief of the *Encyclopedia of World Dress and Fashion*.

NOTES

Adapted from Erekosima and Eicher (1981, 48–51, 87).

1. Eicher met one man who said he had cut pelete bite, but this seemed an exception. A few respondents indicated that they knew of some boys who had learned to cut cloth and sell it (Eicher 1980b).

2. We use the term *openwork* to describe the process of cutting threads from the cloth to make a new design. Irene Emery (1966, 247–248) distinguishes cutwork and drawn work as openwork embroidery in which two steps take place: (1) parts of the fabric are cut away or withdrawn, and (2) stitches are used to prevent fraying of cut edges and for embellishment. The Kalabari cloth has the first step alone. Therefore, we call it "cut-thread" and "pulled-thread" cloth, a subcategory of openwork.

3. The late King Charlie's nickname was Cane because he long supported his aging father King Abbi before the latter's death. Kieni, is a vernacular adaption of Cane.

4. When used to symbolize exclusive group identification, pelete bite and fimate bite serve more to delineate the modern form of Kalabari lineage: one based not on blood but on free bonding.

5. In the transition from mere European trade print into socially valued cloth of regular textiles exported continuously to West Africa, either the family selection of a particular design for recognition or the individual bestowing a name provides the crystallizing impetus for characterization. The indicators of textile acceptability as personal property within any community, arising at any time, appear unpredictable. Ruth Nielsen found in interviewing heads of three European firms exporting wax print textiles to West Africa that "classic designs" take years to produce, with "no fixed rules or directions on how to produce an exceptional African design." Sales records indicate the design's success, particularly when African consumers name it, whether nonAfricans see any connection with the design. She concluded that any design's popularity "is the result of the totality of the African culture, language, geography, and environmental conditions of the people" (reported in Eicher 1980a, 10, 11).

3

Cut-Thread Cloth Characteristics

Otto Charles Thieme

KALABARI TERMS *pelete bite* and *fimate bite* name one of their most beloved textiles, made from a process far more complex than at first inspection, requiring consideration of the madras pattern, the techniques of cutting, and underlying design concepts. Further considerations involve the age of the finished cloth, its use as clothing, and finally, imitations. The following comments covering the above points are based on close inspection of (1) the textiles in the 1980 premiere exhibition seen in figure 3.1, (2) hundreds of Eicher's slides taken in Nigeria, and (3) Eicher's field notes.

Madras used for cutting pelete bite is called *injiri*: a closely woven, plain-weave cotton of warp stripes, large-scale conventional plaids, and large-scale plaids with large square centerfields. Warp-striped fabrics are often used, such as *kieni* and *igodoye moru*, with patterns of thin stripes of red, yellow, dark blue, and white-and-dark-blue wefts. The fact that fabric nearly identical to the nineteenth-century igodoye moru cut by Osonta JohnBull (see fig. 3.2) still exists in Kalabari cloth markets attests to its continuing popularity and demand. Over time, the original color sequence remains constant, but the width of the stripes in the sequence may vary, as seen in examples of old and new kieni.

The two other types of cloth used to create pelete bite are plaids. The first type of pattern is a conventional plaid, either symmetrical or asymmetrical. Although available in many color combinations, the cloth most suitable for cutting is generally brilliant red, maroon, dark green, dark blue, or black, often highlighted with narrow lines of white or bright color. Closely related is a plaid

Top, Fig. 3.1. Pelete Bite Exhibit, Goldstein Museum of Design, 1982. Red ikata cloth pattern, center; blue and green golminji pattern, right. Photo: Robert Burningham.

Bottom, Fig. 3.2. JohnBull wrapper cut by Osonta JohnBull, mid-1800s.

pattern arrangement, subdivided into large square units using the full width of the fabric. The arrangement of the plaid pattern within each unit forms a large centerfield surrounded by four borders. Often a narrow band of white weft threads separates each of these large squares from the others, as shown in both textiles in figure 3.1. The Kalabari name many of these plaid fabrics. For example, when the plaid with a large square centerfield consists of a dark blue ground subdivided by a fine plaid of narrow white lines of equal width, the fabric is called *ikaki mgbe* (tortoise bones). When the white lines of the plaid are of unequal width and yellow is introduced into the borders, the cloth is called *amasiri* (tiger's paws).

Physical characteristics of the pelete bite aid the women in cutting the motifs and planning the allover design. First, the fabric must have a relatively high thread count, which allows threads to be removed without substantially weakening the cloth. Second, small-scale stripes, checks, and plaids are necessary, because removal of only a few groups of threads changes the overall grid pattern of the original fabric, allowing design by subtraction to be more noticeable. Third, the color itself and color sequence of the thread are important. Usually, a dark or intense color dominates the cloth. With the removal of lighter and brighter colors, the resulting dark-colored areas contrast with the remaining uncut areas, leaving a shadowy pattern, as seen in figure 3.3.

The cutting of pelete bite and fimate bite requires selecting appropriate cloth. The designs are made by removing the lightest and brightest colors from the fabrics, sometimes cutting only two threads—other times, areas up to one centimeter wide. For example, if the warp color sequence is six blue, two white, two blue, two white, and six blue, the white threads must be severed into segments without disturbing the blue and without cutting the weft. After the thread segments are removed, a gauzelike, same-colored shape remains. Great care must be taken not to sever threads that leave weak spots or even holes. On both pelete bite and fimate bite, cutting ceases about half a centimeter from the selvedge of the cloth, thus preserving its structural soundness.

The cutting of the cloth directly relates to the underlying design conceptualizations of the pelete bite artists. Logic may suggest cutting one motif at a time and carefully pulling threads before proceeding to another. One artist, Wariba Kula, showed Eicher a piece employing this method. In other cases, however, the entire design may be fully conceived before cutting begins. For example, another artist, Amonia Akoko, cut all the threads she thought necessary to form the pattern but did not simultaneously remove them. When Eicher visited her, she had begun work to remove them, but half of her thirteen-foot piece still

Fig. 3.3. Cloth pattern called ikaki mgbe by Amonia Akoko: cut pattern at top and left. 1981.

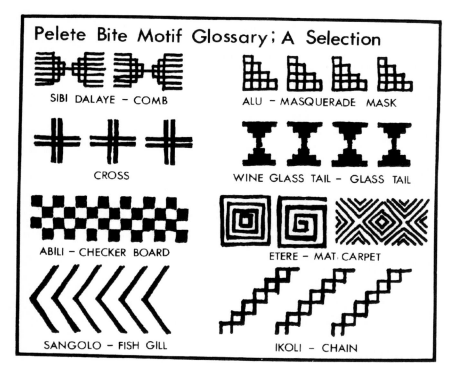

Fig. 3.4. Drawing of Pelete bite motifs. Otto Charles Thieme.

had cuts ready for pulling threads. She agreed to sell the piece, understanding it would be used to show her method.

The shapes of most motifs depend on the geometric grids of the cloth because the stripes and plaids guide the cutting. Curved motifs that ignore this guide demand special design and cutting skills, as in the case of the igodoye moru cloth cut by Osonta JohnBull shown in figure 3.2. This curvilinear motif, cut like a snake, demanded a high degree of design proficiency. Its many graceful curves are formed by removing the red and white warp threads from small rectangular areas of the igodoye moru stripes. A glossary displays some of the common motifs found on pelete bite (see fig. 3.4).

The removal of the lighter colored threads is a basic component of the pelete bite design conceptualization. This concept is so ingrained that when Eicher asked one Kalabari woman to cut pelete bite on a plaid dominated by beige, not the usual dark colors, the woman pointed out that the cloth, named "Johnny Walker," was unsuitable. Proving her point, the woman cut and removed segments of the beige threads, leaving no noticeable change in the plaid pattern. Had she cut and removed the maroon threads, she would have disturbed the dark grid, leaving only the beige ground.

Dates are difficult to assign to cut-thread cloth for several reasons. First, few pelete bite have specific dates ascribed to them by the Kalabari. Although Osonta JohnBull was credited as the originator of a piece in the 1800s, the year of the cutting was not remembered. Second, highly prized cut cloth is handed down through generations. While a cloth may have a detailed history of family ownership, a specific date of cutting and the artist's name are often missing. Third, some cloth colors and patterns have become classics. Their constant demand and continuous supply obliterate possible dating through a fabric's appearance or disappearance from the market. Last, imported, woven cloth became barred from Nigeria to protect its developing textile industry, but it continued appearing on the black market. People also keep older cloth in family cloth boxes; one man told Eicher he kept one for twenty-five years before having it cut.

Both men and women wear pelete bite and fimate bite wrappers. The usual Kalabari man's wrapper is reportedly about two yards. A woman's wrapper set generally has two parts: an "up" wrapper, about a two-yard length, wrapped from waist to midtorso; and the "down" wrapper, from waist to ankle (sometimes a full-width piece lengthened with an additional piece sewn across the top, depending on the wearer's height), covered by the "up" wrapper.

Woven imitations of pelete bite and fimate bite appear in Kalabari markets. With designs copying traditional cut cloth, the imitations are not easily recognized; close inspection, however, reveals the loom-controlled techniques that produced it. Fimate bite imitations are easiest to recognize; the open areas imitate the area of withdrawn weft threads obtained during weaving by placing wide gaps between groups of weft threads. Woven imitations of pelete bite are more difficult to discern. This effect is achieved with both weft and warp threads woven in some areas and others with weft threads that float freely along the back in other areas. When these floats are snipped off, only minute examination of the cloth reveals the lack of tiny irregularities made by the pelete bite artist.

OTTO CHARLES THIEME (1943–1996), MA, formerly curator, Cincinnati Art Museum, helped mount the 1980 pelete bite exhibit in the Goldstein Museum of Design. As my graduate research assistant, he had become fascinated with pelete bite and was first to recognize that the light or bright threads were always those being cut to make pelete bite designs. Publications include *Simply Stunning: 200 years of Fashion from the Cincinnati Art Museum* (1988) and *Avant Garde by the Yard: Cutting Edge Textile Design, 1880–1930* (1996).

NOTES

Adapted from Thieme (1982).

4

"Our Great Mother . . . Tied This Cloth"

Pelete Bite Cloth, Women, and Kalabari Identity

Elisha P. Renne

"Our women are very fanciful."
—COMMENT OF A KALABARI MAN

INTRODUCTION

In the praise song for the mythical Kalabari heroine Owamekaso, singers refer to her magical cloth, decorated with the variegated images of all the *oru nama*, children of the *oru* (mythic heroes and heroines; Horton 1965, 32). Each oru nama, which include most common reptiles and amphibians in the home of the Kalabari people, are referred to in subsequent verses of this praise song, for example:

> The fearfulness of the tortoise in your cloth, is in your cloth, big woman,
> Our great mother, the persistent one, tied this cloth.
> The fearfulness of the python in your cloth, is in your cloth, big woman,
> Our great mother, the persistent one, tied this cloth (Horton 1965, 32).

The oru nama animals mentioned in this song—tortoises and pythons, among others, are also depicted or referred to in the patterned Kalabari cloth known as *pelete bite*, as shown in and discussed in the previous chapter. While it is unknown precisely what type of cloth this magical cloth was, the song suggests two themes that will be explored in this chapter.[1] First, the connection of Kalabari women's creativity with cloth production will be examined. Owamekaso, the leader of the village heroes/heroines, was said to have introduced trade to the Kalabari people and to have performed many other miraculous "feats with the aid of a magic cloth" (Horton 1965, 32). In mythic traditions elsewhere, protagonists are armed with other magical objects. For example, Monkey in the Chinese classic *The Journey to the West* has a gold-tipped iron rod as an aid. Why is cloth so important for a mythic Kalabari heroine? And how is this power to perform "miraculous feats" related to the heroine, Owamekaso, being hailed as "Our Great Mother"? Used in this context, this phrase is an honorific title, but it may also refer to the value placed on motherhood in Kalabari society and the vital connections between mothers and their children. Oru nama, literally "children of the mythic hero/ines," are depicted on Owamekaso's magic cloth as well as on the pelete bite cloths that Kalabari women produce and name. What is it about cloth and the tendency for it to be named that makes it a particularly appropriate object for making these kinship connections?

Second, in this song, Owamekaso is called "the persistent one," perhaps referring to women's continuation of practices and materials that support the cultural identity of the Kalabari people. Indeed, while Kalabari women are considered to be the creators and primary producers of pelete bite cloth, it is also senior women of Kalabari households who are the custodians of boxes of these cloths and other valuables used in family funerals (Eicher and Erekosima 1987). Why is it that Kalabari women are the collectors and conservators of cloth, and why is it that cloth is considered a fitting entity to maintain a Kalabari cultural identity through time?

In discussing these two themes, I focus on pelete bite, an object uniquely associated with the Kalabari. Little had been known about this cloth outside of the Niger delta area in southern Nigeria. One photograph, however, published by P. Amaury Talbot, a British colonial administrator, shows a Kalabari woman wearing a pelete wrapper (Talbot [1932] 1967, 300), but has no information about the cloth or its motifs. Thus, at the time of Joanne Eicher's 1966 visit to Buguma, nothing had been published about pelete bite. It was people's constant reference to this special cloth, of which, as she recalls, she knew virtually nothing, and the consequent gift from the Erekosimas that prompted her interest in researching it: "I was continually shown a particular cloth and was told, 'Madam, this is our own cloth.' I thought it was madras and in the book, *Nigerian Handcrafted Textiles* (Eicher 1976), I called it 'Buguma cloth.' . . . When leaving they asked me to choose a cloth I liked. I chose something with bright, varied colors, I didn't know the name. Later, they sent me the pelete bite cloth, *ikaki mgbe* [see fig. 2.5] . . . I still have it" (Eicher 2000).

It was not until March 1980 when she returned to Buguma that she was able to pursue research on pelete bite cloth, interviewing women pelete bite artists on designs, techniques used, and their training. She also commissioned and purchased several pelete bite cloths for her collection, some of which were displayed in the 1982 Goldstein Galley exhibit, "Pelete Bite: Kalabari Cut-Thread Cloth" (Eicher and Erekosima with Thieme 1982), and which were shown in the Cloth Is the Center of the World exhibit in 2001. Thus, her "discovery" of and subsequent research on this cloth coincided with her development as an African textile scholar and woman collector, a point to which I will return at this essay's conclusion.

MYTHIC HEROINES, WOMEN'S CREATIVITY, AND KALABARI GENDER RELATIONS

The mythic heroine Owamekaso is said to have introduced trade, including the political trading organizations known as *wari* or *polo*, to the Kalabari people (Horton 1969b). The city-state of Owome (or New Calabar) became renowned for its trade with Europe (Horton 1960a, 2). Mythic heroine Ekineba is said to have introduced an additional innovation to Kalabari society, the dancing and drumming of the Ekine Society masquerades (Horton 1975). While the Ekine Society is restricted to men and only men dance the masquerades, as Erekosima and Eicher (1981, 49) have noted, "In deference to the female realm of inspiration and creativity, . . . Ekineba, a goddess and patroness who is believed to be the originator of aesthetic skills . . . [it is] women [who] guard the culture's creative impulse." Thus, myths that celebrate the creativity of women deities—who introduced many innovations to Kalabari society associated with other realms (whether they be spiritual or overseas)—persist despite changes in Kalabari traditional religious beliefs. As the historian E. J. Alagoa has observed, "To reinforce the strength of the feminine image in the religious thought of Niger Delta communities, we note that many groups worshipped or still venerate female guardian deities or national gods. . . . Among the Kalabari of the Eastern Delta with their almost total change to a masculine idea of the Supreme Being, the creation of the political system was still ascribed to the goddess Awomekaso" (Alagoa n.d., 2).[2]

This recognition (and celebration) of the creativity of women is reflected in another aspect of Kalabari social life; in particular, in women's role as mothers, critical in perpetuating the family group and its name. The elaborate rituals performed for new mothers (Daly 1984a; Iyalla 1968) are testimony to the importance of women and their childbearing ability. As in other West African societies, wealth is constituted, in part, by having many people in a family (Guyer 1995). This need for children and the associated value attributed to women's childbearing supports a set of complementary gender roles in Kalabari society, in which men are seen as producers of wealth through corporate trading, and women are seen as reproducers of wealth through their fertility. This complementarity is evident in distinctive dress styles for men and women, as when women's dress and demeanor are said to be "staid and refined," as opposed to men's, which is described as "dashing" (see chap. 2). Similarly, women and men have distinctive roles to play in the funeral performances, as described in later chapters. Associated with these complementary roles is the idea of unity, of women and men coming together for the mutual benefit of society. This may also be seen in women's production of pelete bite cloths used not only by family members accompanying a corpse from the mortuary to the house during funeral observances but also by Ekine Society members as face cloths in their exclusively male masquerade performances (Renne and Eicher 1994). Thus, while the Ekine Society is restricted to men, who perform their masquerades, playing men, women, and their children in these dances, women who largely control the production of pelete bite cloth make reference to the names and designs of particular water and nature spirits depicted in Ekine Society masquerades.[3]

"TORTOISE BONES," CLOTH, THE TORTOISE MASQUERADE, AND CHILDREN

This complementarity may be seen, for example, in portrayals of the nature-spirit *Ikaki* (Tortoise), which the Kalabari sometimes call the "Old Man of the Forest" and Horton (1967, 226) refers to as "a kind of supernatural super-tortoise." Ikaki is featured both in an Ekine masquerade named in his honor and in a particular pelete bite cloth, such as the one given to Joanne Eicher in 1966. This pelete bite cloth is called ikaki mgbe ("tortoise bones"), one of the most popular madras (injiri) cloths used for cutting pelete bite designs (see fig. 3.3). Each two-yard length consists of two distinctive indigo and white finely checked centerfield panels, surrounded by broad blue bands. It is the foundational checked-and-striped design that Kalabari women say inspires and makes possible the pelete bite designs that may be cut (Eicher and Erekosima with Thieme 1982, 15). That this particular cloth was named ikaki mgbe was probably because when selected white threads are cut and pulled, the resulting overall design resembles the scales of a tortoise's shell. The specific named patterns cut in her cloth included *sangolo* (fish gills), *ikoli* (chain), and *alu* (masquerade triangle), referring to the water and to nature spirits (*owuamabo*), of which Ikaki (Tortoise) is one (Horton 1967, 226).[4]

It should also be recalled that Tortoise was one of the fearful oru nama portrayed in the mythic heroine Owamekaso's cloth. Aronson (1980b, 65) refers to the fact that Ikaki-Tortoise "to the Rivers people is a very wise and cunning creature" whose image is depicted on cloths "often associated with kings, chiefs, and the priestly class." While Aronson is referring to the depiction of ikaki motif in Akwete cloths, handwoven by Igbo women to the north, she notes that ikaki is "a Rivers term for tortoise," suggesting that Igbo weavers produced these cloths for the Kalabari and other delta groups. She also proposes that these Akwete ikaki cloths were preceded by earlier cloths, sometimes called *ikaki bite*, and were woven by Ijebu Yoruba weavers. These cloths were so valuable to Kalabari patrons that they commissioned copies of the cloth from Akwete weavers when the Yoruba cloths became difficult to obtain. As Aronson (1980b, 66) observes, "It is conceivable that ikaki was at one time extremely important to the Rivers people."[5]

Tortoise is a memorable character in Kalabari masquerades performed by the Ekine Society. With his insatiable greed and great cunning, Tortoise attempts to acquire everything he can and trick all those with whom he comes into contact. However, his excesses are his downfall. This theme is shown quite literally in the masquerade story that has him climbing up a palm nut tree and greedily sucking palm nuts as one of his sons, the feckless Nimiaa Poku, playfully begins to cut the tree down. When Tortoise sees this, he throws a cutlass at his son but instead hits his favorite son, the comely Kalagidi, whom he thinks he has killed. Meanwhile, his wife, Aboita, and her favorite son, Nimiaa Poku, dance together, rejoicing at Tortoise's misfortune. After Kalagidi is revived, Tortoise climbs down from the palm tree, lamenting, "Ye, a bad wife kills a man, a bad wife kills a man, I am finished-o, Kalagidi" (Horton 1967, 235).

THE IMPORTANCE OF CHILDREN AND CLOTH

Tortoise's wife, Aboita, is unflatteringly portrayed by Ekine masqueraders as a foolish flirt who favors her equally foolish son, Nimiaa Poku, who continually undermines his father's efforts. In this Ekine Society masquerade, men assert their own ties to sensible children and women's favoring foolish ones, yet what this masquerade story suggests above all is the vital importance of children to both men and women.[6] Women's power would seem to derive from their ability to bear these children who will perpetuate Kalabari society. Similarly, women's production of pelete bite cloths, represented with names and symbols relating to the Kalabari people's cultural past, also confers them with a certain "cultural capital" (Bourdieu 1977, 184) as stories about the mythical heroines such as Owamekaso and Ekineba suggest. Furthermore, cloth in general, because of its intimate contact with the human body (Schneider and Weiner 1986, 178),

Fig. 4.1. Pelete bite entirely covers the bed in family funeral room (biokiri) enhanced with head tie of pelete bite, 1988.

and pelete bite cloth in particular, with its specific named patterning referring to Kalabari mythology, lend to the visual identification of individuals as Kalabari. As such, these cloths are critically important in several life-stage events, such as those marking birth and death. For example, during Kalabari funerals (see chap. 18 and 19), the corpses will be displayed on beds in a series of rooms in the house of the deceased that have been elaborately decorated by women specialists (*ededapu*). The second decorated funeral room, known as the *biokiri* or "family room," may have the bed entirely covered with pelete bite cloths, as seen in figure 4.1.

However, according to one informant, "only the funeral beds of the very wealthiest women (usually elderly), who have had time to accumulate enough cloths, are decorated with pelete bite" (Renne 1985, 112). Similarly, during the Buguma Centenary celebrated in 1984, the first child born during the year was honored and swathed in a pelete bite cloth (shown in fig. 4.2). Women's creative power, as the song about Owamekaso and her magical cloth suggests, is situated in the "miraculous feat" of bearing children and in their innovative use of objects and actions that constitute Kalabari cultural identity.

Fig. 4.2. The firstborn child of the Buguma Centenary year, wrapped in pelete bite, officially recognized at the Centenary Awards Ceremony, February 1985. Photo: Elisha P. Renne.

CONSERVING KALABARI IDENTITY IN A GLOBAL UNIVERSE: WOMEN CLOTH PRODUCERS AND COLLECTORS

Indeed, the mythical heroine Owamekaso is said to have introduced trade that has allowed Kalabari women to obtain the madras cloth, steel needles, and knives that they needed to create pelete bite cloth. Thus, ironically, the Kalabari people's participation in the global economy (they have had trade relations with European traders since the fifteenth century; Alagoa 1972) served to strengthen their reproduction of a particular Kalabari identity, reflected in the production of a type of cloth unique to them. The antiquity and explanation of how pelete bite cloth came to be produced by Kalabari women is unknown. However, one cloth documented as having been made by Osonta (see fig. 3.2), one of John-Bull's wives, whom he married in about 1860, has been dated to sometime after that and before her death in 1892 (Eicher and Erekosima with Thieme 1982, 5). Women continue to produce hand-cut pelete bite cloths, even as such cloth

Fig. 4.3. Madam Amonia Akoko (left), with three apprentices, Igbiki Idere, Aliaba Clark, and Ebenbon Wokoma. This unanticipated encounter marks the first time that Joanne Eicher met the pelete bite artist and oru kuro specialist, who subsequently provided the Eicher collection with several fine pelete bite examples. Buguma, 1980.

designs have been copied and are now called "machine-cut" or "English-cut" by the Kalabari (Eicher and Erekosima with Thieme 1982, 10).

One such woman, Amonia Akoko, who continues the hand-cut tradition, is not only an extraordinary pelete bite artist and teacher but also a traditional religious specialist, preserving ideas about Kalabari spiritual beliefs as well. As such, she is a powerful and persistent conservator of Kalabari heritage. It was in March 1980, when Joanne Eicher returned to southern Nigeria to conduct research on pelete bite and its production, that she first met Amonia Akoko. This trip was extremely productive for, as Eicher described it, "Fieldwork in Kalabari was sort of magical—[I was] just turning the corner and there Amonia Akoko was, cutting pelete bite" (Eicher 2000).

Amonia, a woman in her forties, was seated next to three of her apprentices (fig. 4.3), who were learning to cut pelete bite cloth by pulling threads from cloths with patterns that Amonia had cut (Eicher and Erekosima with Thieme

1982, 10). Amonia herself had learned to cut pelete bite cloth from her grandmother, some of whose cloths she still kept (Eicher 1980b, 154).

Eicher and Amonia became immediate friends, perhaps because of their shared interest in pelete bite cloth and Kalabari culture. In 1981, when Eicher returned to Buguma, she interviewed Amonia about her work and commissioned several cloths from her, including an *amasiri pelete bite* cloth that was featured on the cover of the 1982 Goldstein Gallery exhibition catalog, *Pelete Bite: Kalabari Cut-Thread Cloth* (Eicher and Erekosima with Thieme 1982). Amonia Akoko estimated that it took three months to cut and pull threads for a complete eight yards of amasiri cloth. While she teaches both women who are relatives and those who are not, nonrelatives are charged higher apprentice fees. Her teaching technique consists of having apprentices learn simple patterns such as "cross" first and then more difficult patterns later. As is the case in apprenticeship elsewhere in Nigeria, the cloths these students make are sold and the profits are kept by the teacher, Amonia (Eicher 1980b).

The cloths that come out of her workshop are extraordinary in the breadth of designs used, the inventiveness of their depiction and placement, and the precision of cutting. One such cloth, a predominantly red cotton madras cloth with dark blue and white warp and weft striping known as *ikata*, displayed in the 1982 exhibit, is a virtuoso work with over seven different motifs incorporated into its design, as figure 4.4 shows.[7]

The cloth has been blocked off into design fields, each of which is cut with motifs including "glass *etemi*" (wineglass stem), alu (masquerade triangles), *abili* (checkerboard), *okoloba igila* (broken plate), sangolo (fish gills), *etere* (mat), and cross (Eicher and Erekosima with Thieme 1982; Renne 1985). While some pelete bite artists cut each design area and then remove the threads, Amonia cuts the designs for the entire cloth before removing the threads. For her, the entire piece is conceptualized before cutting commences. As Joanne Eicher observed, "Being an artist was the center of her life" (Eicher 2000).

Amonia's creativity is perhaps related to another important aspect of her life, namely, her participation in traditional Kalabari religious activities. In this sense Amonia's artistic and religious interests overlap as she portrays references to water spirits in the pelete bite cloths that she cuts and in the spirit-possession dances she performs.[8] The Kalabari water-spirit possession cult in which she is an adept is known as *oru kuro ereme*, literally, "spirit carrying women." This form of possession—by local nature spirits (oru)—is almost exclusively the domain of women. While other forms of Kalabari spirit possession associated with mythical or ancestral beings (conducted largely by men) are in decline

Fig. 4.4. Ikata, the predominantly red cotton madras (injiri) with dark blue and white warp and weft striping, cut by Amonia Akoko. Each blocked-off design field has a distinctive motif: glass etemi (wineglass stem), alu (masquerade triangles), abili (checkerboard), okoloba igila (broken plate), sangolo (fish gills), etere (mat), and cross. Eicher Reserved Collection. Photo: Petronella J. Ystma, 2001.

(Horton 1969a, 29), oru kuro possession is very popular and may be increasing. During spirit-possession sessions, the adept, having been consulted by a client wishing to contact a water spirit and after making the proper sacrifices, will be possessed by male water spirits, who speak and dance through her.

In March 1985, Amonia performed an oru kuro dance at the request of a woman whose daughter had recently returned to Nigeria having just received a degree at a British university. The dance, which I was able to attend, took place at night at Amonia's shrine in Abalama, to the immediate northwest of Buguma. The dance ground was festooned with multicolored triangular flags, and as people (mainly women) began to congregate, drummers began playing on a similarly decorated drum. Eventually, Amonia emerged from the spirit shrine house and entered the adjoining dance ground, wearing dress (e.g., real India madras and an Akwete ikaki-style cloth seen in fig. 4.5) associated with water spirits.[9] She danced and then retired to the shrine house several times.

Each time she emerged she was wearing a different configuration of cloths: white lace material in one appearance and red and white *injiri pelete bite*, cut with okoloba igila, abili and etere designs, in another, as seen in figure 4.6.

This oru kuro performance was remarkable, not only because of the distinctive use of particular cloths but also because of Amonia's different portrayals. At times, she was aggressive, at others, gentle, and yet at other times, she was flirtatious. Because these oru kuro possession performances are not restricted to specific dances and traditional presentations, there is a considerable range of creative possibilities open to possessed women. Indeed, Horton (1969a, 43) has argued that this lack of restrictions on the more common minor water spirits depicted in women's spirit possession (as compared with men's more formal avenues for possession) allows for creative innovation. Similarly, one might argue that the ubiquity of cloth in everyday life provides Kalabari women with a medium for the innovative, "fanciful" creativity displayed by pelete bite artists and the ededapu funeral bed designers, one not open to Kalabari male artists who follow certain conventions in their carving of masquerade masks (Horton 1965) and ancestral figures (Barley 1988). Perhaps it is because cloth is viewed by Western researchers as being a less formal component of Kalabari traditional practices (such as masquerade performance and ancestor worship) that until the 1980s, when Eicher and Erekosima began to investigate pelete bite cloth production and use, little had been written about Kalabari women's artistic production and performances. This included women's production of pelete bite cloth, their decoration of funeral rooms and beds with an abundance of cloth, or the use of cloth in marking the respective stages of women's development and debut into motherhood. While Kalabari's women's reproduction—of children and of rituals surrounding their birth, of pelete bite cloth designs, and of Kalabari traditional religious beliefs through oru kuro dances—may be viewed as marginal activities by Western researchers when compared with Kalabari men's political and economic prominence, they are equally critical to the perpetuation of Kalabari society and cultural identity (Guyer 1995, 87). Like the mythical heroine Owamekaso, Kalabari women's "persistence" and "fanciful" creativity complements the contributions of Kalabari men's masquerade performances and sculptures. This gendered complementarity of cultural reproduction and artistic production has parallels in art collected by Kalabari as well as by Western men and women, an issue considered in the following section.

WOMEN, CLOTH, AND COLLECTING

Perhaps it took a woman—Joanne Eicher—to appreciate the artistic contributions of Kalabari women.[10] As women researchers discovered elsewhere (Weiner 1976), women often had their own artistic traditions that complemented men's,

Fig. 4.5.
Amonia Akoko at an oru kuro dance. Wearing injiri and ikata cloth, March 1985, Juju Abalama. Photo: Elisha P. Renne.

Fig. 4.6.
Amonia Akoko at an oru kuro dance wearing pelete bite cloth, March 1985, Juju Abalama. Photo: Elisha P. Renne.

but because researchers were predominantly male, these traditions were often overlooked. At times, this was because male researchers could not participate or were denied access to information and at other times because of their own interests.[11] Sometimes, women's artistic abilities were not seen as important, discounted by men and a male-dominated ideology that cast women as dependent reproducers, rather than as creative producers (Ortner 1974).

The media with which women and men worked—as well as whether their productions were considered functional craft or nonfunctional art—have also affected whether women's artistic endeavors have been recognized.[12] For example, collectors recognized African ivory sculptures (Ben-Amos 1995, 37) as art from the sixteenth century on. However, with a few exceptions, it was not until 1972 when Roy Sieber (1972) organized the show "African Textiles and Decorative Arts" at the Museum of Modern Art that the works of women textile artists (as well as men) came to be taken seriously and were widely displayed in museums and galleries. Nonetheless, cloth continues to be relegated to the category of "decorative arts" in Western art history surveys and is associated with the domestic sphere and women.[13] It is hard to say how the cultural construction of this categorization began. Did textile art come to be marginalized in the Western commercial art world because of its association with manufacture and domesticity, or was it marginalized because of its association with women?

The tendency to associate textile arts with women carries over into the activity of collecting itself, which, in the United States, is gendered in several senses. The act of amassing a collection itself has historically been considered a masculine activity, requiring the characteristics ideologically attributed to men—competitiveness, acquisitiveness, and serious professionalism. Women might collect, but it was interpreted through the lens of dominant gender ideology. That is, women's collecting was said to be done nonprofessionally, as a hobby without serious intent, and as part of their everyday domestic activities as consumers (Belk and Wallendorf 1997, 9). While this gendered characterization of collecting has changed with the feminist movement's questioning of various unexamined assumptions about the roles of men and women in American society in the 1960s and 1970s, and with women's increased access to income-generating employment, gendered associations with particular types of objects collected continues. For example, in a study of 192 American collectors, "the categories in which there are more women than men collectors include animal replicas, housewares (dishes, silverware, utensils), and jewelry. In contrast, more men collect antiques, books, automobiles, sports-related objects, and tattoos" (Belk and Wallendorf 1997, 12).

The gendered configuration of collecting in the United States should not be taken as the baseline of collecting elsewhere in the world, nor does the phenomenon of the collection exist universally (Stewart 1984). However, in the case of textiles, both American and Kalabari women share this particular interest. While there are many differences in midwestern US and Kalabari social life, there are certain similarities in the experiences of some American and Kalabari women, such as Eicher and Amonia, that help to explain their interest in collecting cloth.

COLLECTING CLOTH AND THE EICHER COLLECTION

Amonia learned to cut pelete bite cloth from her grandmother and kept several of her grandmother's cloths. In the Kalabari area, accumulations of cloth are kept in large boxes that are kept in storerooms and under beds, their contents only removed when a special event requires their use. Thus, when I was cataloging the different cloth types and patterns used in pelete bite cloth in 1985, I sometimes waited for some time as the women pored through their cloth boxes, looking for a particular cloth to show me (Renne 1985). While I did not see Amonia's cloth boxes or their contents, the varied and extensive collection of cloth that she wore during the oru kuro ceremony suggests that she owned and kept many cloths.

Eicher also has a family background associated with cloth. Both her mother and maternal grandmother were seamstresses and loved cloth. "My childhood was spent looking through pattern books," she observed. While Eicher never sewed, she did learn to weave in high school, and her mother also wove. In an interview with Eicher, she says, "My mother was a marvelous weaver! She was the kind of person who was so creative, she couldn't do production work. She also loved buying drapery material and was an innovative clothing designer. You know, I grew up when they went to proms, my mother could just make me prom dresses by looking at a picture, she would know how to cut the pattern" (Eicher 2000).

Perhaps it was growing up with this background in textile arts that led Eicher to an appreciation of Nigerian textiles, which she began to purchase when she first moved to Nigeria. In the 1978 Goldstein Gallery catalog that accompanied the exhibit "West African Art and Textiles" she wrote, "The textiles [in my collection] were collected primarily from 1963 to 1966 when I was resident in Enugu, Nigeria and traveled extensively throughout the country. Many fabrics were purchased from traders who came to my door; some were bought in local markets as I traveled in Lagos, Ibadan, Bida, Kano, Onitsha, Port Harcourt, and Calabar. Others were purchased directly from craftsmen in Abeokuta, Akwete, Ijebu-Ode, and Oyo or were gifts from friends (Eicher in Smith and Eicher 1982).

While these cloths were initially purchased for use in her home and for clothing, her cloth acquisitions shifted as she learned more about them. Stewart (1984, 166) has noted the serial nature of collecting: "This seriality provides a means for defining or classifying the collection and the collector's life history." As Eicher's career as a textile and clothing scholar developed, her collecting began to focus on textiles used by the Kalabari people. This included pelete bite cloths as well as Akwete cloths (Aronson 2001), wax-print commemorative cloths (Spencer 2001), and a range of indigo resist-dyed textiles (Wolff 2001).

When collecting pelete bite cloths in southern Nigeria, Eicher not only paid special attention to the techniques and motifs used by Kalabari women but also recorded information on each woman's training and the circumstances surrounding the making of certain cloths. Thus, the names of the women artists who cut the particular pelete bite cloths in her collection are often documented along with a brief summary of their histories. The uniqueness of these cloths is also seen in their named patterning, reflecting the historical and physical environment in which they are made.

In her own way, Eicher has contributed to the continuity of Kalabari identity through her research on and collection of pelete bite cloth. Her close relationship with the Erekosima family has been critical to her understanding of the importance of cloth in Kalabari society; her role as an honorary "daughter" of the house underscores the ways that women, through their collection of cloth, foster extended social and international relations.

CONCLUSION

When Eicher first visited Buguma, she was repeatedly told that pelete bite was "our cloth," the cloth most closely associated with the cultural identity of the Kalabari people. Perhaps it is not coincidental that the first pelete bite cloth she acquired was an ikaki mgbe cloth given to her by the Erekosima family. As discussed earlier, Ikaki-Tortoise was probably extremely important to the Kalabari people (Aronson 1980b, 66). Precisely why ikaki was so important to the Kalabari, and particularly to "kings, chiefs, and the priestly class" as well as certain wari-houses, is suggested by the following story cited by Talbot ([1932] 1967) about Ikaki-Tortoise. In this story, recounted by Mrs. A. K. B. Manuel, the wife of the Native court clerk at Degema, the appearance of "jujus" or nature spirits in the delta was attributed to the devices of Ikaki-Tortoise after having had a quarrel with the Kalabari goddess Tamuno. According to Mrs. Manuel,

"Now one time, at the beginning of the world, Tamuno called Tortoise and several other people to make farm for her. Also she told Tortoise to send a he-goat to look after the vegetables already planted—bidding him choose a goat which would be quick and bear plenty of kids for her" (Talbot [1932] 1967, 63–65).

Tortoise replied in anger, asking the goddess Tamuno to accomplish an equally impossible feat (as in, asking for a he-goat that would bear many kids). She responded by making him work on her plantation without feeding him for several days. Angry and hungry and frustrated, Tortoise went to the bush and cut several sticks. After decoratively carving them, he gave each a name for the various "jujus," spirits that were said to reside within each of the sticks. Shortly after, a woman sent by Tamuno passed by the spirits sticks, for which Tortoise demanded a sacrifice since "no woman may pass by these jujus!" (Talbot 1967, 64).[14] When the woman consulted Tamuno, the goddess instructed her to make the sacrifices since "even the goddess could not stop juju, now it had come. So they took yams and fish and gave to Tortoise, who cooked these and set them out before the carved sticks, saying he was now making good the wrong done by the woman. That is how jujus first came to earth—because Tortoise was angry with Tamuno and wished to set up another power beside her" (Talbot 1967, 65).

This story suggests the ways ideas about mythical deities and nature spirits have been fundamental to the cultural construction of gender relations and domains in Kalabari society. It is not surprising that the Kalabari men's Ekine Society should honor Ikaki-Tortoise with a masquerade-play in his name, as it was Tortoise who introduced a form of spirit worship that challenged the power of women, represented by the goddess Tamuno. This story may also explain the importance of the depiction of Ikaki-Tortoise in Akwete and cloths associated with male kings, chiefs, and priests. Yet it is also necessary to recognize the importance of myths about goddesses such as Tamuno whose power Tortoise sought to circumscribe as well as of the work of Kalabari women who—as creators of life and of pelete bite cloth—contribute to the power of these men but also who have their own domain of dominance. Thus, while the pelete bite cloth known as ikaki mgbe ("tortoise bones") refers to the exploits of Tortoise, it may also be seen as representing the creative power of Kalabari women who have the ability to depict his image in cloth. It is through the research of Eicher, her students, and Erekosima, with their focus on cloth and dress, that the complementarity of women's and men's respective powers in perpetuating Kalabari identity and society may be more clearly seen.

ELISHA P. RENNE, PhD, conducted fieldwork in Buguma for her University of Minnesota MA: *Pelete Bite: Motifs and Meaning* (1985). Eicher originally published that the finely woven madras used for pelete bite was commercially produced, but as a weaver, Renne identified the madras selvages as being handwoven. She continued her research in southwestern Nigeria for her PhD at NYU. Publications include *Cloth That Does Not Die: The Meaning of Cloth in Bunu Social Life* (1995), *Yoruba Religious Textiles* (2005), *Veiling in Africa* (2013), and *Veils, Turbans, and Islamic Reform in Northern Nigeria* (2018).

NOTES

Adapted from Renne (2001).

1. According to some myths, her cloth is said to be a "print" trade cloth (Eicher 1993, 253). According to Samuel Bob Manuel, cited in Talbot ([1932] 1967, 74), "The name of the cloth is *okpokpointa* (or juju cloth as foreigners call it)."

2. Also spelled "Owamekaso."

3. Although few young men were mentioned as having cut *pelete bite* briefly in order to pay school fees (Eicher 1980b), it is only women who regularly produce this cloth. However, while women control this aspect of cloth production, Ekine Society members have historically had trade access to other types of indigo resist-dyed ritual cloths used by them. They are also depicted in ancestral family screens (Barley 1988; Horton 1960a).

4. "*Ikaki mgbe* cloths characteristically displayed at least one of the three most common geometric motifs cut by *pelete bite* artists—namely, *etere* (matting), *abili* (checkerboard squares), and *alu* (masquerade triangle). The two most common motifs cut on these cloths were *abili* and *etere* or *abili* and *sangolo*" (Renne 1985, 50).

5. For example, one Kalabari royal family kept an Ijebu Yoruba cloth that they called *ikaki bite* as a family emblem (Eicher and Erekosima 1995, 149), a name that literally means "tortoise cloth."

6. *Egwa* and *iya* forms of bridewealth payments to the bride's family, the former is small and less prestigious, giving the husband conjugal rights; the children belong to both the mother and father's families. With the large *iya* type bridewealth payment, the husband obtains conjugal rights and the child belongs exclusively to his lineage (Talbot 1967, 437–438). More recently, *egwa* payments are now more common, although Christian weddings may also be performed that confer family affiliation of the children with the husband's family (Michelman and Erekosima 1992, 169).

7. This cloth also is stamped in yellow ink with the trademark INTORICA, a mark used by an Indian textile manufacturer that derives from the phrase, "India to Africa" (Evenson 1991, 20).

8. This situation is similar to Horton's (1963) point about the Ekine Society, whose members have both religious and artistic concerns.

9. Horton (1969a, 18) notes that this combination of cloth is also used by the male priest of the spirit, "Head-of-the-Canoe-Prow," who is possessed during the Fenibaso festival.

10. Eicher was instrumental in documenting Kalabari women's textile artists, and she encouraged her graduate students, who researched other aspects of Kalabari women's art including ritual (Daly 1984a, 1987), India-Kalabari madras trade (Evenson 1991), Kalabari women's societies (Michelman 1987, 1992), and *pelete bite* motifs (Renne 1985).

11. Robin Horton's extraordinary work (e.g., 1960a, 1963, 1967, 1969b, 1975) on the Kalabari focused primarily on the Ekine Society and masquerades.

12. See Hardin (1993, 265–283) for a discussion of these issues.

13. Three examples of West African robes were collected by the German trader C. Weichman "from the Benin coast of Nigeria, some time before 1659" (Lamb 1975, 86–87); cloth was also given to traders and missionaries as gifts.

14. Eicher (1993, 254) reported in her fieldwork that Kalabari women are not permitted to enter the Ekine Society drum house.

5

The Economics of Making Pelete Bite

Joanne B. Eicher, Tonye Victor Erekosima, and Carl Liedholm

THIS CHAPTER ANALYZES the economics of the transformed cloth called *pelete bite* and *fimate bite* from imported Indian madras (*injiri*) that involve cutting and removing existing threads to create a new design. Artists who cut cloth can make either type. Since the fimate bite designs have little variation (other than width of stripe), we focus on the intricately cut pelete bite.

Ordinarily, each patterned madras has a specific name, frequently that of the first trader (traditionally male) who introduced it into the Kalabari market, which accounts for the named cloths such as *kieni, owunari, oruwari, anabraba, okpominaolu*. However, some names are epigrammatic such as *ngeritubo* (an only child), *golminji* (gold-flecked, literally, "gold water"), *ikaki mgbe* (tortoise bones), and *amasiri* (tiger's paws).

THE TOOLS AND THE CLOTH

The imported tools used for making pelete bite, a needle and a cutting blade of penknife or razor, were commonly and inexpensively available in local markets in the early 1980s. Similarly, the imported cotton fabrics were readily available but expensive, depending on such factors as quality of fabric and whether purchased in a competitive urban market like Port Harcourt or in a local village market with higher prices. Generally, the brighter examples are called injiri, and the darker ones, *krukrubite* ("black" or "dark" cloth). Kalabari men and women prefer injiri and krukrubite over printed cloth for wrappers, even when uncut; these become even more prized after a Kalabari woman imposes additional design elements on them.

The technique for cutting the cloth is generally the same: lifting one or several threads with a needle and severing by cutting. If using a razor blade, the woman ties heavy string to the needle so as not to lose it. Some women cut and pull threads for one motif at a time. Still others cut a large section of a cloth and then pull the threads or have someone else pull them.

THE MOTIFS

The motifs cut on the patron's cloth can be either requested specifically by the patron or selected by the woman as appropriate for the cloth. Although certain motifs are traditionally cut on certain cloths, new motifs can be created. Generally, inspiration for the motifs comes from shapes of objects or creatures found in Kalabari culture and habitat. These motifs can be grouped into categories. Motif examples drawn from the physical environment with Kalabari names are *amgbo* (millipede), *odum ikelekele* (python), *sangolo* (fish gill); from the masquerade: *alu* (triangle shapes in a masquerade veil), *igbiri* (rattles); or from the household: *etere* (mat or rectangle-faced carpet), *sibi dalaye* (comb, or literally rake, for the hair). Other motifs appear European in origin but have Kalabari names, for example, *abili* (checkerboard surface or "draughts") and *ikoli* (chain). Still others carry English names such as "cross," "wineglass"—or a hybrid term of English and Kalabari—"*glass etemi*" (meaning wineglass tail, the shape of its stem). Figure 3.4 illustrates motif examples, and figure 4.4 shows blocks of motifs.

HIERARCHY OF CLOTH

Kalabari rank pelete bite in a hierarchy of types, which includes both hand-cut and machine-made copies. At the top of the hierarchy, three cloth patterns appear to have existed for well over a hundred years: amasiri, ikaki mgbe, and *igodoye moru (igodoye omuaru)*. The artists agree that these three are the most frequently purchased by their patrons for cutting. These three cloths often have particular motifs cut on them because of the characteristics of each cloth regarding pattern and color. The cloth called amasiri is one of the most difficult to cut because it is a tightly woven, tiny indigo and white plaid. The design called etere, meaning "mat," is often cut on amasiri. Etere motif describes the rectangles produced from interlacing strands in a handwoven mat, sometimes cut as a maze. The cloth called ikaki mgbe, an indigo and white checked cloth, has a variety of designs cut on it, most usually geometric and symmetrical. The cloth called igodoye moru, a somber indigo, red, and white cloth of narrow stripes, usually has asymmetrical designs cut on it. However, some designs, although symmetrical, are placed asymmetrically on a cloth.

In the middle of the hierarchy are the other cloths hand-cut by the women. A variety of cloth patterns exist with a variety of motifs cut on them. The artists share a core of known motifs, but additional new designs emerge or old ones are modified as a woman becomes inspired by a specific cloth and its pattern and colors.

At the bottom of the hierarchy are the imported, manufactured cloths, which provide competition to the hand-cut ones, referred to by the Kalabari as "machine-cut" or "English-cut." The most frequently purchased is the copy of fimate bite. Copies of pelete bite have originated by manufacturers replicating some designs of traditional pelete bite cloth patterns. They have very regular repeat and float threads on the reverse, which make the cloth heavier than the hand-cut ones. Customers generally favor the hand-cut pelete bite because of its appearance and lighter weight. However, innovation has also emerged in regard to the imitation pelete bite. Women use scissors to cut off the float threads on the back of the cloth, giving the machine-cut cloth an almost authentic hand-cut appearance.

An important but frequently overlooked element of textile arts, however, is their underlying economic viability. If the economic underpinnings of Kalabari textiles are weak, prospects for continuing production of this art form could be bleak.

ECONOMIC CHARACTERISTICS

One of the major determinants of the economic viability of Kalabari textiles is the demand for the finished cloth. Our 1980s investigation revealed an excess demand for the hand-cut pelete bit and fimate bite cloth. Virtually all the producers had a backlog of unfilled orders; customers usually had to wait several months before receiving their finished cloth. As a consequence of this excess demand, the producers also did not experience the seasonal fluctuations in demand that face most other textile producers in Africa. The vast majority of cut-thread cloth is produced in response to specific orders; consequently, in these cases, no inventory of unsold finished cloth is generated. A few producers might speculate on occasion with a two-yard men's wrapper, but rarely will they do so on the standard eight-yard lengths.

Pelete bite and fimate bite are not homogeneous commodities; their differences are reflected in the market prices. The hand-cut cloth is uniformly higher priced than the imported substitutes. Among the hand-cut products, three pelete bite cloth patterns at the top of the hierarchy (i.e., amasiri, ikaki mgbe, and igodoye omuaro) command a premium price because of the time involved in cutting. The fimate bite cloth prices are lower than all the hand-cut pelete bite patterns. The inputs on the supply side also are important determinants of economic viability of Kalabari cloth production. Labor is the major input, followed by material and capital.

The fixed capital requirements of the Kalabari textile producers were rather modest in 1980. The needles cost five Kobo ($0.09 USD) each, with only two required to produce eight yards of cloth. Razor blades were fifteen Kobo ($0.27 USD) each in Buguma, with approximately ten needed for eight yards of cloth, because the blades become dull. Consequently, the fixed capital cost per yard of finished cloth amounted to only twenty Kobo ($0.36 USD). Working capital (i.e., the cash, accounts receivable, and inventories), on the other hand, is often a more important capital cost element for small textile producers than is fixed capital. For Kalabari textile producers, however, even the working capital requirements appear modest. Most customers bring their own cloth, so material inventories or cash to pay input suppliers are not needed. Moreover, few sales are made on credit; indeed, some producers even required a 50 percent advance for their labor! Finished goods inventories, as noted, are minimal. Material inputs are important only in those instances when the customer does not provide the producer with cloth fabric. In such cases, the imported cotton fabrics are expensive.

The most important input in all cases, however, is labor. The bulk of the labor is provided by the entrepreneur herself and to a lesser extent by apprentices. Hired labor is virtually nonexistent. The production of Kalabari cloth is a labor-intensive activity. Cutters can take over a month, for example, to produce eight yards of the amasiri design. Complete data on the actual time required to produce various types of Kalabari cloth are unfortunately not available. The amasiri and other more complicated designs took about twice as long to produce as the more standard pelete bite designs. A skillful producer cut standard pelete bite at a rate of four yards per week but was said to cut amasiri type designs at a rate of only two yards per week. A less skillful artisan, however, may have cut one yard of amasiri per week even when working "full time," which appears to have been around thirty hours per week.

The crucial economic issue is whether the return to the entrepreneur or enterprise is sufficient to ensure that the activities are economically viable. Once again, the paucity of data makes it difficult to provide a definitive answer. Nevertheless, sufficient preliminary evidence framed some tentative conclusions. For those producers who only cut cloth brought by their customers, it appears that the labor charge per yard for cutting amasiri cloth was, for example, approximately seven naira, written ₦7 ($12.60 USD). If a producer cut two yards of amasiri per week, she would earn ₦14 ($25.00 USD). For those cutting amasiri who purchased their cloth inputs, the return for a similarly skilled artisan appeared to be somewhat higher, from ₦15 ($28.00 USD) to ₦18 ($32.40 USD) per week.

How do these returns compare with the other types of activities in Nigeria and elsewhere in 1982? In Nigeria, the return from the cutting of pelete bite appears to have exceeded that generated by other women's activities. For example, producers of *kasa* (racks for drying fish) earned only ₦7 ($12.60 USD) per week. Nevertheless, the return was below the 1982 urban minimum wage of ₦37 ($66.00 USD) per week. Thus, our preliminary finding is that the return from cutting cloth is high compared with the alternative income-earning opportunities for women in the area but is below the earnings that could be generated in the "formal" sector.

From our sample of thirty entrepreneurs, the majority were young (because sharp eyesight is needed and older women's eyesight tends to fade), with two-thirds less than thirty-five years old and three less than fifteen years old. Not surprisingly, most of them were relatively new to the activity. Slightly less than half had less than five years' experience in the business. The majority of the entrepreneurs learned how to cut cloth from friends or relatives, while some paid to apprentice under a teacher/producer and others were self-taught. The cutting of pelete bites, while an old art, appears to be a dynamic, growing activity in the area.

Kalabari artists have contributed to the new organizational structure of an "open" society in which apprentices do not necessarily come to them based on traditional relationships such as daughters, sisters, or relatives by marriage. Instead, the criteria of ability, interest, industry, and teachability appear to be the ones that have been applied in selecting their protégés, thus spreading through the population of women and especially younger generations values of personal achievement and a way of producing income.

JOANNE B. EICHER, PhD, is Regents Professor Emerita in the Department of Design, Housing, and Apparel at the University of Minnesota. She is coeditor of *The Anthropology of Dress and Fashion: A Reader*; coeditor of *The Visible Self: Global Perspectives on Dress, Culture, and Society*, 4th ed.; and editor in chief of the *Encyclopedia of World Dress and Fashion*.

TONYE VICTOR EREKOSIMA (1940–2008), PhD, native-born Kalabari, lived in the Igbo towns of Owerri and Umuahia, because his father was an educator and secondary-school principal, until Erekosima's university years in the United States. He was steeped in Kalabari cultural tradition, however, thanks to his family's routine travel to Buguma, his parents' birthplace, for holidays and significant events like funerals. Following his PhD, he served as Director, General Studies, Rivers State College of Education, and Director, Instructional Resources Center, University of Port Harcourt. He coedited *A Hundred Years of Buguma History in Kalabari Culture* (1984) and *Buguma 1984 Centenary Symposia on Kalabari* (1991).

CARL LIEDHOLM, PhD, was on leave from Michigan State University from 1965 to 1967 as faculty at EDI, University of Nigeria, Enugu, researching Nigerian rural nonfarm employment and small enterprises. Publications include coedited books *Growth and Development of the Nigerian Economy* (1970) and *Small Enterprises and Economic Development* (1999).

NOTES

Adapted from Eicher, Erekosima, and Liedholm (1982).

6

Indian Madras Plaids as Real India

Sandra Lee Evenson

MANY PEOPLE RECOGNIZE this expression: "If it walks like a duck and quacks like a duck, it is probably a duck." The expression summarizes the logic behind identifying an object based on its characteristics. For the Kalabari, the cloth called *injiri*, or Real India, was just such a duck. By thirteen characteristics, the knowledgeable Kalabari consumer distinguished the authentic from the ersatz.

The term *Real India* defines a type of Indian madras. It is a yarn-dyed, plain weave, cotton, checked, or plaid fabric handwoven in South India, almost exclusively for export. Real India has been known by several other names over the last four hundred years, from Guinea Stuffs and Callowaypoose to Real Madras Handkerchief (Evenson 1994). As a term specific to the Kalabari, *injiri* is the most accurate; one suggestion is that it refers to the seventeenth-century weaving village of Injerum, located north of present-day sites of Real India production, and another is that it relates to Kalabari pronunciation of India, as noted in chapter 1. For the purposes of this study, the term *Real India* best captures the Kalabari measure of authenticity. My chapter traces the trade history of Real India to determine at what points in its history its characteristic features entered the Kalabari aesthetic.[1]

The Kalabari love of cloth expresses itself within a critical constraint. The primary Kalabari deity is the goddess Owamekaso. She introduced trade to the first Kalabari and taught the Kalabari trading skills useful with Europeans

Fig. 6.1. "Chief Jim Jack with wife and the two daughters" from a Kalabari Historical Album. Four family members wear the same Indian madras. Members of a compound wearing the same pattern express family power and influence, n.d..

(Horton 1962). Owamekaso strictly prohibited the Kalabari from using specific trade cloths that Manuella Daba BobManuel-Meyer Petgrave identifies as cloth printed with vines, flowers, or leaves (Petgrave 1992). Thus, the Kalabari had a cultural predisposition for selecting checkered and plaid cloth.

From an economic perspective, amassing large quantities of this exotic textile became, in part, a telling indication of the Kalabari trader's prowess. A man would demonstrate his success to the community when his family and his compound members displayed cloth wealth in the form of daily dress. Kalabari traders who introduced Real India with unique and aesthetically satisfying patterns named the cloth after their families. When worn by members of the same household, Real India visually communicated wealth and community influence. As Kalabari participation in the slave trade expanded, Real India became a local currency and identified the Kalabari as an economic force in the Niger delta. When Kalabari power waned in the late nineteenth century and the "scramble for Africa" placed most black Africans under white European colonial rule, Real India channeled the might and wisdom of ancestors and river deities back to the colonized Kalabari. In the late twentieth century, Real India used as dress and as display powerfully expressed Kalabari ethnic identity within the larger independent state of Nigeria. Thus, over time, the cultural authentication of these Indian trade cloths into both ritual and daily life demonstrates "the capacity of cloth to encode kinship and political histories" (Schneider and Weiner 1986, 179).

TERMINOLOGY

The history of the Indian textile trade is well documented (Chaudhuri 1978; Irwin 1955, 1956; Irwin and Schwartz 1966; Watson 1866, 1873). Many secondary sources contain glossaries of textile trade terms, which I used to compile a glossary of synonyms for Real India over time. From this Real India glossary, I identified the following terms that could be traced, one to another, through time, to Real India:

"Guinea Stuffs" describes several different cotton fabrics, usually striped or checkered, that capitalized the West African slave trade from the seventeenth to nineteenth centuries as both currency and dress. While early references to Guinea Stuffs describe them as cheap, their quality ranged from coarse to fine. Callowaypoose, Nicanees, and Populees exemplify better-quality varieties of Guinea Stuffs.

Rumal, translated from the Persian word for face towel or handkerchief, describes a one-yard-square format with borders and a central field filled with printed, woven, or embroidered motifs. Jasleen Dhamija (1994) reports that a rumal, when folded into a triangle, was used by Muslim men to cleanse the hands and face before prayer.

"Madras Handkerchiefs" and "Ventapollam Handkerchiefs" originated as a blend of the checked weave of Guinea Stuffs and the bordered format of rumals.

"Real Madras Handkerchief," called RMHK in the export trade, contrasts with imitation Madras Handkerchiefs woven on power looms in Europe.

Many secondary sources assumed Guinea Stuffs were synonymous with Real Madras Handkerchief or Real India. An examination of the primary and secondary sources confirms this hypothesis, but it would be more accurate to state that Guinea Stuffs appear to be the antecedent form of Real India.

CHARACTERISTICS OF REAL INDIA

Between the seventeenth and twentieth centuries, a wide variety of brightly colored cotton fabrics were shipped from India to West Africa. Analysis of findings synthesized from earlier research, including both library research and interviews, reveals thirteen characteristics of Real India:

Colors: primarily indigo blue, madder red, and off-white, with some yellows, browns, greens, and violets.

Dyes: natural dyes, including indigo, until the 1960s when synthetic dyes replaced most natural dyes in an effort to standardize colors and reduce costs; however, indigo use continued.

Fiber content: 100 percent cotton.

Fabric width: consistently described as one yard wide.

Fabric length: three eight-yard lengths, or twenty-four yards, dates from the late 1920s; sixteen-yard warps were the norm prior to this time (Amalsad 1926).

Unique odor: indigo and natural dyes produced a unique odor and taste, contributing one layer of scent to Real India. In addition, the warp yarn was sized with rice starch to ease its handling during weaving (Brunnschweiler 1957). One source noted that the sweat of the weaver as he bent over his loom in the humidity of South India contributed to the unique odor (Fröhlich 1981). An RMHK exporter in Madras added that household cooking odors contributed to the scent of the cloth because the pit looms used to weave Real India were located in weavers' homes.

Yarn-dyed checkered or plaid motif: primary documents described checkered using two colors (e.g., indigo blue and off-white) or plaid using three or more colors (e.g., indigo blue, off-white, and red). Authors did not specify the number of colors or how complex the color palette. Most primary sources used the term check or checkered, regardless of the number of colors used. The term *plaid* has changed in meaning since the seventeenth century from its original definition as the large shawl or wrap that predated the kilt as Scottish ethnic dress. Visual images of Kalabari men and women wearing examples of Real India dating from at least the mid-nineteenth century establish that both checkered and plaid motifs were in use (see fig. 6.1).

Thirty-six-inch-square repeat: the pattern was not a simple balanced check like modern gingham. Patterns may have used only two colors but were complex and visually distinctive, accounting in part for the naming of Kalabari cloths.

Rumal format: some Real India lengths exhibited only a thirty-six-inch repeat, but most featured yarn-dyed checkered or plaid borders enclosing a central field. Eight rumals equaled one piece—three eight-yard pieces per warp.

Yarn count: two-color or three-color Real India is the foundation fabric for *pelete bite*. Pelete bite is a Kalabari textile art in which the light and bright threads are cut and subtracted from the whole cloth. Yarn size and thread count must be sufficient so that threads can be removed without compromising the integrity of the final pelete bite fabric.

Handwoven: in South India, as contrasted to imitations woven on power looms in Switzerland, France, and England. Tentering holes in the selvages distinguished Real India from power-loomed imitation madras.

Distinctive fold: most trade cloths in the later nineteenth and early twentieth centuries were folded accordion-style. Real India was folded in halves, then quarters, then thirds to enclose the raw edges. Later, with the introduction of the INTORICA line by a Swiss trading company, the cloth was folded to display the INTORICA name woven into the selvages (Evenson 1991).

Yarn dividers: Norman Fröhlich (1981) and D. B. Fröhlich (1993) specify the presence of white weft yarns floated or woven into the cloth between pieces to mark the cutting line.

Many early Indian trade cloths were described in the records as having one or more characteristics listed above. In the years before the industrial revolution, for example, all cloth was handwoven, looms were narrow, dyes were natural, and rice-starch sizing was a common finish. It is the accumulation of characteristics listed above, taken together, that define Real India. Each of these characteristics was incorporated and carefully retained over time so that Real India cloths produced for the Kalabari in the late twentieth century were yarn-for-yarn reproductions of named Kalabari cloths revered for generations (Michelman 1992). Each characteristic speaks to the trade history of Real India and its cultural authentication into Kalabari life.

THE TRADE OF REAL INDIA

Based on the wide-ranging patterns of the overseas Portuguese textile trade, it is possible that the Portuguese exported Real India from South India and imported it into West Africa as early as the sixteenth century (Vogt 1975). Between 1410 and his death in 1460, Prince Henry the Navigator sponsored several voyages down the coast of West Africa, in part to capture a portion of the Arab spice trade. Once Vasco da Gama rounded the Cape of Good Hope (after Bartholomew Diaz) and landed on the western coast of India at Goa in 1498, the eastern sea route between Europe and Asia expanded. For the first time, European and Asian trade routes converged into a global trade network.

As Portuguese traders entered the South Asian trade system, they participated in an existing trade pattern in which cotton cloth was the currency of choice in the spice trade. Traders exchanged gold bullion for brightly colored cotton textiles in South Indian ports, and then the textiles were exchanged for spice in the Malay Archipelago and the Moluccas, the fabled Spice Islands. Ships laden with spice returned to the Red Sea and Persian Gulf ports of the Ottoman Empire, where they were converted to bullion for another round of the same journey. Meanwhile, caravans led by Asian and North African Muslim merchants left Hormuz and Aden for ports of the eastern Mediterranean, such as Alexandria and Beirut. Once in the Mediterranean, the spice changed hands and was carried throughout Europe by Italian merchants from Florence, Genoa, and Venice. The price of spice increased with each change of hands, accounting for the intense interest of the Portuguese in capturing a portion of this lucrative trade. When the Portuguese established a trade route around the Cape of Good Hope directly to Europe, they began to usurp the successful and long-standing pattern of gold-for-textiles-for-spice developed by the Arab traders (Subrahmanyam 1993; Wolf 1982).

The spice merchants of the Malay Archipelago were savvy traders. They did not produce cotton textiles and favored the bright cotton cloths from India. It is possible that as the Portuguese made their way up and down the West African coast, stopping for water and supplies along the way, they recognized that merchants like the Kalabari were equally savvy and might also appreciate the Indian textiles preferred by the spice merchants. The Portuguese regularly traded a South Indian fabric called Salempores to the Spice Islanders. Salempores were described as white and dyed with indigo, possibly checkered, and measuring one yard wide and sixteen yards long. The Portuguese naturally would have selected textiles whose sales were successful elsewhere, so perhaps it was this cloth that first entered the Kalabari aesthetic. If so, the introduction of six of the thirteen primary characteristics of Real India occurred at this time. Salempores were all cotton, dyed with natural indigo with its unique color and scent, and measured one by sixteen yards. In fact, images of pelete bite dating from the late twentieth century feature an indigo-and-white-checkered pattern as the foundation motif suggesting an early cultural authentication of these elements (Eicher and Erekosima 1987). In addition, based on field observations of Real India being woven for the Nigerian market, warp-winders brushed rice starch onto the warp to ease handling. It is possible that this practice was quite ancient and might have been a characteristic of Salempores. The rice starch contributed to the special fragrance of the cloth, adding another smell to the Kalabari aesthetic concerning Real India. In any case, by the early seventeenth century, one chief market for Salempores was the Guinea coast, as the bight of West Africa was known (Chaudhuri 1978; Irwin 1956).

Over the next four hundred years, the Portuguese, Dutch, and English who followed usurped the successful and long-standing pattern of trade developed by the Arabs. Each of the European East India Companies engaged in extensive trade of a wide variety of Indian cotton textiles, referred to by dozens of names. Sorting through the glossaries of trade textile terms reveals some names were synonymous for the same cloth, and some names were applied to fabrics of widely varying description. Because Indian cotton textiles acted as a currency in the spice trade and later in the slave trade, the competition for control over textile sources was fierce. It is hardly surprising that primary trade documents offer only ambiguous cloth descriptions, lest these corporate secrets fall into the wrong hands. Adding to this ambiguity, there was little agreement on the spelling of many textile terms, most likely because Europeans interacting with speakers of many languages were attempting to phonetically duplicate the indigenous textile terms as they heard them.

Descriptions of what was purchased in different West African ports of call help clarify matters. For example, in the glossaries, the term *Guinea Stuffs* consistently identifies "the generic term for a wide range of cheap, brightly-coloured Indian calicoes, mostly striped or chequered, and very popular with the negroes" (Irwin and Schwartz 1966). French explorer Jean Barbot (1655–1712), writing of his voyages along the Guinea coast in the late seventeenth century, offers useful details about color. He reports in 1678 that "Guinea Stuffs or cloths" were in demand in Sierra Leone. "Broad and narrow nicanees fine and coarse" and "narrow Guinea Stuffs chequered, ditto broad" were in demand on the Gold coast and were used to make "clouts to wear round their middles" (Barbot cited in Kingsley 1899, appendix). Barbot does not include any cloth in his discussion of New Calabar, the ancestral home of the Kalabari, but reports

Old Calabar preferred "striped Guinea clouts of many colours." His references to color throughout his report indicate that more than blue and white Salempores were for sale. Guinea Stuffs are defined by their many colors. Red dyes were very popular in East Asian markets, as were yellows, greens, and violets. All dyes were natural and, like indigo, carried unique odors. Stripes and checks were yarn-dyed until the industrial revolution. Thus, Barbot's report is evidence that by the end of the 1600s, the Kalabari had a wider range of colors from which to select a preferred color palette in yarn-dyed fabrics woven into a checkered or plaid design. The Kalabari aesthetic for Real India had become more defined.

Furthermore, Barbot reports in 1700 that trade goods popular in the Congo and Cabenda included "Guinea Stuffs, 2 pieces to make a piece" (ibid.). The meaning of this description is unclear, but it might be evidence of the introduction of the bordered rumal format into the Kalabari aesthetic for Real India. North Indian Gujarati weavers wove Indian cotton rumals for the Islamic market. Rumal distribution expanded as Islam expanded throughout North India and into East Asia. The Victoria and Albert Museum has two uncut handkerchief pieces excavated at Fostat, Egypt, dating to fifteenth-century Gujarat. They are coarse compared to nineteenth-century Real India and their borders printed instead of woven, but their bordered format around a central field is unmistakable. Gujarati weavers also produced Guinea Stuffs for the East India Companies. It would have been only a matter of time before the rumal design made its way to the Guinea coast. Following a devastating famine in Gujarat in the mid-seventeenth century, weavers and weaving traditions moved to South India to villages along the Coromandel coast. It is possible that cotton rumals formerly woven for the Islamic market, closer to North India, worked their way into West African trade, where they found acceptance and popularity. When weaving for West Africa moved to South India, the rumal tradition went with it.

Meanwhile, the apogee of the Indian textile trade occurred in the years between 1670 and 1700 (Lawson 1993). Throughout the sixteenth, seventeenth, and eighteenth centuries, the East India Companies were major purveyors of both spice and slave trades, financed with Indian cottons (Wolf 1982). Demand increased in Europe generally and in England specifically because of the fast colors, bright prints and patterns, and overall comfort of this fascinating new textile compared to English wool and linen. When the Portuguese and Dutch introduced sugar production to Brazil and the West Indies, demand for sugar resulted in increased demand for West African slave labor, which in turn led to increased demand for textiles to both procure slaves and to clothe them. By the end of the seventeenth century, specific types of Guinea Stuffs (such as Callowaypoose, Chelloes, Hussanees, and Populees) appeared regularly in the records (Hill 1927). As competition intensified for ever-increasing numbers of able-bodied slaves, greater efforts were made to meet West African middleman/ customer tastes. The generic "anything goes" blend of brightly colored cotton stripes and checks was no longer a successful strategy. Evermore specific textile terms would be used hereafter.

From an examination of the trade dispatches between Madras and London, evidence suggests that the progression of Real India terminology away from the generic term *Guinea Stuffs* to more specific terms continued. In addition, diversification in textile products expanded. For example, between 1744 and 1755, thirty-seven varieties of "piecegoods" (average-length cloths, as compared to "longcloths") were exported out of Madras for London (Dodwell 1920). Guinea Stuffs was not one of those categories, but Salempores, Callowaypoose, and four types of rumals were specified. Of the rumals, the types described as "Red & White" and "Masulipatnam" are of particular interest. Red and white implies a check or stripe, and Masulipatnam is near Ventapollam, a central distribution center for the East India Company in the late seventeenth century. By 1850 the trade cloths called Ventapollam Handkerchiefs were a significant textile product exported from Madras. The height of the handkerchief trade was 1853, with several kinds of handkerchief fabrics exported from Madras: Ventapollam Handkerchiefs, Lunghie Handkerchiefs, and Madras Handkerchiefs. Middlemen in the textile trade possibly simplified the terminology by grouping checkered or plaid rumal- or handkerchief-style cloths into a name reflecting their port of origin. Thus, Ventapollam Handkerchiefs appear to be a link between the generic term *Guinea Stuffs* and the specific Real Madras Handkerchiefs. Taken together, the evidence from Fostat and Ventapollam lend credence to the idea that sometime in the late 1600s, checkered Guinea Stuffs and the rumal format coalesced into what is still known as the Real India of the late twentieth century. A ninth Real India characteristic entered the Kalabari aesthetic with the introduction of rumal borders.

The steady demand for Indian cottons as currencies in the spice, slave, and sugar trades would inspire the industrial revolution. As demand for Madras Handkerchiefs in West Africa increased, new European cotton mills attempted production of the first power-loomed imitations of Madras Handkerchiefs, using raw cotton imported from India. An early English effort at domestically producing Guinea Stuffs was attempted and abandoned in 1706, prior to the industrial revolution. Apparently, West African middlemen preferred East India Company goods to imitations (Irwin 1955). In other words, by the early 1700s, the intrinsic and extrinsic characteristics of Guinea Stuffs / Madras

Handkerchiefs had been culturally authenticated into West African life so thoroughly that imitations were readily detected and rejected.

During the late 1700s, the English East India Company became the governing force in India, at the expense of its earlier trade activities. The company appears to have lost focus on the tastes and needs of its customers, and private traders filled the gap because they could respond to individual market tastes more quickly. Abolition of the British slave trade in 1807 meant a sharp reduction in demand for Indian trade textiles. Competition to supply the remaining customers was fierce. For the Kalabari the slave trade was replaced by trade in palm oil, which was used as an industrial lubricant in the textile mills of the industrial revolution. Private traders made every effort to retain the business of these West African middlemen. In the early and mid-nineteenth century, once again, terms for specific types of textiles crystallize. In an appendix to his 1823 *Remarks on the Country Extending from Cape Palmas to the River Congo*, Captain John Adams listed and briefly described those cloths that sold best in particular West African ports. He included specific types of Guinea Stuffs—Chelloes, Nicanees, Calawaypores (Callowaypoose)—as well as Guinea Stuffs generally, which Adams said should be checked, without any border. This implies that Guinea Stuffs routinely featured borders, suggesting that the fusion of checked Guinea Stuffs and handkerchief-bordered rumals had already occurred prior to his report.

Adams also listed Lungee Handkerchiefs and Pullicat Handkerchiefs (originating on the Coromandel coast) along with Chelloes and several types of rumals, all of which are "esteemed at Calabar." His context appears to refer to New Calabar, home of the Kalabari (Jones 1963). The Guinea Stuffs listed as cheap and coarse were not preferred by the Kalabari; Callowaypoose and rumals were Kalabari best sellers. Adams's comments suggest that by this time, if not before, a higher thread count and better-quality yarn and weaving fulfilled, in part, the Kalabari aesthetic for Real India. When Kalabari artisans first created pelete bite is unknown (Renne 2001). One crucial characteristic of Real India, however, is a thread count of sufficient density to permit the subtraction of threads without compromising the integrity of the cloth. Adams's report documents an eleventh component of Real India.

Throughout the late 1700s, as the capabilities of power spinning and power weaving in Europe improved, mills in England, France, and Switzerland produced imitation Madras Handkerchiefs. In 1836, imitation Madras Handkerchiefs constituted the main manufacture of Montpelier, France (Brunnschweiler 1957). One example of a private trader entering the Madras Handkerchief trade at this time was A. Brunnschweiler and Co. (also known as ABC), a family-owned Swiss weaving company. By 1872, it manufactured power-loom woven imitations of Madras Handkerchiefs for the West African market because of the popularity of Madras Handkerchiefs in West Africa generally (Van der Laan 1983). Imitation Madras Handkerchiefs proved popular and profitable, but not as much as Real Madras Handkerchiefs. West African customers skillfully identified one from the other. One way African customers determined authenticity was the presence of small holes along the selvage of the fabric. Weaver use of lateral tension (tentering) bars to help maintain the fabric's full width during weaving creates these small firm holes. In an attempt to add "genuineness" to early ABC imitation Madras Handkerchiefs, a member of the Brunnschweiler family designed a "hole making machine," which apparently carried out a very complicated mechanical movement involving pins set into a roller, piercing the fabric. The experiment was unsuccessful as West African customers were not deceived (Fröhlich 1981). Thus, tentering marks became evidence of handweaving and defined a critical component of the Kalabari definition of Real India. The meaning of the term *Real India* becomes clear.

At first, ABC imported Real India and other cottons from South India, then reexported their wares via a sales office in Manchester, England. But by the turn of the twentieth century, the company had established offices in Port Harcourt and Lagos to better understand and to communicate local tastes directly to master weavers in Madras. Norman and D. B. Fröhlich were members of the Brunnschweiler family and acted as ABC's agent in Rivers State, Nigeria, and in Madras. During the first half of the twentieth century, innovations like use of "artificial silk" (rayon) embroidery and chain stitch embroidery were introduced, but for the Kalabari market, "Reals," as they were by then called, remained the best-selling product.

One popular innovation to Real India involved a new way of folding the fabric that enclosed the cut edges and created a tidy square packet. In 1925, ABC introduced a line of trademarked Real India called INTORICA, from the phrase India-to-Africa. The Kalabari respected the INTORICA name for its quality Reals, which suggests that the Fröhlichs were well versed in the Kalabari aesthetic for Real India. The fold of the fabric was modified to display the INTORICA name woven into the selvage and became a twentieth-century mark of value—and a twelfth characteristic of Real India.

In 1993, D. B. Fröhlich confirmed Norman Fröhlich's description of Real India, emphasizing the importance of handweaving. He notes that on Real India, floating weft yarns indicated where to cut apart the handkerchief squares.

Indeed, an examination of Real Madras Handkerchiefs dating from 1855 held in the Victoria and Albert Museum bore this feature, a final characteristic of Real India.

D. B. Fröhlich reiterates the Kalabari specification for natural dyes. He refers to these as "running dyes." The warp was wetted and woven while moist, so the colors slightly melted into each other. Moreover, he articulated the importance of the unique odor of Real India, as described earlier. Another attempt to deceive African customers with imitations included sprinkling "aromatic powders" to impart the fragrance of Reals. Again, it did not fool West African customers. Agents at one export office in Madras reported Kalabari customers went so far as to taste the fabric to verify its authenticity.

Did Real India need to "taste like a duck"? Certainly, by the late twentieth century, Real India carried at least thirteen discrete characteristics, color and weave being the most prominent. Tasting the fabric seems superfluous. Perhaps the agent was attempting to reinforce the idea that his customers were very particular and this export house could satisfy any demand. Perhaps this idea of tasting fabric originated with a linguistic confusion about Kalabari customers having specific aesthetic tastes. Jasleen Dhamija (personal communication 2005) reports that market women in many societies taste cloth for the presence of salt used to set indigo, because artificial dye processes do not use salt. Can the Kalabari be included in this practice? Tasting cannot be corroborated in published sources, so documenting this practice is a fascinating avenue for future research. In any case, tracing the history of Real India illuminates the origins of its characteristics.

Within the Kalabari aesthetic, Real India is identified by the way it looks, the way it feels, the way it smells, and some say by the way it tastes. The physical senses were a crucial set of tools in determining the authenticity of imported textiles. The sensual nature of Real India played an important role in the enculturation and perpetuation of identity for the Kalabari as they used Real India in daily and ritual life. The production and use of Real India exemplify discussion of the role our five senses play in the aesthetics of dress. Our aesthetic involvement with textiles creates associations profoundly linked to memory and meaning.

SANDRA LEE EVENSON, PhD, has a BA from University of Minnesota and extensive commercial and personal knowledge of textiles, dress, and fashion. She reviewed export documents and interviewed government officials on madras in Delhi for her MS at University of Minnesota, then researched primary documents on madras in London for her dissertation. She is coauthor of *The Visible Self* (2000, 2008, 2014).

NOTES

Adapted from Evenson (2007).

1. I use the term aesthetic to refer to a set of characteristics that summarize an ideal informally agreed on by a group of people. In this case, Real India is an object with characteristics that are appreciated by the senses. It captures the spirit of a people and communicates what it means to be Kalabari (Eicher et al. 2000).

Ecological Systems Theory and the Significance of Imported Madras Cloth

Joanne B. Eicher, Tonye Victor Erekosima, and Manuella Daba BobManuel-Meyer Petgrave

MANUELLA DABA BOBMANUEL-MEYER PETGRAVE found Urie Bronfenbrenner's ecological systems model (1979) useful in analyzing madras with an individual interacting with four interconnecting ecological systems: the micro-, meso-, exo-, and macrosystems throughout life.[1] She expanded his model to analyze Kalabari culture as a larger ecological system by focusing on madras, with its significant use and meaning from birth through death. Madras's significance to the Kalabari begins when the newborn's father delivers it ceremoniously as a gift to the mother for carrying the child and ends when it adorns the corpse (Eicher and Erekosima 1987, 44).

Petgrave claims that every Kalabari owns at least one madras wrapper. Family trunks contain madras from deceased ancestors to use at celebrations; thousands of yards of madras constitute a significant part of the Kalabari material environment, emanating from their years of global trade. Petgrave used Bronfenbrenner's model to analyze the importance of madras (*injiri*) to the Kalabari. By the late twentieth century, European intermediaries no longer transported madras between India and Africa because Nigerian trade embargoes made English trade of madras unprofitable (Eicher 1988; Evenson 1991; Evenson 1994). Instead, in the late 1970s, West African traders directly imported from India, risking being caught with illegally transporting it into Nigeria, knowing that customers would pay premium prices.

SIGNIFICANCE OF MADRAS CLOTH AND ITS
RELATIONSHIP TO THE BRONFENBRENNER MODEL

In the early 1900s, Talbot (1932), a colonial officer assigned to the southern Nigerian territory, noted the significance of imported madras in Kalabari life. He believed the Portuguese brought it into the area where chiefs adopted it for their dress.

> [Madras,] which was first introduced to these regions by the Portuguese, was for many years the finest material obtainable and therefore became the dress of Kalabari chiefs and is still worn on ceremonial occasions. It is also often used to screen *juju* and sacred images. Such pieces of cloths are family heirlooms, and the older they are, the more valuable they become. As much as four pounds is often paid for one, though save for their sentimental value, it is difficult to understand why these old cloths should be rated as much more highly than the modern ones, only slightly coarser in texture and of almost identical patterns—a kind of check or plaid which may be purchased for as many shillings as these cost pounds. Yet, when the property of a late Abonnema chief was being divided out in 1916, the thing which his successor was anxious to obtain above all others was a piece of . . . [madras] . . . discolored by age. So soon as this was taken from the box he stood up and said: "I should like to have that piece for my share of the house property, because it is the one with which I covered the faces of my ancestors at the Nduein Alali [ancestor screen]." (Talbot 1932, 279)

Petgrave's research analysis of using madras confirms Talbot's observation, enhanced by Bronfenbrenner's model. He focused on "changes triggered by life events or experiences that may originate in the external environment or within the organism" (Bronfenbrenner 1979, 201). Origin, the critical feature of these life events, alters the existing relation between the person and environment, creating a dynamic that may instigate developmental change (ibid.).

Bronfenbrenner's four concepts—microsystem, mesosystem, exosystem, and macrosystem—capture the complexity of the ecological system for an individual's development through life. Petgrave realized that madras, as the most significant textile used in Kalabari life, illustrated his concepts and analyzed Kalabari examples. She applied his model by first asking: How is the cloth used? Who uses it? How does use impact the life course of the individual? What social relations connect the several individuals interacting during the occasion?

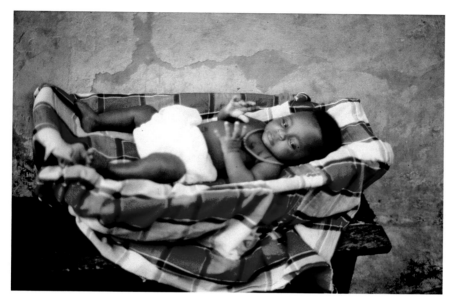

Fig. 7.1. Madras in a carrier surrounds a newborn, 1988.

MICROSYSTEM

Bronfenbrenner's microsystem is a pattern of activities, roles, and interpersonal relations experienced by an individual in a face-to-face setting with other persons (1979, 227). The Kalabari mother documents a microsystem with the birth of her first child; she becomes a woman, completing the final stage, *iyi-iria*, literally meaning, "seclusion after the delivery of a child," which safeguards the mother's and baby's health postnatally. Not every woman goes through this expensive and time-consuming stage (Petgrave 1992, 66). Female family members provide support to the new mother and her baby with special care and attention. They ritually bathe and massage her twice daily, dressing her in a special madras, called *torusima* (meaning to spoil, disfigure, disguise, or deface a surface), usually pale yellow, tan, or rust plaid, sometimes discolored with age (Petgrave 1992, 67). Thus, the child's first important person is constantly dressed in madras during the first few months after birth.

Madras also touches the newborn child placed in the baby carrier, illustrated in figure 7.1. Thereafter, whenever madras surrounds the individual at any age, its wearing or use indicates being Kalabari. In all subsequent microsystem events, the individual can and will wear madras both for informal and formal wear, constituting a microsystem event, one taken for granted.

MESOSYSTEM

Bronfenbrenner's mesosystem comprises the linkages and processes taking place between two or more settings containing the developing person (e.g., the relations between home and school, school and workplace, etc.). In other words, a mesosystem is a system of microsystems (1979, 227). The Kalabari naming ceremony, in contrast to the baby's use of madras after birth, forms mesosystem linkages semiformally. Family and friends gather with the mother, father, and child. The mother receives gifts of cash; family members and intimate friends bestow a variety of names on the child. Only the father, the central figure, gives a two-yard gift of madras, in presenting it to the mother. With great consideration, he also chooses and formally assigns a name. This visible ceremonial interaction signifies the mesosystem linkage; the two parents and Kalabari community identify and recognize the newborn.

The madras serves to socialize the baby into the family, with its specific length making the presentation significant. A two-yard piece ordinarily remains when six yards are cut from an eight-yard piece for a woman's two-piece "up-and-down" wrapper set. The two-yard pieces are stored in family cloth boxes for use in several ways: as head ties for women's specific ensembles, as wrappers reserved for male family members, or for the father's gift to the newborn, thus becoming the center of a triangular social process involving a woman, a man, and their child. The meaning given the cloth differs among the three. The gift declares that the child is Kalabari, born of the union between the mother and the man acknowledging himself as father (Petgrave 1992, 63). The gift marks a mesosystem linkage: members of two lineages unite in the procreation of the child, who can, as a result, claim rights to financial support vis-à-vis the father.[2]

The madras gift signifies the baby becoming formally incorporated into the family. When the Indian madras is a named pattern, the baby becomes identified with a particular family, carrying the name of the first trader who brought it into the community (Petgrave 1992, 54). The named cloth symbolically announces that the baby shares a culturally recognized bond both with the father and the ancestor giving the textile its name. Named madras is prized and valued for presentations; it embodies family, lineage, or clan history linking the present microsystem and mesosystem of the child with past microsystems. Madras presentation associates the worth and value attached both to the cloth and to the child. The best material gift of the environment (madras cloth) is offered to the best gift of nature (the child). One Kalabari informant summarized the importance of the madras gift by the father:

The injiri (madras) cloth was the first cloth that came to Elem-Ama. It had high value. A child is the greatest thing a man can ever have, and materially speaking, the injiri is the greatest treasure a man can ever possess, at the early times. So, traditionally a man's happiness at the birth of a baby is measured by the presentation of a most cherished material gift—a piece of injiri—to the cherished child. This will be used to carry the baby, until much later when it will be removed and kept in the box, and brought out again at puberty for the child to wrap. (Petgrave 1992, 62)

EXOSYSTEM

The exosystem encompasses the linkage and processes taking place between two or more settings, one of which may not ordinarily contain the developing person, but with events, however, that influence processes within the immediate setting of the person. For a child, this might be embodied by the relation between the home and the parent's workplace, and for a parent, this could be embodied by the relation between the school and neighborhood (Bronfenbrenner 1979, 227). As example, nearing seclusion's end, the Kalabari new mother graduates from wearing the dull madras to bright and cheerful patterns of red and indigo madras for everyday wear. "[She] is expected to dress in more colorful madras to show off her lovely skin" (Petgrave 1992, 68). The seclusion and transition ensembles indicate the social and economic status of the mother's family and her changing role from daughter and wife to parturient mother, shown in figure 7.2. Her family's ability to provide appropriate madras and jewelry for the occasion documents wealth marking the thanksgiving ceremonies for families of the child's father and mother, even if relatively poor. They stand together to support the newborn's mother who brought the child, a precious gift, to both the families.

The seclusion period closes with the ceremony of the new mother dressing as an *iriabo* (see chap. 11) to parade to her relatives and husband's homes throughout the community. Cloth boxes provide the textiles dressing her (see chap. 11) in a series of outfits. Her ensembles highlight her physical attributes culturally defined as sexually attractive, relating to her fecund role in the childbearing stage.

For the final stage of presentation, the mother dresses in a gorgeous traditional outfit that identifies her as a mature woman, featuring rich accessories and textiles externally: coral and gold jewelry with velvet and silk wrappers. However, a wrapper of madras is always worn underneath, to fill out the woman's torso, accentuating her fertility. If Christian, she attends Sunday church

Fig. 7.2. Iriabo in madras with her newborn and carrier beside them, 1988.

services in her velvet or silk ensemble and gives thanks for her baby's safe delivery and health. Upon reaching the church and being seated, her attendant covers her legs with a piece of madras for the sake of propriety and modesty. After their community presentation, whether Christian or non-Christian, she goes to her husband's house, resuming a normal pattern of activities.

The iriabo community parade illustrates an exosystem event vis-à-vis her newborn child. The child, though not on parade with the mother, is identified and raised as Kalabari, and if Christian, is brought under the educational and social service umbrella that the Christian community provides to its members.

MACROSYSTEM

The *macrosystem* consists of the overarching pattern of micro-, meso-, and exo-systems characteristic of a given culture, subculture, or other broader social context and is thought of as a societal blueprint for a particular culture, subculture, or other broader social context (Bronfenbrenner 1979, 228). Madras in Kalabari life demonstrates macrosystem linkages when used in a full week of Kalabari funeral celebration events for a deceased elder. Madras ensembles on the living and the dead indicate gender and symbolize status. The specific ensembles worn incorporating madras also designate the relationships of the surrounding community members and the ancestors to the deceased.

DRESSING THE CORPSE AND BEDS-OF-STATE

Family and community members hope that the departed one, as an ancestor, will view the living with beneficence. To help ensure this, the deceased is sent off to join the ancestors amid pomp, ceremony, and much madras cloth (see fig. 7.3). The deceased may be dressed in madras with distinctions of gender and age observed. In life as in death, the madras gown called *ebu* is meant only for males of old age and high distinction. This is paralleled for a deceased female of old age and high distinction by using dark indigo pelete bite to decorate her bed-of-state as Renne mentions in chapter 4.

Although the madras cloth ushering the newborn child into Kalabari society identifies the family of the child's father, madras associated with the corpse at funerals marks status achieved by the individual within the larger society. This differentiation that occurs at death is a function of the passage of time for an individual. For example, madras adorning the walls and the bed-of-state as described in chapters 18 and 19 may have been obtained years ago in the family's trading days and prized by extended family members or may have been purchased recently by a family of new wealth, but most essential to the successful

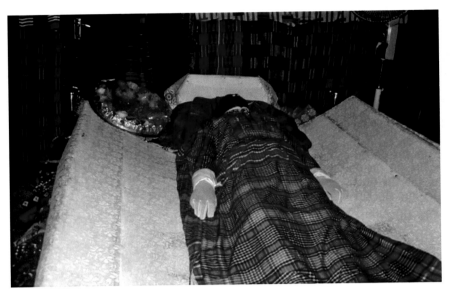

Fig. 7.3. The deceased, in madras gown, lies in an open coffin embellished with white lace, 1983.

funeral celebration, the madras must be brought from the family cloth boxes and storage room.

DRESSING THE MOURNERS

Whether new or old, pieces of madras will dress the family members of the deceased during the funeral celebrations elaborated in chapters 18 and 19. After burying the deceased, family mourners at subsequent events in the funeral celebration wear the cloth removed from the decorated beds. Mourners from the larger community also draw on their families' cloth boxes for their dress. Various madras ensembles are deemed appropriate for both male and female mourners of the deceased's family. Particularly dark-colored pelete bite, often worn by immediate family members for funeral celebrations, indicates the high esteem held for this most valued form of Indian madras.

For example, female mourners on the first day of a funeral for their male or female elder wear pelete bite in escorting the corpse from the mortuary to the family house; immediate family male mourners usually dress in a long white shirt and dark madras wrapper. Pelete bite worn at funerals identifies the wearer as an immediate family member of the deceased. Such fabric in general emphasizes kinship ties (Erekosima 1979). At funerals the pelete bite is equated and correlated to the funeral event, transforming an earthly matter into a spiritual one, emphasizing the somber occasion.

On the last day of the funeral celebration week, mourners parade through the community. They follow one after the other according to their relationship to the deceased with dress coordinated to communicate relationship to the deceased. Women in the immediate family lead the parade wearing bright red madras cloth. Males of the immediate family wear a range of ensembles, often madras wrappers.

The multiple acts of lending, borrowing, using, wearing, returning, and storing the madras cloth, which accompany preparation of the viewing rooms and beds-of-state and dressing the corpse and mourners, activate a multitude of interconnecting social relationships in a grand week of bustle and celebration. The events comprising a funeral celebration offer opportunities to illustrate an individual's place within the Kalabari ecological system. The funeral celebrations make visible, through the use of madras and other imported cloths, many of the important Kalabari societal structures.

Though initially developed to understand child development, Bronfenbrenner's ecosystem model serves for assessing the significance of an item of material culture, like madras, to a society. Petgrave's analysis demonstrates how Kalabari use madras to celebrate and affirm links within a complex web of social relations. These links connect Kalabari individuals to others in their immediate sphere of social interaction and to those outside this sphere. Wearing madras at funerals becomes part of a blueprint of the Kalabari social world.

EXTENDING THE BRONFENBRENNER MODEL

Bronfenbrenner's model helps construct a complex picture of sociocultural life, illuminating the importance of madras to the Kalabari people. Madras also connects individuals to other Kalabari with whom they have little or no face-to-face contact, because each Kalabari recognizes other Kalabari wearing madras. Named madras cloths connect Kalabari individuals to their ancestors and the generations that will follow. Ultimately, using madras connects Kalabari individuals to overarching cultural beliefs and the Kalabari worldview. When madras is handed down through the family across generations, material culture items pass from one generation to the next, linking contemporary microsystems to those of the past, extending mesosystem and exosystem linkages forward and backward in time.

Madras, used throughout a Kalabari individual's life course, ties any one Kalabari to another. Madras is so critical in the structure of relationships among Kalabari people that smuggling cloth and paying high prices have become common acts. Applying Bronfenbrenner's model to analyze how the Kalabari use madras reveals its importance in Kalabari society. By implication, the social relations connecting the Kalabari consumers of madras to Indian producers are also extremely vital to the Kalabari.

Recognition of the exporter-importer links forces an extension of Bronfenbrenner's model. He proposes that the macrosystem, synonymous with ethnic boundaries, is the highest network of social relations through which a Kalabari individual's life can be affected. To the contrary, trading networks supplying the valued cloth lie beyond the macrosystem, yet their failure can deprive an individual of those fabric symbols necessary to a successful living of Kalabari life. We suggest that the study of the use of madras by the Kalabari therefore requires the creation of another level within his ecosystem model—a level of global structural relations.

JOANNE B. EICHER, PhD, is Regents Professor Emerita in the Department of Design, Housing, and Apparel at the University of Minnesota. She is coeditor of *The Anthropology of Dress and Fashion: A Reader*; coeditor of *The Visible Self: Global Perspectives on Dress, Culture, and Society*, 4th ed.; and editor in chief of the *Encyclopedia of World Dress and Fashion*.

TONYE VICTOR EREKOSIMA (1940–2008), PhD, native-born Kalabari, lived in the Igbo towns of Owerri and Umuahia, because his father was an educator and secondary-school principal, until Erekosima's university years in the United States. He was steeped in Kalabari cultural tradition, however, thanks to his family's routine travel to Buguma, his parents' birthplace, for holidays and significant events like funerals. Following his PhD, he served as Director, General Studies, Rivers State College of Education, and Director, Instructional Resources Center, University of Port Harcourt. He coedited *A Hundred Years of Buguma History in Kalabari Culture* (1984) and *Buguma 1984 Centenary Symposia on Kalabari* (1991).

MANUELLA DABA BOBMANUEL-MEYER PETGRAVE, MA, native-born Kalabari from Abbonema, lived in Kalabari communities until 1989, met Joanne Eicher in Buguma after completing her BS in textile science in Nigeria, and came to the University of Minnesota for her MA, *The*

Significance of Indian Madras in the Life Cycle of the Kalabari (1992), on which this chapter is based. Her father's family, Bob-Manuel, is one of the four major groups on the island of Abonnema. Her paternal grandmother, Fanny Bob-Manuel, was the first Western-educated Kalabari woman.

NOTES

Adapted from a paper presented at the "Workshop and Seminar on Real Madras Handkerchief" in Madras, India (now Chennai), February 4–11, 1994. Published as Eicher and Erekosima (1997).

1. Bronfenbrenner's work was influenced by that of Kurt Lewin (1935, 73), especially a formula that Bronfenbrenner reworked with t as the time at which a developmental outcome is observed and t-p as the period or periods during which the joint forces from the person and the environment were operating to produce the outcome. The process producing developmental change is not instantaneous but one that takes place over time and can change over time. Therefore, the processes that operate as an individual ages will not necessarily be the same as those taking place earlier (Bronfenbrenner 1989, 190).

2. If, later on, the father celebrates the most prestigious form of marriage, called *iya*, with the mother of his child by transferring property to her, his rights in the child increase. An iya ceremony includes a grand public celebration involving the presentation of madras from the husband to the wife. The couple's prestige rises with offspring gaining more rights in the father's lineage. An iya marriage also constitutes a mesosystem event for offspring.

India and West Africa

Transformation of Velvets

Barbara Sumberg and Joanne B. Eicher

THE KALABARI WEAR and use embroidered velvets called *india*, one of their internationally imported cloths. Through the study of cloth and dress, their global trade history comes into focus. Kalabari use of imported Indian cloth draws attention to trade history and cultural contact among Africans, Indians, and Europeans since the fifteenth century. By studying the manufacture of gold- and silver-embroidered velvet in India and its Nigerian use, we add to the historical knowledge of world trade from the fifteenth to the twentieth century. We outline Kalabari use of these cloths, speculating on the connection of these early Indian velvets to those worn by the Kalabari in the late twentieth and early twenty-first centuries.

TECHNIQUE AND PRODUCTION

Velvet woven on the handloom has a supplementary warp that requires an additional warp beam on the loom. The extra nonstructural warps are drawn up from below the structural warp, a thin metal rod is inserted, and the warp is lowered, leaving a row of loops in place. This pile formation is repeated every three rows. As the weaving progresses, the rods are removed by cutting the loops, permitting the cloth to be wound on the cloth beam.

Velvet has been woven in many parts of the world, and many variations on the plain pile weave have been developed. It was first produced in the Middle East in Persia as early as the ninth century. By the sixteenth century, Sassanian velvets had reached their technical and artistic peak, with the production of fine, figured silk velvets using a number of different colors in the supplementary warp. These fabrics were often woven with gold or silver threads and occasionally flat strips of metal (Wilson 1979, 119). *Kemba,* velvet brocaded with many colors, and *catma,* a velvet with gold thread, were woven in Bursa, Turkey, in the sixteenth century; in the Far East in China; and in Japan, where velvet (*birodo*) was made from the sixteenth to nineteenth centuries in the periods known as late Momoyama and early Edo (Wilson 1979, 138, 191).

Italy was the acknowledged center of the European velvet industry in the medieval and Renaissance periods, with Lucca, Florence, and Venice all known to produce fine silk examples. Spain and Lyon in France have also been identified as locations for production in Europe. The techniques most commonly used were varied pile heights, gold and silver brocade, and voided velvets that used a combination of cut and uncut pile achieving a textural pattern.

In India, voided *ikat* (textiles with extra warp dyed in a resist pattern before weaving), plain, and figured velvets were the most frequently woven (Dhamija 1989). Production centers were Ahmedabad, Kannauj, Gujarat, Lahore, Lucknow, Punjab, and Central India during the Mughal period, at the craft's peak. Akbar, the Mughal emperor from 1556 to 1605, encouraged highly skilled weavers from all over Central Asia to settle in India and spread their knowledge and contribute to the development of even more refined weaving. Silk velvets were primarily produced for use by members of the courts because the costly textile was affordable only to the wealthiest patrons, who surrounded themselves with velvet tents, cushions, hangings, elephant trappings, and some for their royal clothing (Smart and Gluckman 1989).

The velvet we discuss relates to plain single-color velvets with gold and silver embroidery, important in Kalabari ritual apparel. Further research in the Niger delta might reveal older Indian velvets with a wider range of techniques, as elaborated above.

VELVET IN WEST AFRICA

The Kalabari rank the cloth they use in a hierarchy according to differential prestige to imported cloth types. The velvet called india, at the top of the hierarchy, specifically displays community wealth and position. For males, wearing india indicates achieving the rank of chief and having considerable wealth and social standing, and wearing an embroidered velvet *attigra* gown, worn with a matching fan and the highly decorated hat (*ajibulu*), displays economic success and stature. Men may also wear it during the stately dance when ending a masquerade (*ada seki*).

Women use india primarily during the last stage of the process of *iria*, as Daly indicates in chapter 11. Bearing children confers a position of high status, equaled only by great age (analogous to that of male chief), similarly expressed by wearing india adorned with coral, gold jewelry, and a hat appropriate for the velvet wrapper. A woman's and her family's position within the community is visually shown by wearing india.

India also has a place in the celebration of the death of a person of substance. An extravagant presentation of heirloom cloth for a funeral honors the deceased's long and successful life and the family's social standing when india is used on walls and bed in the third room (see chap. 18). A designated chief mourner wears velvet to lead the funeral promenade and at the last funeral dance. In figure 8.1, both the male and female chief mourners wear embroidered velvets.

According to respondents, for many years velvet was used only in these prescribed situations. With changes in the Nigerian economy, its use in the 1980s and 1990s was extended to the situation of women becoming more heavily involved in the economic support of themselves and their families. Chapter 12 describes the members of the women's social and dance clubs known as *eremne-ogbo* choosing wrappers of matching velvets to make a group statement.

Such use illustrates that Indian embroidered velvets have come to play an important role in Kalabari culture, where both old and new cloths are highly valued. Velvets are kept in cloth boxes with other treasured family textiles, guarded by women elders who keep Kalabari heritage and standards alive. Some velvets may date to the nineteenth century, just as some *madras* has been dated to that time.

Because the Kalabari cherish cloth, they take pains to preserve old pieces from decay for continued use by coming generations. Their determination to retain and display wealth appears to offset the climatic conditions in the Niger delta inconducive to preserving cloth. Cloth use is carefully monitored, stored in boxes and trunks in locked rooms, aired after use, and seldom washed because only briefly used.

Evidence of the embroidered velvet's source links these remote island communities of the Niger delta to India via Portuguese traders (Vogt 1975). Through studying textile trade records between India and West Africa, velvets apparently arrived sometime after the Portuguese trade began. The earliest citations we have found of velvet being a West African trade item are Barbot's description of trade goods destined for Ghana and Benin in 1678 (Kingsley

Fig. 8.1. Two chief mourners wear embroidered velvet (india) at Saturday evening funeral dance. Male mourner in red and female in black. 1983.

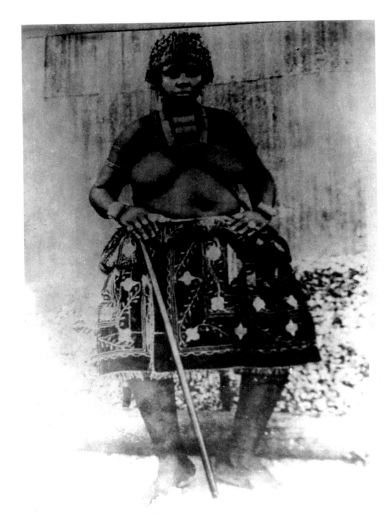

Fig. 8.2. A 1903 photograph of a young woman wearing a gold-embroidered velvet wrapper, large coral beads, and gold jewelry.

1964) and a description of its use in the Nembe king's 1898 funeral (Tepowa
1907) in the Niger River delta. Neither citation indicates the source. The earliest
visual evidence of velvet use in this part of Nigeria is a photograph dated 1903,
found in a Kalabari family album and seen in figure 8.2, in which a woman is
wearing an embroidered velvet wrapper.[1]

VELVET IN INDIA

Documentation on the expensive, handwoven silk velvet fabric displayed by princes in the Mughal court abounds. The making of embroidered-velvet robes of honor known as *khilats* was an early practice introduced possibly during the Sultanate period. These khilats were presented by royalty to honor a member of the royal court or an ambassador to the court (Dhamija 1989, 13).

R. N. Mehta (1956) describes two velvets from the Mughal period, lasting from the mid-sixteenth to the mid-nineteenth century, in the Calico Museum collection. These are Jain hangings to be draped behind a *suri* when he delivers a sermon. They are embroidered with *kalabatun* (gold thread) on a velvet ground. Both pieces are attributed to the Gujarat area, dating to the first twenty-five years of the eighteenth century, which places them toward the Mughal period's decline. They are very similar to other velvets made during the mid-seventeenth century; Mehta attributes the late date to the time lag in styles between the provinces and the metropolis. The embroidery technique used in the couched *zardozi* work is said to be introduced by the Portuguese (see chap. 9 for further elaboration) (Bhushan 1990).[2]

Velvets were used for cushions, hangings, curtains, and animal trappings (Smart and Gluckman 1989). Jamila Bhushan cites an eyewitness account of Sir Thomas Roe at the court of Jahangir in which he describes a palanquin covered with velvet and embroidered with pearls, and wall hangings of fine brocaded velvet (Bhushan 1958). Roe states that the city of Lucknow is famous for its excellent quality of gold and silver embroidery on heavy velvet, generally used for elephant clothes; couch covers; bolsters; and waistcoats, caps, and shoes to be worn at state occasions. The work is very heavy and, consequently, very expensive. It was in demand at the native courts, but with the integration of the states in the Indian Union, the demand has almost died out (Bhushan 1958, 42).

The *band-gale-ka-coat* of the Hindu at the turn of the century was sometimes made of "heavy velvet embroidered richly with gold and silver thread and spangles" (ibid.). Shanti Swarup cites tent panels embroidered in silk and gold on velvet and velvets painted in gold as extant textiles from the Mughal period (Swarup 1968). John Irwin and Margaret Hall catalog embroidered velvets from the Calico Museum collection (Irwin and Hall 1973). Jain book covers, a game board, and hangings attributed to Gujarat are among the pieces described. When the Mughal reign declined in power, so did the courtly arts that it supported (Dhamija 1989). Yet the making of embroidered velvets did not die out as completely as the art of handwoven velvets.

While no evidence of voided or brocaded velvet production in contemporary India was found, gold-embroidered cloth is still produced (ibid.).[3] Farida Jalees, in a study of contemporary *zari* workers (see chap. 9), notes the revival of the hand embroidery on luxury cloths of silk, wool, and velvet in response to overseas demand. A parallel example of cloth use and documentation may be that of the handwoven checked and plaid cloths from Tamil Nadu and Madras known for export as Real Madras Handkerchief or RMHK. Evenson states that little attention is paid to madras production in India because it is almost exclusively an export item. Since Indians do not use the patterns, colors, and widths woven for export to West Africa, they have exhibited little interest until recently in documenting it.[4] Could the case for embroidered velvets be similar if produced primarily for export?[5] Hazel Lutz in chapter 9 states that the Muslim *zardozi* workers have been producing cloth embellished with metallic thread for centuries. Jasleen Dhamija states that woven and embroidered velvets were not made by the same artisan communities. The embroidered velvets of the Mughal era are well documented (ibid.). Sparse research on Muslim communities may account for the lack of information on twentieth-century, machine-made embroidered velvets from India.

R. N. Mehta reviews the textile arts of India, both historical and contemporary. Though he does not mention the weaving of velvet, he does report on the couched embroidery, zardozi: "Famous also is Lucknow's zardozi and *Kamdani* work, embroidery in gold and silver that for long dazzled the courts of the Nawabs of Oudh—every design a piece of originality and imagination. Both types are of ancient origin and most probably originated there, coming into prominence during Mughal times. At present, apart from Lucknow, this kind of embroidery is also done in Bombay, Banaras, Bareilly, Agra, Aurangabad, Delhi, Hyderabad, Surat, and the Gujarat region" (Mehta 1968).

He goes on to say: "Today, beautiful curtains, bedcovers, table centers, cushion covers, etc. are produced in silk, satin, and velvet, and embroidered in colored silks, with a sparing use of gold and silver" (ibid.).

Sukhdev Chib (1978) also cites Lucknow as a center for contemporary zardozi work that is sold in markets abroad. The industry has its historical roots in the patronage of the court of the noblemen of Oudh at Lucknow. The final evidence of embroidered Indian velvet is a photograph in the Italian periodical *FMR* (the periodical of Franco Maria Ricci International from Milan) *with* a detail of black velvet, embroidered with gold thread and sequins. The caption reads: "*Choga* (man's ornamental coat), detail, Chamba, twentieth century. Velvets with gold zardozi" (Ricci 1985).

The photograph and caption in the periodical indicate that gold and silver embroidery on machine-made velvet was still being done in India in the twentieth century, even though no evidence is given regarding date or place of manufacture. In fact, Lucknow is still a center of zari, where the work is done almost exclusively by Muslim men and women and marketed by Hindu middlemen (Jalees 1989).

CONCLUSION

Because of the name india, the embroidered velvets used in the Rivers State of Nigeria, in the city of Port Harcourt, and in remote island communities in the delta of the River Niger are apparently from India. We have seen embroidered velvet in use and have photographic documentation of its display at funerals, centenary celebrations, and rites of passage. In a personal communication in June 1992, Jasleen Dhamija revealed that a close examination of details of these photographs shows that some pieces are obviously contemporary and machine embroidered, while others use materials and techniques that indicate handwork. Recent field research in Madras has shown that machine-made velvet is hand embroidered with gold thread as well as machine embroidered, primarily for export to Nigeria. The choice of colors and patterns is based on the demand of the Kalabari market and is quite distinct from gold embroidery, zardozi, sold in local Indian markets.

Possibly these remote island communities in Nigeria may be the resting place of handwoven and embroidered velvets produced in the final days of the Mughal era. Only a detailed analysis of the cloth boxes of Kalabari families could confirm this. Export records need to be perused to discover whether other West African destinations existed besides the specific sites of the Kalabari and Nembe peoples. Additional research among the Niger delta peoples and documentation of velvet use in other parts of West Africa could provide further insights into the appeal of these luxurious textiles.

BARBARA SUMBERG, PhD, former curator of Costume and Textiles at the Museum of International Folk Art, published *Sleeping Around: The Bed from Antiquity to Now* (2006); *Material World: Textiles and Dress from the Collection* (2010); and *Young Brides, Old Treasures: Embroidered Macedonian Dress* (2011).

JOANNE B. EICHER, PhD, is Regents Professor Emerita in the Department of Design, Housing, and Apparel at the University of Minnesota. She is coeditor of *The Anthropology of Dress and Fashion: A Reader*; coeditor of *The Visible Self: Global Perspectives on Dress, Culture, and Society*, 4th ed.; and editor in chief of the *Encyclopedia of World Dress and Fashion*.

NOTES

Adapted from Sumberg and Eicher (1995).

1. This photograph was found in a Kalabari family album, typical of a rich source of data yet to be fully plumbed.

2. Couched embroidery involves using two threads: threads of the top stitching hold the bottom thread in place.

3. Voided and brocaded velvets have patterns made by varying pile and nonpile areas.

4. Dhajima (1993) documented the relationship between this cloth and rumals made in South India. The Madras Craft Centre in Chennai sponsored a symposium on Real Madras Handkerchief in January 1994.

5. The difference between madras and velvet being documented in India is that madras is a variation of common textiles used in India known as rumals. These rumals were used by Muslim men to cover the head during prayer and to wipe the hands and face after washing in preparation for prayer. With the propagation of Islam, rumals spread all over the world (Dhamija 1993).

Designed for Wrapping

Changes in Indian Embroidered Velvet Produced for the Kalabari

Hazel Ann Lutz

INTRODUCTION

I analyze some changes in design of embroidered velvets made in India during the period from 1980 to 1997 for the Kalabari and neighboring, culturally related communities residing in the Niger River delta and Nigerian diasporas around the world. These textiles are still used within the communities in 2019, as in the past, as wall hangings and the like and as three-dimensional wrapped dress. In previous research (Lutz 2003), I termed this cloth *zari-embroidered velvets*. Zari is a northern Indian word for gold and silver embroidery and related embellishments decorating the surface of textiles and apparel.

Such embroidered velvets belong to a long Indian tradition of decorating velvet textiles with gold and silver embroidery for uses in Indian nobility homes and for ceremonially decorating their transport animals, especially elephants and horses. From at least the early twentieth century, the Kalabari employed the imports in two-dimensional forms and used them in their formal dress, turning them into a three-dimensional form. In the last two decades of the century, Kalabari importers came face-to-face with the Indian manufacturer-cum-exporters for the first time, ending the era of colonial control of the textiles' design. The arrival of Kalabari wholesale buyers in India inaugurated an era of change in the export textiles' design to better suit them to use in Kalabari wrapped dress.

I conducted research in and around Chennai, India (formerly Madras), in 1997 on the production and trade of embroidered velvets bound for West

Africa. I also examined (1) photographs of domestic Indian embroidered velvets (Gupta 1996), (2) zari-embroidered contemporary Indian women's fashion published in magazines and clothing catalogs, and (3) published and unpublished photographs from Eicher's and Daly's fieldwork. In St. Paul, Minnesota, I observed dress worn by West African expatriates at an annual IgboFest celebration.

I define design for the analysis of the embroidered velvets as the total physical description of the textiles in question—that is, fiber content and weave of the component ground, base, and appliqued fabrics; dimensions of the finished textile; color; surface design patterns; production techniques; materials of surface embroidery and embellishment; and edge treatment. Design changes began to occur from approximately 1980 and were continuing in late 1997, when I observed the production and trade end of the Kalabari-Indian trade relationship. In this chapter, I focus on the changes in the materials, the patterns and techniques of embellishment, the dimensions of the finished textiles, and their edge treatment. I document the intimate connection of these ethnic Kalabari textiles with the global system of textile design, production, and trade that brought them into Kalabari communities, those nearby, and their global diasporas.

BACKGROUND

To understand the design changes I analyze, I provide a historic and cultural background for viewing the zari-embroidered velvets. I include a brief history of Indian zari materials and zari-embroidery techniques, the parameters of the Indian design tradition in embroidered velvets for Indian consumption, and Kalabari cultural uses of imported textiles as funeral furnishings and personal dress established before 1980.

DESIGN AND USE OF EMBROIDERED VELVETS IN INDIA

The tradition of production and consumption, both historic and contemporary, of Indian-made, embroidered-velvet textiles for dressing the home and ceremonial transport animals consists of several elements, which have remained constant through centuries (Gupta 1996). A thin plain-weave cotton, of the type which Americans call "cheese cloth," is glued to the back of a piece of solidly napped, plain-colored velvet fabric. This cloth "sandwich" is then stretched within a large wooden embroidery frame that accommodates from one to six embroiderers working at a time.

Embroidery patterns embellishing such velvets consist of several motifs of floral imagery, much of it abstracted. Some of the floral imagery has over time

Fig. 9.1. Zari-embroidered velvet on elephants in India. Courtesy of Faraz Usmani via Wikimedia Commons.

developed into shapes, which in English are called "paisley." Animal imagery occurs rarely. Borders on all four sides of the velvets are embellished in zari embroidery and zari fringe. The center of the textile can be left plain or filled with repeated motifs called *buti* in Hindi and Urdu languages, in a grid pattern filling the area or with a large central motif with coordinating smaller motifs filling the corners and oriented diagonally toward the center. The whole pattern is characterized by a two-way or four-way symmetry, always visible when the textiles are used. In Indian nobilities' homes, they are hung in their flat form on the wall for decorative purposes or to create a worship space. They are also used as luxurious floor coverings and spread to cover valued objects. Semi-open areas of the home or palace are hung with such zari-embroidered velvets to make temporary walls as the seasons dictate for protection from the sun, wind, or cold. While the nobility traveled or celebrated life course rituals, drawing hundreds of guests, outdoor tents created with zari-embroidered velvets formed the walls and sometimes the canopy and ground covering. All such uses display the entire mirror-symmetric patterns of the embroidery. The embroidery pattern symmetry is also obvious when the textiles dress animals, as in figure 9.1.

In many parts of the world and within India, gold and silver threads and related metal elements have been used for fabric weaving or embellishment since ancient times (Higgins 1993). In the Hindi and Urdu languages, they are called zari. These various precious-metal threads and related elements, which in England are called bullion, are created in two different ways. The metal, when forced through a very fine hole, makes a wire in a variety of thicknesses, depending on intended use, as is in embroidery and the braiding or weaving of fabric trims and fringes. It can also be wound into lengths of tiny coils, like the much larger coils of the American children's toy called Slinky. These tiny wires can also be formed into coils with right-angled corners.

The wires can also be flattened and used in the same applications described above. Thicker flattened wires have a point cut into the end, forming its own needle for direct embroidery on fabric. In another application a thin wire is flattened and then wrapped around a core, historically silk or more recently a cotton, to make a thread called gimp. Gimp is primarily used in embroidery and weaving fabric trims and fringes.

Flattened sheets of gold or silver are cut into a variety of sequin shapes. In ancient times in some regions of the world, gold sheets were created by adhering the precious metal onto very thin leather parchment, which is then cut into thin "threads" or into a variety of sequin shapes.

All these threads and related elements have contained varying proportions of real gold or silver through the centuries, the proportions changing with development of the galvanizing technique—gold on silver, later precious metals on copper. The proportions also changed with the price of gold and silver and with the income of the niche markets for these complex embellished textiles.

Lurex, a completely faux type of "gold" and "silver" thread, actually a "tape yarn," was invented in the mid-twentieth century. These faux precious-metal "threads" are cut from extremely thin sheets of polyurethane layered with any of a variety of aluminum-based metallic colors. Lurex-type tape yarns used in India, as elsewhere, wrap the core of the golden and silverine gimp threads. Sequins are also cut from sheets of the metallic polyurethane. Unlike the earlier metal wires, these modern elements do not tarnish.

In India the polyurethane "threads" and sequins are distinguished from real precious-metal zari by the name *plastik zari*. The entire class of real and faux metal threads and related elements are together referred to simply as zari, a practice which I follow here. During the more than one hundred years of Kalabari importation of embroidered velvets, the metallic materials underwent the same change in metal composition as occurred elsewhere in metallic textile production in the world.

Asli, "real" zari embroidery, like British bullion work, is executed with a straight, eyed needle by artisans known as *zardoz* (feminine, *zardozi*). The zardozi technique couches all the precious metal onto the top, or right side, of the cloth.

From at least the mid-twentieth century, a new embroidery technique displaced much of the straight-needle zari embroidery production for products for the growing Indian middle class and foreign markets. The *ari*, a hooked needle embroidery technique, is generally valued for the speed with which the work is done. This greatly decreases the price of the finished goods.

Ari embroidery is produced by a different set of craft workers (Haynes 1986; Nissim 1976). The technique creates both a chain stitch line of zari on the right side of the cloth and a single-thread line of zari on the wrong side of the cloth. Thus, ari embroidery only uses faux precious-metal threads, as it is undesirable to place expensive gold and silver on the back side where it will not be seen. Additionally, in ari embroidery the variety of zari elements of the Indian gold and silver embroidery tradition are reduced to just gimp thread, sequins, and fringes; however, ari has added in the new element of beads and cloth appliqué, both applied to the cloth with the chain stitch.

Concurrent with this change in embroiderers and threads in producing for the Kalabari market, the designs of the embroidered velvets also changed, but in a manner that is not simply traceable back to the changes in zari threads and elements, the embroidery technique, or the embroiderers employed to make the export textiles. To focus my analysis on the other sources of design change in zari-embroidered velvets, I refer to them all simply as embroidered velvets.

DRESS AND HOUSEWARE VELVET PRACTICES OF THE KALABARI IN THE TWENTIETH CENTURY

Additional context for my analysis is provided by published research results into the distinctive mode of dress the Kalabari have created with Indian and other imported textiles as other chapters describe. Not making their own cloth, they rely on imported textiles, many from India, to construct their ethnic ensembles and high fashion.

Chapter 8 discusses an early photograph from the beginning of the twentieth century found in Talbot (1926, fig. 95), in which an *iriabo* wears a gold embroidered velvet over her upper torso. Chapter 8 also discusses the use of the embroidered velvet worn by a Kalabari woman in 1903 (see fig. 8.2), congruent with the Kalabari female dress protocol as an iriabo. The woman wears an embroidered-velvet covering her lower torso and thighs for her formal coming-out ceremony following her child's birth. The designs of these two early imported Indian velvets follow the design tradition evidenced in historic Indian embroidered velvets.

In chapter 2, Erekosima and Eicher analyze the process by which the Kalabari culturally authenticate Indian textiles for their own culturally prescribed dress and funeral celebration decor discussed later (chap. 18 and 19). The embroidered velvets for funerals are employed as two-dimensional wall hangings, canopies, bedspreads, or as folded decorative shapes placed on funerary bed surfaces. When the embroidered velvets are spread out as a canopy, on walls and as bedcovers, the cloth's entire embroidery pattern remains visible, like those in Indian households and as animal trappings. When folded on the bed, only the shiny embroidery thread and the velvet's rich nap are visible, symbolizing the life successes of the deceased. When the cloth is folded and draped over the head or footboard, borders and diagonal corner motifs show to good effect.

Kalabari women also dress in velvet as iriabo for other important celebrations, like the 1984 Buguma Centenary. The velvet cloth, doubled over and tied at the waist, hangs slightly above the knee. The folded-over thickness of the cloth enhances a new mother's horizonal girth, celebrating her fecundity. The embroidered borders running horizontally across the body also emphasize the girth of the wearer, following the Kalabari female ideal. The congruence of the 1903 photograph with Eicher's and Daly's 1980s field photographs and Daly's chapter 11 analysis of Kalabari female dress protocol in the last quarter of the twentieth century indicate that the Kalabari culturally authenticated the Indian embroidered velvets more than one hundred years ago to use as wrappers and to construct this important gendered ideal.

DISRUPTION OF THE COLONIAL TRADE NETWORK

The Kalabari embroidered velvets of the twentieth century originate from somewhere in India, perhaps several locales over the century, as the zari embroidery industry shrank and changed in response to the decline of the Indian nobility. The search for new wholesale customers within and outside India occurred together with employing cheaper labor (Nissim 1976; Haynes 1986) and materials in producing both zari elements and the embroidered velvets themselves. Yet until around 1980, the Kalabari embroidered velvets, like the Indian symmetric embroidered velvets, were always based with cotton and edged with fringe, and they followed the Indian tradition of embroidered border, motif placement, and pattern content. After 1980 the design of the velvets for the Kalabari began changing.

The Nigerian government instituted a ban on textile imports in 1976, sixteen years after its independence from the British, to stem the outflow of Nigerian currency and support its own textile industries. This greatly disrupted the India-West Africa trade in all the textiles so important to the Kalabari cultural community. On the one hand, British-, European-, and Indian-owned import offices located in Nigeria shut down their now-illegal operations or moved across the Nigerian border to continue the textile trade. The wholesale buyers of the latter smuggled the many Indian textile imports into Nigeria. On the other hand, two groups of West African businesspeople began searching in India for the source of these banned imports. West African men, seeing new economic opportunities in the trade disruption, and "market women," wholesale buyers who had long controlled the retailing of Indian textiles in West Africa, flew to India's major cities and asked where they could find the several types of Indian textiles so important to the construction of the Kalabari ethnic identity. This included wholesale buyers living in the Kalabari diaspora who imported the embroidered velvets for members of their expatriate communities in the USA and the UK. Quickly, Chennai "head weavers" and manufacturer-exporters of the textiles precious to the Kalabari posted advertisements for their products in the Mumbai airport and major hotels. Some of them regularly looked for West African wholesale buyers in Chennai hotels.

Though India had gained independence from the British in 1947, followed by Nigeria in 1960, the Indian manufacturer-exporting firms founded under colonialism had maintained complete control of the flow of design information after independence until 1976. By buying directly from the Indian manufacturers and even buying direct from some Indian head weavers, who had started up their own export businesses in the wake of the trade disruption, the Nigerian wholesale buyers circumvented the control of design by the colonial manufacturer-exporters. The new Nigerian wholesale buyers soon learned that the important handwoven plaid cotton *injiri* cloth and other Indian cotton textiles used by the Kalabari were exported out of Chennai. The two groups of people, West African and Indians, finally met each other and began designing the textiles in consultation with each other.

This change in Nigerian government import laws unintentionally opened the era of face-to-face interactions between Nigerian wholesale buyers and Indian manufacturers, both the established firms and those head weavers using the trade disruption as an opportunity to establish their own export firms in competition with the firms to which they had previously sold their products.

Design information was now being communicated directly between Nigerians and Indians. During the colonial era, textile design information had been controlled by British, European, and later some Indian manufacturer-exporter firms all founded during India's colonial era. After 1976 the colonial control began disintegrating.

DESIGN DEVELOPMENT OF EMBROIDERED VELVETS PRODUCED IN CHENNAI FOR WEST AFRICA, 1980–1997

Once in direct contact with the makers and manufacturers-exporters, enterprising Kalabari market women began asking if other, noncotton textiles could also be produced in the Chennai region. One woman brought to her Chennai trading partner an old, deteriorating, zari-embroidered velvet that the Kalabari generally call *india*. She asked if similar embroidered velvets could be produced in Chennai. This Chennai manufacturer had not previously dealt in the embroidered velvets for the Niger delta cultural markets, yet by religion he was connected to the Muslim workforce that produced asli zardozi. He agreed to take on the contract.

Zardoz embroiderers were well established in Chennai, a city of relatively high Muslim population. Also, ari embroidery workshops in Tambaram and other villages south of Chennai had been embroidering Real Madras Handkerchiefs (RMHK), plaid textiles in colored threads (see chap. 6), bound for West African cultural communities from at least the first quarter of the twentieth century. Additionally, newer ari embroidery workshops had been established in villages west and northwest of Chennai by semi-migrant embroiderers who had been leaving their villages seasonally to train and work as embroiderers in Mumbai (previously Bombay). The initial zari-embroidered velvets produced in Chennai for the Kalabari were made with asli zardozi. Quickly, however, a switch was made to ari embroidery.

This direct connection between West Africa and Indian businesspeople initiated the era of truly postcolonial trade in which the subsequent design innovations that I analyze herein could flourish. Competing manufacturer-exporters in Chennai ignored the embroidered-velvet market in West Africa until it became so large that it became financially feasible to enter into competition with the initial Chennai manufacturer-exporter of the embroidered velvets.

With many Indian competitors now producing the velvets, many textile design changes occurred in all those produced for the Kalabari market. About half of the changes responded to forces ranging in scale and specificity from the actions of national governments controlling the international import of handcrafted textiles into the countries where expatriate Kalabari lived, down to individual consumers' design requests for special occasion wear.

I turn now to analyzing those design changes arising in response to the altered use of the embroidered velvets from an Indian flat household textile to a specific Kalabari women's wrapped dress ensemble, the *bite sara*, as described in chapter 11.

The first Chennai-made embroidered velvets were manufactured in large rectangular symmetric designs. These paralleled the large velvets used as funeral bed canopies and worn by Kalabari iriabo as thigh-revealing wrappers, seen on the women dancing in velvet wrappers at the 1984 Buguma Centenary. Their designs follow the historic Indian tradition in household textiles.

A Kalabari market woman resident in the UK, working in cooperation with a Chennai manufacturer of embroidered velvets for West Africa, redesigned the size of the velvets to form them into two-piece wrapper sets for the Kalabari woman's bite sara ensemble. Other West African wholesale buyers and Indian manufacturers of textiles for the West African market watched the sales of these new wrapper sets. When they saw the textiles' market success, they designed their own competing versions and entered the market.

The initial change in the size and relative dimensions of the velvets to accommodate wrapping the velvets for the bite sara style set the stage for significant breaks with the Indian embroidered-velvet design tradition. Kalabari earlier uses of the Indian embroidered velvets, to decorate or canopy funerary beds or to hang on funeral room walls, primarily displayed the textiles in a fully flat form, showing the design symmetry; folded velvets placed on funerary beds showed too little of the cloth to exert any new design direction.

Kalabari rectangular, embroidered velvets of the 1980s had also been culturally authenticated into formal dress for chiefs, but this exerted no new demands on the design. The men's ankle-length gowns consisted of two embroidered velvets sewn together at the top and the sides, leaving spaces for arms and head, as seen in figure 8.1, continuing to display the Indian textile's four-way symmetry.

Producing embroidered velvets used for the bite sara ensemble required resizing the textiles and using them in a particular three-dimensional form that exerted a consistent new design direction for the velvet embroidery. A series of changes was thus set in motion going beyond the mere change in dimensions and creating a double set of wrappers, one slightly smaller than the other. With the major new influence for design alteration of the Indian velvets now coming from their use in Kalabari women's bite sara ensembles, the changes initiated served to enhance the textile's aesthetic interaction with women's bodies, as

Fig. 9.2. Asari Tomina Ereme members wearing bite sara of zari-embroidered velvets. Variations in size and design of crown motifs, double or single borders, and diagonal versus orientation of larger corner crowns. Buguma, 1984.

seen at the Buguma Centenary celebrations in figure 9.2. The ankle-length bite sara wrapping style, like the iriabo ensemble, enhances a woman's expansive middle girth with multiple layers of velvet on her lower body. In addition, placement of the borders of the two cloths horizontally across the body at ankles and knees further exaggerates width, rather than height. The members of women's clubs often order new, matching wrapper sets for participation in important events. Failing this, they coordinate the colors and embroidery patterns of their wrapper sets, as figure 9.2 illustrates. This image shows six changes in placement and size of embroidery motifs and borders that occurred:

(1) The corner motifs underwent a change from the typical Indian diagonal placement to a placement that appears vertical when the cloth is wrapped in the bite sara style.
(2) The motifs placed in the area enclosed by the embroidered borders were enlarged, further emphasizing and drawing attention to the female wearer's ideal bulky lower torso.
(3) The orientation of motifs within the embroidered borders on the long edges of the textiles changed to accommodate the perspective from which

the cloth is viewed when wrapped in the bite sara style. The motifs' new orientation within the short end borders also brings them into vertical alignment with the wearer's body.

(4) The same change was made in the orientation of motifs embroidered in the central ground inside the four borders.

(5) In some wrapper sets, the embroidered borders were doubled, but only on the long sides—those wrapped around the body. This increases the number of horizontal lines crossing the ankle, calf, knee, and middle thigh areas of the wearer's body, again emphasizing her width and girth.

These five changes destroy the complete symmetry characterizing the majority of embroidered velvets of Indian tradition. The new Kalabari borders merely maintain a mirror or left-to-right symmetry, that is, across the textiles' length, wrapped horizontally around the body.

(6) A sixth change from the Indian tradition is also visible in the content of some of the embroidery motifs of the wrapper sets. In the Indian tradition, motifs are largely restricted to abstracted imagery of flowers and trees. For the Buguma Centenary, the women's group wrappers are embroidered with images of human-made crowns. Such iconic, symbolic motifs are consistent with a widespread West African tradition of surface design on textiles. The progress of all these changes is visible in Eicher's field photographs.

In addition to the large central motifs seen in figure 9.2, other West African icons and phrases began to appear on the embroidered velvets. The design of such motifs originated in West Africa, not in India.

As Nigerian market women traveled to India year by year to design and order new bite sara embroidered velvets, edge and border treatment continued to change. Beaded fringe replaced zari fringe, and imitation cloth-of-gold appliqué were introduced about the same time, inspired by new developments in Indian women's fashion, called "Ethnic Chic" by Tarlo (1996, 284–317), drawing on folk embroidery designs produced and used within the domestic spheres of Indian cultural minority groups. Indian manufacturers serving the Kalabari market consulted Indian women's fashion catalogs for new design inspirations. The new beaded fringe, only used on the lower of the two long edges of the wrappers, drew attention to the wearer when walking or dancing and exaggerated her movement. The other three borders were edged in the usual, more rigid, short zari fringe or trim, as seen in figure 9.2, further destroying the symmetry originating in the Indian tradition.

In a 1997 IgboFest celebration in Minnesota, a woman wore the fully developed Ethnic Chic up-and-down wrapper set with appliqued faux cloth-of-gold and beaded fringe. In a celebration in 2018 (see fig. 22.7), two Kalabari women dancing at a diaspora event wore iriabo ensembles again with Ethnic Chic velvet wrappers. By appliqueing the faux cloth-of-gold with ari embroidery, a significant amount of gold surface pattern was increased without adding much production cost in either iriabo or bite sara style. The convergence of all the above changes in the embroidered-velvet design arose when this complex textile became wrapped in the bite sara style of Kalabari women's dress.

Some very lush designs of Ethnic Chic velvets included velvet appliqués on top of the cloth-of-gold appliqués, making the embroidered velvet a four-layered textile. Also, fine-gauge grids of ari-applied faux pearls covered the entire central surface of some of these velvets. Such textiles increased the insulation value and weight of the bite sara ensemble.

Single, heavy, zari-embroidered velvet had been tolerable to wear in the high temperatures and humidity of equatorial Africa when worn in the iriabo ensemble, which exposes the legs from ankles to lower thighs. The change to use as paired wrappers for bite sara, which covers the legs entirely, probably made the velvet wrappers uncomfortably hot to wear. I surmise that this led to the next generation of embroidered-velvet design change.

Several Chennai manufacturer-exporters described them as "a lighter velvet." These "lighter velvets," or "Jet Age Velvets," as one manufacturer in consultation with his Kalabari wholesale buyer branded and identified with hang tags, consisted of a multilayered, embroidered textile like the original Indian velvet, but with a great difference. First, the base cloth consists of a polyester plain-woven cloth, similar to a china silk, usually in a solid or shot—that is, warp and weft threads are different colors—golden or related warm color. This base supports the top layer of polyester cloth. Second, the top layer is either a plain weave, as in the base cloth; an imitation cloth-of-gold; or a similarly thin, dobby—that is, small-figured—weave. In all cases the color is a solid golden or related warm hue. The ari embroidery is applied through both layers, as in the embroidered velvets of Indian tradition.

These innovations occurred after the Indian government lifted its 1980s ban on Indian production of polyester yarns and cloth with high customs duties. Previously to this, all polyester cloth had been imported into India since the advent of the newly independent government's Ministry of Textiles's rules within the government's Five-Year Plans scheme of national economic development. High custom duties had been applied to this "luxury" cloth. In the mid-1980s the ministry lifted the polyester ban in order to free up more land from cotton agriculture for food production so that the nation could become independent in food production. Polyester spinning and weaving mills opened, and the cloth became affordable and fashionable within India. In consultation with their Kalabari trading partners, the Indian manufacturers, serving both the Indian and Kalabari markets, brought polyester cloth into the production of Kalabari embroidered velvets.

The two layers of cloth are also no longer held together with glue. In part, the absence of glue between layers derives from the nature of the fabrics used—the glue would penetrate the topmost fabric and destroy its appearance. Using lighter-weight fabrics, woven from thin synthetic yarns and lacking velvet's nap, not only reduces the weight and insulating properties of the original velvet textiles but also contributes to a less stiff drape, as does the absence of glue. The innovative textiles became cooler, lighter to wear, and easier to wrap around the body. Kalabari acceptance of these lighter "velvets" may have also occurred under the influence of European and American idealization of a thinner feminine silhouette.

Most significantly, in the "lighter velvets," the actual velvet has been relegated to the position of appliqué rather than ground cloth. In the Ethnic Chic design described earlier, polyester cloth-of-gold was appliquéd onto the velvet ground to replace some of the gold embroidery. Velvet was now used as appliquéd borders and pattern motifs on the polyester ground cloth. The reversed positions of velvet base and appliquéd cloth made this three-layered textile much lighter. Yet these complex textiles are still called "velvet." In some even more complex textiles, a layer of synthetic tulle was placed on top of the fabric sandwich before adding the embroidery and appliqués and contributed an additional visual and physical shimmer and depth to the gold-colored wrappers.

All the many separate changes in the generations of velvet design were produced in a variety of different combinations, for as new ideas arose and design experiments were made, different textiles were produced in a seeming constant stream of design innovation, emanating from many competing manufacturer-exporters' workshops. They resulted in the production of a large assemblage of textile designs that are barely recognizable as deriving from their historic Indian roots.

All these new, less expensive wrapper sets became popular among two groups of women. They appeal to those Kalabari not wanting to borrow from senior family members' cloth boxes, as in Kalabari historic practice, for special occasion dress; they now can buy their own. They have also become popular with women in the diaspora communities who live far from their families' cloth boxes.

The change in the base and ground cloth served as an opportunity to change the finishing technique for the edges of the wrappers from the early zari fringe trim. These fringes were attached to the edge of the velvet ground and cotton base cloths sandwiched by embroidery with the hooked needle. They hid the raw cut edges of the velvet and cotton cloths. The use of a polyester base and ground cloth facilitated the adoption of a melt-cutting technique that embroiderers were already using to create cutwork needle lace embroidery in handwoven, cotton RMHK and RMHK Fancies (woven with jacquard borders rather than in plaids) and the newer, fully synthetic RMHK Fancies, called "Washwash." Both the handwoven and synthetic textiles were destined for West African markets. A line of embroidery is first worked around the edge of the polyester sandwich of the so-called velvet, usually in a decorative line such as a scallop or sawtooth (zigzag) line. Then, an electrically heated device melt-cuts the textile just outside the embroidery line. The glitter of the zari embroidery line outshines the rough, but secure, edge created by the melted fibers as they coagulate with each other during cooling. The congealed polyester fibers at the edges will never unravel. The creation of the outside edge by this method reestablished the complete design symmetry in some of these lighter velvets, showing the continuing strong pull of the Indian tradition.

Nevertheless, another design change counteracted this return to the Indian tradition. The most altered and elaborate form of the lighter velvets I observed in production in Chennai for the Kalabari market in 1997 was a three-dimensional textile, reclaiming the thickness of the original velvets' nap without sacrificing the light weight or adding much heat insulation. "Feather velvet" consists in the basic structure of a lighter velvet, with the addition of feather-shaped attachments over portions of the surface. Strips of feather shapes are constructed using the melt-cutting technique in conjunction with an embroidered line for edge finishing and then embroidery-appliquéd onto the ground cloth in overlapping rows. The whole area so treated appears to be covered with individual fabric "feathers," or scales, reestablishing the thickness of the hot and heavy nap of the original velvet in a lightweight, cool, thick textile. Their overall design is also new. For example, a large peacock was embroidered in an approximately two-foot-high equilateral triangle midway between the two shorter borders. The area outside this triangle was covered in "feathers." These most elaborate forms of the new zari-embroidered velvet continue to serve the Kalabari female ideal of a thick torso. They bear little resemblance to the textile of Indian tradition from which they began to emerge less than twenty years previously.

CHANGES OF IDENTITY THROUGH PRODUCTION AND TRADE

The embroidered velvets changed their names as their designs changed. The Indian embroiderers named the West Africa–bound textiles "Africa cloth" and "that thick cloth" because their thickness—and in the case of the cotton RM-HKs and "lighter velvet" polyesters, their dense weave—is harder to embroider than the generally thinner fabrics embroidered for Indian consumption. Manufacturer-exporters and their wholesale buyers developed their own names for the various generations of design change: "jet age velvet," the descriptive "lighter velvet," and "feather velvet." Between the Kalabari wholesale buyers and their customers, the embroidered velvets are called "india" and "Bala India" and names specific to the embroidery pattern of various designs, such as "elephant," "peacock," and "crown."

When the embroidered velvets were exported, they came under the jurisdiction of the Multi-Fiber Arrangement (MFA) which governed world trade in textiles and apparel. Established in 1974, the MFA set quotas on the export of textiles and apparel from developing countries into developed countries. In addition, an India items list of textiles and garments was negotiated by the Indian and American governments. The items listed could be imported into the US despite quota restrictions—handcrafted and ethnic textiles and apparel destined for Indian expatriates living in the US. Such items would not compete with American industrial manufactures. The United Kingdom also made use of this same list of India items. The names of the listed items were recorded and described in some detail. For example, a woman's kameez (i.e., tunic) could not have a zipper.

The Indian gold-embroidered velvets destined for the Kalabari market and its diaspora were not included in the exemptions list. However, the list's description of *orhni*—a handcrafted, rectangular textile with borders, considered a type of veil or shawl—did not specify the textile's thickness. So the gold-embroidered velvets changed their name and identity again for export/import purposes. On the international trade paperwork they became orhni.

The MFA was superseded by the Agreement on Textiles and Clothing (ATC) negotiated at the General Agreement on Tariffs and Trade Uruguay Round. ATC established a slow process of dismantling the MFA quotas between 1995 and 2005. So the thick and multilayered gold-embroidered velvets acquired another name, as exporters and importers identified them as orhni on international trade paperwork.

CONCLUSION

In light of the dramatic design changes to a textile originating in the Indian tradition, redesigned for and still manufactured in India for the Kalabari and their neighbors, a question emerges that is important to understanding ethnic or cultural textile traditions and the global society to which the Kalabari belong. Whose cloth are these zari-embroidered velvets? Do they belong to India? The Indian embroiderers call them "Africa cloth" and "that thick cloth." Does it belong to the Kalabari and their culturally close neighbors? The Kalabari call some of them "india" or "Bala India" after a specific Indian manufacturer. Or do these velvets constitute a form of ethnic dress that belongs within a global society—a global society in which many separate cultural traditions in textiles are dependent on multiple geographically divergent cultural sources, places of production, and cross-cultural communications between users and wholesale buyers, on the one hand, and exporters and manufacturers, on the other, in a constant interaction circumscribed by the specificity of governments' economic controls of textile manufacture and trade?

Indian textiles traded to West Africa, particularly to the Kalabari, began as Indian designs and became selected, characterized, and incorporated into male and female Kalabari ways of dress during the colonial period. The textile designs were transformed by Indian manufacturers-exporters and handicraft workers when they began face-to-face interaction with Kalabari wholesale buyers. This freed the textile designs from colonial business control. Individual embroidered velvets' identities continued to change throughout the production, trade, and sale to facilitate the process and evade or take advantage of government controls. The new designs of embroidered velvets attracted the attention of Kalabari residing in the diaspora as well as those residing in the Niger River delta. The history of the long use and later design changes in these velvets provides evidence that the Kalabari have developed a distinctive— that is, ethnic—form of women's dress as they participate in the global system of textile manufacture and trade. The frequently changing designs occurring within the confines of the Kalabari cultural aesthetic, at the same time, show the Kalabari to also be engaged in a fashion system. Ethnic dress and fashion are not distinguishable among the Kalabari.

HAZEL ANN LUTZ, PhD, with expertise in both textile and apparel arts, has a BA in South Asian studies, University of Chicago, and an MA in anthropology, University of Minnesota. She researched the path of Indian production and export of embroidered velvets for Kalabari celebrations for her doctoral dissertation, *Design and Tradition in an India-West Africa Trade Textile: Zari-Embroidered Velvets* (2002). She continues to lecture in India. She coauthored *The Visible Self* (2008).

NOTES

Adapted from Lutz (2003).

II

Kalabari Dress

Section II provides eight chapters concerning how the Kalabari use imported textiles, along with imported jewelry and headwear, for their dress, based on the comprehensive definition of *dress* as all body supplements and body modifications (Eicher and Roach-Higgins 1995), which includes more than garments. This concept of dress, explored in *The Visible Self* (Eicher and Evenson 2014), relates to establishing personal and sociocultural identity, found in all cultures. Chapters 10–13 center on the significance of female and male ensembles throughout Kalabari life. Chapter 14 highlights the dress of a contemporary Kalabari businessman who became a chief and was later knighted. Chapters 15–17 present data on beads (particularly coral) and headwear. The Kalabari examples throughout the volume illustrate dressing for the public self in contrast to the private and secret selves (Eicher and Miller 1994; Eicher 2015b).

10

Male and Female Artistry

M. Catherine Daly, Joanne B. Eicher, and Tonye Victor Erekosima

THE DISTINCTIVE AESTHETIC of Kalabari dress, our focus in this chapter, derives from trade providing the resources for the unique and expressive ensembles, assemblages of borrowed and indigenous Western and non-Western elements.[1] The creative composition of these materials and artistic techniques "is their ethnic identity and genius." (Daly, Eicher, and Erekosima 1984, 2).

Typically the ensembles for both males and females may include cloth in the form of wrappers, blouses, head ties, shirts, and handkerchiefs along with (1) accessories of coral, gold, and glass beads fashioned into jewelry such as necklaces, bracelets, rings, armbands, kneebands, and earrings; (2) sandals and shoes; (3) cosmetic chalks and pomades; and (4) handheld items—purses, fans, canes, elephant tusks, umbrellas, and the like. To the Western eye, perhaps some dress combinations may seem haphazard or without thought. Yet, conscious choices are made and justified, based on knowledge of not only what is aesthetically pleasing but also what is culturally correct.

The basic ensemble for adult women includes an imported lace or eyelet blouse (Plankensteiner and Adediran 2010) worn with what is called an "up-and-down" wrapper combination of a knee-length wrapper worn over an ankle-length one (see *bite sara* in fig. 11.1). The wrappers come in a variety of materials such as striped imported Indian madras (*injiri*), printed woolen flannel (*blangidi*), handwoven Ewe strip cloth (*accraa*), and striped Indian silk (*loko*). For men, trousers or an Indian madras wrapper combined with a loose jumper or shirt known as *woko* is standard. More expensive and complex assemblages are usually the privilege of age for men and women, as figure 10.1 illustrates. Older women may add accessories such as head ties, jewelry, and purses. Older men may also wear costly jewelry, don a distinctive hat like a bowler or top hat, and carry a cane or walking stick.

According to Kalabari respondents, color, rather than pattern or texture, is often the critical factor in unifying ensembles. A green lace blouse with a multicolored print or striped wrapper is considered coordinated if green is repeated in the wrapper. Other factors, like comparable cost, may link the diverse elements in an outfit: lace blouses, worn with blangidi, *Akwete*, and accraa or loko wrappers, are equivalent in price.

A dress assemblage may also be unified through the combination of various items of historical significance to the family. Members often dress in wrappers and other heirlooms that have been brought forth from the ancestral cloth boxes for funerals, chieftaincy installations, or traditional womanhood ceremonies. Many of these are the corporate property of a lineage group and are especially prized because of the length of family ownership.

Learning how to dress as a Kalabari begins early. Within the household, conversations about attire are frequent. Children observe men and women planning their wardrobes and hear them discussing, for instance, whether a wrapper is tied correctly, whether the fabrics used are complementary, whether the selection of accessories is suitable. Through such socialization, each person internalizes the group standard of dress.

In ordinary situations a person may dress alone, and self-appraisal of one's attire may precede the assessment of others. Before going out, however, members of the family, usually female elders, but sometimes male elders as well, check the ensemble. Their approval is important because the individual is also representing the family, lineage, and even ancestors to the community, and elders are respected as experts and considered repositories of knowledge. For special occasions, other individuals attend the person dressing and guarantee that the individual's appearance is meticulous and aesthetically pleasing. When formal dress is required, elder women in the family, considered knowledgeable arbiters of taste because of their age and experience, are summoned as consultants. They help select items of attire for both sexes and execute or oversee the process of putting together an ensemble for women. Their presence is especially important when other women are being dressed for important occasions.

The female elders also act as the final judges of male attire. Though men do confer with each other and seek the advice of respected older men, almost all will defer to the judgment of these women before stepping out the door into the public domain of village or town. In public, challenges are heard between

Fig. 10.1. Tonye Erekosima, wearing woko with injiri wrapper. Stella Kintebe, left, and Bekinwari Elebe, right, both wearing bite sara with lace blouses; cotton *Akwete* wrapper on Kintebe, silk loko wrapper on Elebe. Buguma, 1984.

rival War-Canoe Houses (*wari*) regarding the appropriateness of a member's dress. For various men's and women's club events, a feature of Kalabari social life, attire is often uniform, as illustrated and described for the *eremne-ogbo* in chapter 12, and members regularly critique each other's appearance.

Part of the aesthetic of Kalabari dress is scrupulous attention to detail. The local expression, "Take time," applied to one's demeanor and dress, illustrates this concern. Other factors affecting the art of assembly concern the differentiation of sex, age, status or role, socioeconomic position, family, and lineage affiliation.

The materials used in dress are manipulated into characteristically Kalabari ensembles in several ways. This wide variety of processes is especially evident during *iria*, the traditional womanhood ceremonies. At each stage, specific processes used in the proper assemblage of dress are learned; these processes, when understood and correctly executed, are featured in each rite of passage. Cloth is tied; items are carried; ears are pierced; hair is shaved, plaited, and combed; arms, legs, and torso are colored; the body, fattened through diet and cleansed by washing, is adorned with jewelry. Knowledge about dress materials and processes is cumulative and in the final stage of iriabo culminates in the ultimate expression of femaleness.

The Kalabari worldview, which incorporates the ancestors, the water people, and the community deities (Horton 1960a; Horton 1962; Madume 1976), is reflected in the complementarity of male and female artistry in Kalabari dress. The ancestors, as founders of lineages who are honored, represent the communal nature of Kalabari society, in which the basic necessities like food and compound space are shared for the welfare of the group. The clothing of deceased family members becomes corporate property as well. Wealth is displayed through the donning of generations-old cloths and precious ornaments such as gold or coral beads. Cut-thread cloths are an example of treasured items worn to venerate the ancestors who bequeathed them. Artistry in dress is determined not only by the contents of the cloth boxes but by access to them: as guardian of the family cloth boxes and dispenser of their contents, the eldest female controls the male lineage property and its use.

The water people, the spirits inhabiting the rivers and streams, mold and control the environment from which the Kalabari have made their living historically by fishing and trading. They also are responsible for a person's good or bad fortune and his creativity, including creativity in dress. Their power extends to almost any economic activity, one example being artistic services provided by the knowledgeable elder women, who are often financially compensated. The coral, gold, and rare clothlike madras and embroidered velvets and other items used to create a typical Kalabari ensemble have come by water as a result of successful commercial ventures. People who wear these fine objects may have acquired them through personal enterprise, attributable to the water people, as well as from the ancestral cloth boxes (Erekosima 1989).

Unusual fashions and clothing innovations are also linked to the water people. In the past the acquisition of coral beads, imported cloth, hats, canes, handkerchiefs, and other Western paraphernalia that the Kalabari combine in innovative ways was the result of male commercial activity from which women benefited in their kinship roles; the man's success or failure in obtaining these items was ascribed to the water people, as was the aesthetic influence of the water people on women, which they exercise in making cut-thread cloth, decorating funeral rooms, and being arbiters of dress. Successful and affluent Kalabari women, however, are also recognized for their economic pursuits and business acumen. Through their own efforts they may extend their wardrobes with traditional costly items of dress and pay for the services of the female elders.

Acting as intermediaries between the ancestors and water people are the community deities, who are concerned with the welfare and culture of the group. For example, Owamekaso, head of the community deities, is said to have taught the people their skill in trading. We posit that the deities, as the bearers and guardians of culture, are responsible for Kalabari identity as reflected in dress. The distinctiveness of Kalabari dress is epitomized by the opulent ensembles that women wear for postnatal practices associated with iria.

Because of the role of dress in communicating wealth, status, and prestige, both Kalabari men and women are meticulous in their assembly of items. Both draw from the heritage of heirloom textiles and accessories from the family cloth boxes, and both defer to the expertise and aesthetic advice of female elders, the gatekeepers of Kalabari culture, and the women who also have created the subtle designs of cut-thread cloth. Naturally, some differences occur between the sexes in form, process, technique, and intent. For example, women wear a double set of wrappers while men wear one. Arrangement and meaning differ as well. Women wrap their bodies to emphasize the girth of the abdomen and suggest fecundity. In contrast, the wrapper and woko worn by men give an impression of linearity and imply social stature and power. The Kalabari dress ensemble is a symbol of the "fabric of culture [in which] the warp of the revered past and woof of the opulent present are woven into a seamless whole through a creative commitment to the society's future or persistent well-being" (Erekosima 1982. Many other peoples in and outside Africa are known for creative assemblage in their attire; analyzing the nature of Kalabari artistry in dress allows insight into both Western and non-Western cultures.

M. CATHERINE DALY, research associate, Eoin McKiernan Library, has extensive skills in the textile and dress arts. She completed research in Nigeria for her MA degree at Michigan State University and moved to the University of Minnesota for her PhD on the Kalabari topic of the female maturation process and dress called *iria*. She conducted her fieldwork primarily in Abonnema. After her PhD, she pursued research on Afghan dress, published in the *Encyclopedia of Dress and Fashion* (2010). She currently researches lumberjack wear in North America.

JOANNE B. EICHER, PhD, is Regents Professor Emerita in the Department of Design, Housing, and Apparel at the University of Minnesota. She is coeditor of *The Anthropology of Dress and Fashion: A Reader*; coeditor of *The Visible Self: Global Perspectives on Dress, Culture, and Society*, 4th ed.; and editor in chief of the *Encyclopedia of World Dress and Fashion*.

TONYE VICTOR EREKOSIMA (1940–2008), PhD, native-born Kalabari, lived in the Igbo towns of Owerri and Umuahia, because his father was an educator and secondary-school principal, until Erekosima's university years in the United States. He was steeped in Kalabari cultural tradition, however, thanks to his family's routine travel to Buguma, his parents' birthplace, for holidays and significant events like funerals. Following his PhD, he served as Director, General Studies, Rivers State College of Education, and Director, Instructional Resources Center, University of Port Harcourt. He coedited *A Hundred Years of Buguma History in Kalabari Culture* (1984) and *Buguma 1984 Centenary Symposia on Kalabari* (1991).

NOTES

Adapted from Daly, Eicher, and Erekosima (1986).

    1. See Aronson (1980a) for a summary of the history of cloth and related items in the delta.

The Stages of Traditional Womanhood

M. Catherine Daly

IRIA, THE KALABARI TERM for the traditional stages of developing Kalabari womanhood within the female life course, formerly had five stages, referring to ways of dress corresponding to female maturation (iria) as seen in figure 11.1: *bite pakiri iwain* (half-length of a piece of cloth), *ikuta de* (bead display), *konju fina* (waist tie), *bite sara* (blouse and ankle-length wrapper) and *iriabo* (ensemble for a woman who has borne a child).

Fig. 11.1. Drawing 1: The stages of traditional womanhood. Courtesy of M. Catherine Daly, drawn by Sylvia Ruud.

117

These stages in the twenty-first century are practiced in varying degrees depending on the social situation and celebratory events, with bite sara commonly worn by adult women.[1]

Historically, these five stages consisted of females of the same age-set experiencing a sequenced rite of passage that spanned the female life course from late childhood through childbirth. Each stage was defined in terms of a young woman's role and responsibilities to her kin group, her developing sexuality, her marriageability and relationship to men, and her residence pattern. Sequencing these stages depended on the external signs of physical maturity of the young girl and her parents' public acknowledgment of these changes. In the case of a young girl being betrothed at an early age, her future husband took responsibility to acknowledge her maturity publicly. In either circumstance, Kalabari custom *demanded* that she appear in appropriate dress during a series of public occasions. Each stage of her growth specifically emphasized various aspects of her appearance that corresponded not only to her developing and altering female body form but also to her changing sex-role status within Kalabari society. As the young girl moved from one transitional stage to the next, her parents furnished her complementary items of clothing and adornment, items initially obtained through trade and representative of her lineage or family.

Several criteria determined not only which young girls participated in these rites of passage but also when they started these progressive stages. One criterion was usually the onset of a young girl's menses. Menstruation qualified her to begin the sequence, which in turn was followed by subsequent signs of physical growth and development of the female body form. Since growth and development is individual, however, the sequenced rites of passage within an age-set varied from one girl to the next.

Another criterion was the parents' financial ability to obtain the appropriate clothing and adornment for each stage. Although the use of clothing often figured as a prominent indication of the stage of female development, adornment and other body modifications were also important; many of these other forms were both time-consuming and costly activities involving the services of the community's knowledgeable women.

Both the cloth or wrapper (bite) and upper body covering of a blouse (called *kappa* or *buba*) identify the life course stage of the wearer. The important features of the cloth focus on the:[2]

- Length or position between waist and ankle. For example, the term bite kpuluma refers to wearing the cloth from waist to knees while bite sara refers to wearing it waist to ankle

- Number of wrappers worn at one time, ranging from one to more than three, designated as "set"
- Cloth type, referring to the "named" cloth types (Talbot 1932, 190); the Kalabari use some stored in the family cloth boxes for traditional occasions
- Mode of tying such as gathered or "wavelike" (*sengi*) or the common form worn on a day-to-day basis (*ebre*)
- Sequence and duration of wearing each cloth type
- Dimensions (length and width) of each cloth type.

Initially, the cloth wrapper was chosen first with the upper-body clothing selected to "match" or coordinate with the wrapper in three ways: comparable costliness, corresponding colors, and similar ornateness.

Additional forms of adornment corresponding to the clothing worn included jewelry, head ornamentation, and foot treatment.[3] Different types of jewelry were worn at the various stages: bracelets, upper armbands, kneebands, rings, necklaces, and earrings. Head ornamentations included hair treatments, head coverings, and additives to the hair. The girls had bare feet or wore shoes or sandals.

BITE PAKIRI IWAIN

The first stage, bite pakiri iwain (now only ceremonially practiced), meaning "half the length of a piece of cloth," referred to the time young girls started their menses.[4] In the past practice, parents would guard their daughter's sexuality once she was considered physically mature and potentially fertile, and they expected her virginity to remain intact. This was also the time when parents approved a betrothal to take place. The girl's roles and responsibilities were expected to parallel those of other children living in the family compound, engaging in learning and contributing to domestic activities like housekeeping, marketing, and child-rearing of younger siblings, and she was held accountable for her activities to older relatives.

When a girl's menses started, she went through her first short seclusion period, followed by the first formal ceremonies or "coming-out" rituals known as bite pakiri iwain. During seclusion, she tied a half wrapper, a fathom of cloth cut lengthwise, worn short (bite kpuluma) but long enough to cover the pubic region in front, leaving the navel and buttocks exposed. Christian missionaries, active in the latter part of the eighteenth century in the delta, imposed values of modesty not necessarily held by the Kalabari prior to the pre-Christian era. The Kalabari focused special attention on the development of breasts and female buttocks, emphasizing that only women with prominent buttocks carry a wrapper properly. Change in this physical attribute signified that she was a woman—able to wear a wrapper. In this context, a "small" piece of cloth was considered suitable rather than a cloth of any particular length and was also referred to as a small handkerchief (*bite ankinsi*), folded diagonally, resting below the waist on the hips and tied in back. For this occasion the Kalabari preferred the cloth type *loko*, a handwoven, striped design cloth imported from India that was lightweight and either silk or silk-like. The upper body remained uncovered so that her breast development could be noted.

Her adornment was small, inexpensive, colored, imported strung glass beads (called *aka*), usually white (*pina pina*), blue (*buloo*), or red (*awu*). The same style, shape, and color aka encircled both wrists as bracelets (*nunuma*) and below the knees as kneebands (*buo po*). At the ears small wire dangle earrings (*beri suai*) completed the adornment.

At this time also the typical short, cropped hairstyle of young girls changed to being shaved in an arching design across the forehead from ear to ear (*on-onqo*). A Kalabari girl wore these shaved hair designs up until the time she went to her husband's house (Talbot 1932, 211); after marriage she arranged her hair in a different manner. Despite her linear body form, this stage emphasized her body and celebrated the beginning of her menses and breast development. The importance of breasts is significant since Kalabari considered them the most sacred physical attribute of female appearance, related to Owamekaso, their female deity.

IKUTA DE

When a young girl's breasts "came out" or "filled up" and her buttocks developed, she entered the second stage of iria, ikuta de (bead display). Her increased height and curvaceous figure grew more mature in shape and indicated her physical and social maturity, which in turn attracted male suitors, the main purpose of this stage. Items considered to be indicative of wealth consisted of small, identical, cylindrical, strung beads worn in similar placement as for bite pakiri iwain at the wrist, as bracelets (*nunuma*), and below the knees, as kneebands (*buo po*). One large cylindrical bead necklace worn with two longer but smaller continuous and cylindrical ones (*poko suaye*) adorned her breasts. In addition, two longer bead necklaces of similar style, color, and shape were draped symmetrically and diagonally in front, one from her left shoulder across to her right waistline and the other from her right shoulder across to her left waistline. A final adornment of earrings (*beri suai*) of various styles and materials pierced her ears.

Since Kalabari values stressed the virtues of single and betrothed females retaining their virginity until after marriage, sexual activity was discouraged; a young girl becoming pregnant was considered "spoiled" or damaged and brought a lower bridewealth. Although Kalabari prize fertility, a young girl who established her ability to bear children before marriage did so at a social and financial sacrifice.

After completing seclusion (*ikuta de iria so*) and her "coming-out" display, men admired her "freely" or openly by commenting on her appearance. The young girl's physical attributes implied potential fertility, which made her more desirable for marriage; if suitors found her appealing, they approached her parents concerning marriage (*bibi finjiye*). At this time, the value of the beads worn during ikuta de showed the parents' social status and position in the community. These "tokens were passed down from mother to daughter" and were "collected or traded in [the delta] when the Kalabari chiefs traded with the Portuguese" (Iyalla 1968, 216). If the marriage was arranged when the girl was young, then the husband contributed the beads.

In addition to the physical attributes of the body, the stage of ikuta de emphasized in greater degree the wearing of beads (*ikuta*) and other items of adornment, possibly because their use originally defined the stage prior to the introduction of cloth. Clothing of a wrapper and an upper-body covering figured less importantly since they obstructed the visibility of the female body and its development.

At the numerous coming-out displays, respondents claimed the color (i.e., blue/*buloo*, black/*krukru* or red/*awu*) and shape (round, oval, or lozenge) of the waistbeads expected to be worn distinguished at least four substages of ikuta de:

- Mingi biri ikuta—light-blue beads worn for bathing began the sequence; "everyone knew the young girl's maturity once the system of beads started"
- krukru ikuta—black beads worn during the second substage
- Olombo—red, flat beads worn during the third stage
- Ila—three-inch smooth or faceted agate beads worn during the last stage; "everyone knew that the young girl was no more."

Each of the four substages had a corresponding period of seclusion. After the period of confinement, the bead display started. Each substage with its complementary beads changed every Monday during a three-week period. On this day (*feni bene*), the equivalent to the big market day or big play day, young girls participated in traditional Kalabari dances, songs, and dramatic plays (*seri*) dressed in their beads. They met in the village arena or marketplace to "reveal their maiden build, beauty and youth to the admiration of spectators whose relatives were perhaps anxious to choose a new bride" (Iyalla 1968, 216). After the young girl completed the cycle of beads (*ila ikuta de*), the "time came to cover up."

Formerly, in the pretrade era, young girls wore no cloth, only waistbeads. Later, they covered their buttocks underneath their waistbeads and likewise concealed their breasts. They wore a short wrapper (bite kpuluma) of the loko cloth type but slightly longer and more fitted than the wrapper worn during bite pakiri iwain. The upper cloth, usually a different striped design of loko, tied around the neck, exposed the back and draped over the breasts to below the waist. As mentioned, the high cost and aesthetic value of a prestigious trade cloth like loko supported its use on a ritual occasion, as throughout the sequenced rites of passage for iria.

The amount and quality of a young girl's adornment varied with her parents' wealth and in some cases her betrothed's wealth. P. Amaury Talbot (1932, 179) reported that money must be provided to buy waistbeads for her until the coming of her small breasts and she went into the next stage. Adornment for hair included camwood dye (*awu*) coloring the short, cropped hairstyle typical of ikuta de. Brooches like miniature Christmas balls (*sibi suka ai* or *angra*) dangled from the forehead at the hairline with possibly either one or two decorative hand-carved bone, ivory, or other natural material combs (*sibi dalaye*) in the hair.

KONJU FINA

Entering the third stage, konju fina or waist tie stage, signified that a Kalabari female was mature and could now "put something on the waist" (*konju sua ye*). This distinction often designated her as an engaged woman as well. According to Talbot (1926, 172), "In olden days, among the Kalabari, little maids wore the short cloth called konju fina for some time before their menses." Many of my Kalabari women informants, however, claimed that usually females wore short wrappers after menstruation began. Her "filled out" figure with well-developed breasts and, more importantly, her protruding buttocks indicated her ability to wear wrappers properly. The Kalabari qualitatively judged this development by running the palm of the hand over the buttocks to determine whether they were substantial enough to carry the wrapper.

Whether single or betrothed, the young woman continued to live with her parents until her future husband performed the traditional marriage ceremonies. One such ceremony "bought the mouth of the wife (*bibi fe*)" where the future husband brings food to the bride's family. This occasion could also be expensive since "further sums of money were necessary to purchase several of the small cloths she began to wear at this time" (Talbot 1932). In addition, the type of bridewealth that was paid determined her residence. As a "small" bridewealth (*egwa*) wife, she remained with her kin group; as a "big" bridewealth (*iya*) wife, she usually moved to her husband's compound since he had paid for her and her offspring.

After the period of seclusion for konju fina, the young woman wore a set of one to four short wrappers (bite kpuluma) to the midthigh, longer than the singular wrapper worn during ikuta de. Each set consisted of one outer visible wrapper whose named cloth type classified the set and numerous underwrappers that supported the outer cloth by being simultaneously hand tied, rolled, and tucked underneath the other one. The underwrappers could be of any cloth type, but the more expensive and prestigious, the more status was conveyed.

In the same manner as the waistbead sequence during the second stage (ikuta de), a prescribed order for the outer named cloth types existed. These cloths were ritually changed by color every big market day (feni bene) or eighth day. Sacrifices were also made to ancestors at the family shrine on the eighth day during the next nine weeks (Talbot 1932). In addition, if enough available cloth types permitted, a daily change might be instituted. The cloth types appeared in successive weeks in the following sequence:

- loko—soft silk cloth
- sinini—imported European, commercially woven, pile or velvet-like cloth with varying types of surface decoration
- accraa—handwoven cloth similar to Ghanaian kente cloth
- ikaki—handwoven West African cloth with a specific Akwete cloth design known as tortoise motif

or

- akwa miri (Akwete)—handwoven cloth from the Igbo village of Akwete in Nigeria
- gom—handwoven striped cloth of undocumented origin, possibly England or India
- amatiye (blangidi)—commercially woven, wool flannel cloth imported from England.

The number of named cloth types and sets and the length of time they were worn depended on their availability within the young woman's family, which in some cases reflected its financial position. If the girl was not betrothed or married, her family's responsibilities included dressing her appropriately. Since the "coming-out" display conveyed ownership of these items, one Kalabari woman told me, "You showed your different kinds of cloth according to your means. That's the only way we noted wealthy people" (Daly 1982). A blouse (kappa) with short or capped sleeves covered the upper body and completely concealed the breasts, local fashion dictating the preferred style. The material varied but matched the named cloth type used for the wrapper.

Consistent with the costliness of this display was the monetary value of her adornment. Twin coral-strung bead bracelets and kneebands encircled each wrist and knee, while numerous coral strung bead necklaces in a variety of sizes, shapes, and styles hung from her neck and covered her blouse. Either gold or coral bead earrings pierced her ears. Another costly practice at the time of tying the "first cloth" and on subsequent festive occasions was the application of elaborate indigo dye patterns (buruma) to her body (Talbot 1932, 184).

BITE SARA

The fourth stage, bite sara or cloth tied to the ankle, continues in the twenty-first century, the traditional wrapper ensemble characteristically worn by an adult Kalabari woman. A Kalabari woman going through the stages usually had met several criteria for adult female status before she attained the right, privilege, and responsibility to dress in the bite sara prototype. She had "found a husband," married, and, in most cases, had borne a child. Because of her reproductive capabilities, she qualified as an adult female, a contributing member of the community at large and to either her own or her husband's lineage group, depending on her marriage status. As an adult, the ideal Kalabari female figure continued to be admired when substantial and thick or "plumpy," as stated by my Kalabari informants during my fieldwork. Traditional Kalabari beauty emphasizes well-developed breasts and buttocks. "To be up to a woman," is to be fat; fat in this context refers to well-developed breasts and buttocks.

According to custom, a mature Kalabari woman still wears an outer wrapper ensemble of "named cloth types," usually those initially given to her by her husband and stored in her own personal cloth box (ari i lekiri). The Kalabari considered these named cloth types as more prestigious than "ordinary" cloth because of their cost and high social value. They were trade items originally and later became part of the highly prized Kalabari family heirlooms. These cloths are still stored in family cloth boxes (bite igbe) and reserved for use on ritual and traditional occasions. The choice of named cloth type determines the choice of the articles of dress as well as the manner in which they are worn. An example is the outer wrapper ensemble made up of two wrappers, a traditional Kalabari female ensemble in which the initial "down" wrapper ends at the ankle and the second, or "up," wrapper worn over the longer wrapper ends near the knee. Each

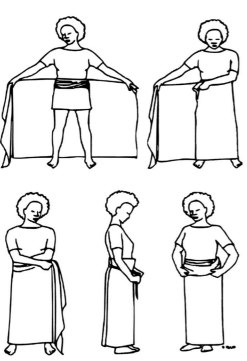

Fig. 11.2.
Drawing 2: Tying the
"down" wrapper. Courtesy
of M. Catherine Daly,
drawn by Sylvia Ruud.

Below, Fig. 11.3.
Drawing 3: Tying the "up"
wrapper. Courtesy of
M. Catherine Daly, drawn
by Sylvia Ruud.

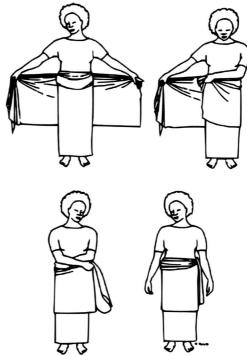

wrapper or named cloth type is a two-dimensional textile that circumscribes the body in the customary Kalabari tying (see figs. 11.2 and 11.3).

To dress herself, the wearer first ties the down wrapper over an underwrapper (see fig. 11.2). Simultaneously, with legs spread to allow for walking ease and aware that the bottom edge or selvedge of the wrapper must remain parallel to the ground, she holds both ends of the down wrapper waist high behind the body with each hand. The left hand holding one end is brought across the front of the body while the right hand, holding the other end, also overlaps the front of the body and extends slightly beyond the left side. A "tie" of string or other available material such as rope, twine, the torn selvedge of fabric, or a scarf secures the down wrapper right below the abdomen in front and at the top of the buttocks in back. After wrapping, the woman makes a final adjustment, which is accomplished by a small tug at the hem or above the tie so that the bottom edges will be even and parallel to the ground. The excess material above the tie is concealed by folding it over the tie and pulling it tightly to the left and right, then tucking it underneath the tie.

The top wrapper follows a similar tying process but instead of being draped to the ankles is hung to the knees. The wearer achieves this shortened effect by gathering the upper cloth edge horizontally by hand behind the body. This tying technique, called ebre, eliminates the excess material of the outer wrapper while also creating the desired bulkiness across the abdomen. To further this effect, the wearer, holding both ends still gathered behind the body, wraps the cloth in the same manner as the down wrapper across the body, but this time she secures the cloth end held in the right hand and draws the end across the body to the left side. The end is either pulled taut and tucked over the top edge of the up wrapper to the inside or gathered and rolled underneath the up wrapper on the outside.

The length of each wrapper creates bulk for the wearer, an amount of style overlap, and a degree of body ease. The width of each wrapper, more critical for the down wrapper, covers the space from the waist to the hem. In spite of these factors, individuals in some situations purchase additional yardage to sew to the original down wrapper only and add the necessary length or width needed because the wearer is taller or fatter than "normal."

The cloth types worn as wrappers generally dictated the length of the material that was bought, as some cloths were only available in certain yardages. The term *piece*, therefore, referred to the customary length sold; the width varied and reflected the typical warp and weft capacity of the commercial and hand-woven looms associated with a particular cloth type, as well as the standards established by commercial activity. Usually, a piece equaled eight yards of fabric, with six yards used for a woman's ensemble (divided into a three-yard up-and-down wrapper) and the remaining two yards reserved for a man's wrapper.

According to custom a mature Kalabari woman wore either an up-and-down wrapper ensemble of any "ordinary" cloth type or the previously mentioned named cloth types. The only exception was madras (*injiri*). Only a Kalabari woman who had given birth wore injiri, the most traditional Kalabari cloth. Ordinary cloth referred to less expensive cloth: "print and wax print" (worn daily) or brocade and lace (for special occasions). These cloths usually included a wrapper ensemble with identical matching blouse. Ordinary cloths worn include the following:

- brocade—a commercially woven cloth imported from England
- "lace"—a commercially woven cloth made in either Nigeria or imported from western Europe and England
- "print" cloth—any commercially woven printed cloth
- wax print—a commercially woven, resist-dyed, printed cloth imported from Ghana, Holland, England, or Switzerland (or China in the twenty-first century)

Other cloths used by the Kalabari include the following:

- okuru—a type of raffia cloth made by the Ndoki people of southeastern Nigeria (Aronson 1982, 164)
- krukrubite—"dark" injiri cloth type
- egenebite—a handwoven indigo dyed and white striped cotton cloth type "possibly originating from Ilorin, a northern Yoruba town" (Aronson 1982, 161).

Some disagreement exists whether the above are considered ordinary or named cloths because they have historical connections. In contrast to ordinary cloths, named cloth types, because of their high cost and great social value, were and still are considered more prestigious. Some named cloth types become family heirlooms when their original owner dies, and they are stored in family cloth boxes and worn on ritual and traditional occasions. As wrapper ensembles, each cloth type contributes to an identical up-and-down wrapper ensemble or is used as a wrapper in the combinations noted below. The first cloth type listed is the "down" wrapper; the second cloth type is the "up" wrapper:

- *accraa/accraa*
- *Akwete/Akwete*
- *aso-oke/aso-oke*—a handwoven narrowband cloth type woven by the Yoruba of southwestern Nigeria

- *blangidi/accraa*
- *gom/gom*
- *ikaki/ikaki*
- design or fancy injiri—a more costly cotton or cotton rayon blend injiri that is similar to brocade
- *onunga/onunga*—a Yoruba handwoven strip cloth similar to aso-oke

Although other West African groups wear the same or similar types of cloth as the Kalabari because of previously established parallel trade relationships, the Kalabari claim their outer wrapper ensembles as distinct combinations and their method of tying as uniquely Kalabari. Unlike ordinary cloth types, these combinations are again reserved for special occasions rather than worn daily. The upper-body coverings "match" the costliness and value of the named cloth types worn as outer wrapper ensembles, which usually means complementing the ensemble by wearing expensive imported lace or beaded blouses. The blouse style varies, with the bodice typically a rectangular shape varying in neckline and sleeve treatment.

Body adornment, although less definitive of the bite sara stage, includes jewelry (bracelets, rings or *ringi*, necklaces, and earrings) made of gold or coral. The styles, sizes, and shapes available are innumerable and seem less indicative of a prescribed order; rather, they add to the overall visual expression of bite sara. Head treatment, including hairstyle and head ties (*sibifina bite*), is more a matter of personal choice. Hairstyles range from short-cropped, traditional West African style (twined, braided, and plaited) to commercial hairpieces, wigs, and chemically treated hair. Sandals or shoes, handkerchiefs, and purses complete a woman's dress.

The following composite lists the articles of dress typically worn for the bite sara prototype (see fig. 11.1, on extreme right). These items are listed in the order in which they are assembled on a woman's body as she dresses—that is, she begins with the undergarments (underwrapper or Western lingerie) and ends by slipping her feet into shoes and picking up a handbag.[5]

BITE SARA COMPOSITE

- traditional or Western-styled undergarments
- blangidi "down" wrapper with accraa "up" wrapper, both tied ebre
- lace or beaded blouse
- bracelets and necklaces of coral beads or gold vary; not a consistent pattern in number of style

- gold rings, one on each ring finger or two on each hand at index and ring fingers
- coral bead or gold, drop pierced earrings
- personal hairstyle or head tie; sometimes a hat
- shoes or sandals and a handbag

In the twenty-first century, with primary education for children and school uniforms normally worn by both boys and girls, the first three stages of female dress are seen only at celebratory events. The blouse and wrapper ensemble (bite sara) is often worn daily by many Kalabari adult women on the islands. The iriabo ensemble continues to flourish (1) when a new mother, her husband, and her family decide that she will be sequestered after the birth of her child, described below; or (2) at celebratory events and rituals such as funerals or in the diaspora.

IRIABO

This final stage deals primarily with the postpartum activities following child-birth. Three separate periods distinguished these activities, each recognized by certain characteristics: (1) the first week of seclusion following childbirth, (2) the one- to three-month period of confinement, and (3) the coming-out process. Predating Western and Christian missionary influence, prenatal prac-tices corresponding to the first, second, and third trimester of pregnancy were undertaken (Daly 1984a, 74–78). If a woman's pregnancy condition indicated restricted movement, she was put to bed at her mother's house, her mother-in-law's house, or a maternity clinic.

The iria tradition as a ritual process was economically and socially expen-sive, involving the iriabo's husband, her mother, the respective lineage groups, chiefs, and the village chief, all of whom collaborated to support such a great effort. "[Becoming an] iriabo is the highest ceremony you can do in Kalabari" and still is the most prestigious ceremony involving female participation. A mother may have felt she "must do it for her daughter," since to have a daughter become an iriabo was the last tribute a mother paid her daughter as she left her family of orientation, established a family of procreation, and became a woman herself. Iria past and present is a ritual system marking the change from one family to another. Although many individuals are involved in helping a young woman "make" iriabo, it is the iriabo's mother who in most cases looked after her during this period, but if the young woman was an iya or "full" wife, thus the property of her husband and his lineage, then his mother cared for her.

The practice traditionally followed the birth of the first child. The first seclu-sion period separated the mother and child from the community who lived in the personal bedroom of a Kalabari house (*kalabio*). Many precautions were taken to ensure both the mother's and newborn's recovery from the birthing process, with the mother being bathed and fed and the child taken care of, most often with others' help. When she bathed, people from her compound prepared her food and washed her wrappers. After bathing, she rubbed camwood on her body and dressed in a "named" cloth, beads, and gold earrings, changing each day into a different named cloth or one of a different color.

As soon after birth as possible, the husband brought gifts of money, cloths, yams, and rum; the money was used to purchase food, chalk, cloth, and other necessities such as rum, with minerals and chalk applied to her skin to add color, texture, and scent for grooming and fatness for her appearance. With changing times, commercial products of creams and oils have been added. The cloths are used to dress her and decorate her bed, the yams as food, and the rum for libations.

After the first six to eight days of seclusion, she moved into the second room, the *biokiri* (family room), a less private space, but not the *wariku* (parlor). She could receive visitors of friends, relatives, and her husband, who remained responsible for her food, drink, and dress, but the couple maintained sexual abstinence. Grooming practices were an essential daily activity that included bathing, sometimes soaking for hours to soften the skin to make it "fine, fine" (Daly 1982).

Older respondents stated that at one time iriabos wore only madras for wrappers and upper-body coverings while in the fattening house. The short wrapper was tied sengi with a draped cloth covering both shoulders, different from the madras prototype to be worn after completing her thanksgiving service. At that time, she covered only the left shoulder, and each separate piece of cloth could be any type of madras, not necessarily identical patterns. During my 1980s fieldwork, madras was still worn often, as it was considered practical and inexpensive, but rules that it be worn were not as strict, except expecting that madras be worn for the last week prior to coming out for her thanksgiving service, as seen on the left in figure 11.4, or if worn after the service, as seen on the right.[6] Adornment expected was kneebands (buo po), bracelets (nunuma), and necklets (poko suaye) of colored beads (aka) similar in size and shape along with gold earrings (beri suai) of various styles.

The "coming-out" process related to making an appearance, becoming more visible or exposing more of the body in relation to the surviving stage of iria, dealt with her gradual reincorporation into her community. She gave birth and was considered a complete female. To supervise the iriabo's dressing for the thanksgiving service, a knowledgeable woman collaborated with the iriabo's

Fig. 11.4. Drawing 4: Injiri iriabo. Courtesy of M. Catherine Daly, drawn by Sylvia Ruud.

mother and husband for the materials and resources used for the occasion, which also required the husband's consent, because his wife tied her wrapper short with her body, legs, and breasts exposed.[7] The amount of time the knowledgeable woman spent on dressing her was directly related to the materials, resources, and the event, and she was paid accordingly.

The materials chosen for the formal coming out came from the mother's family cloth boxes. The contents of the boxes varied from family to family, but most had similar contents. If the family did not own or have access to the proper cloths, then "you borrow, then secretly, pay money. [But it] is a disgrace if someone knows—the family will be abused (criticized)" (Daly 1982). The variety, type, quantity, and quality of cloth boxes varied; thus, potentially the appearance of each iriabo varied. After being dressed, receiving visitors, and informing elders and relations of her intention, the iriabo was ready to go to church on a Sunday morning. She dressed in either the embroidered velvet (india) or silk (loko).

Before leaving for church, however, close female friends and relatives joined her, joined in prayer, then went in a procession led by an older female relative (iria palibo) through the main street of the town to the church. En route, well-wishers "dashed" (gave) her money in the saucer (*efere*) she carried, praising her appearance and what it represented. On arrival, everyone sat in proximity to the prearranged location for her display, someone checking her appearance and posture while her mother or other elder cared for her baby.

The thanksgiving service was included as part of the scheduled Sunday service for the general congregation. The iriabo and her supporters waited for the designated time to approach the altar en masse. Called by name, she stepped forward with her mother, baby, husband, and supporters, all of whom contributed money to the church collection in her honor. At the altar the minister praised and blessed the health of mother and baby and led the group and congregation in psalms and prayers of thanksgiving. The recession home was like the procession through the town; the iriabo may again have been dashed (given money). A private celebration or reception followed, honoring her, her mother, and her husband, where she received her guests.

After this service and reception, she was able to wear bite sara ensembles, indicating that she was now an adult Kalabari woman, a mother who had a child.

INJIRI IRIABO COMPOSITE

(See fig. 11.4)

- Traditional or Western-styled undergarments
- One or more injiri underwrappers worn bite kpuluma and tied senji
- An injiri outer wrapper worn bite kpluma and tied senji
- An injiri upper-body covering
- Simple jewelry of necklet and pair of earrings for before and more elaborate after the thanksgiving service

INDIA OR LOKO IRIABO COMPOSITE

(See fig. 11.1, Iriabo)

- Traditional or Western-styled undergarments
- One or more injiri underwrappers worn bite kpuluma and tied sengi
- An India loko outer wrapper worn bite kpuluma and tied sengi
- Bare breasts, lace blouses, or blouses decorated with beads or sequins
- Coral bead kneebands (sometimes ankle bracelets)
- One to three large singular coral bead necklets, multiple coral bead necklaces in a variety of lengths, gold necklaces

- Large singular coral bead bracelets; multiple small coral bead bracelets, watches
- Coral bead heart or circular motif or coral bead upper arm-bands
- Two gold rings on each hand at index and ring fingers or four rings on each hand on all fingers
- Coral bead or gold drop pierced earrings
- Coral bead, india, or mirrored hat
- Coral bead, brass, or wooden cane in right hand, clear or white saucer with folded white handkerchief in left hand, a piece of folded and draped piece of india over left forearm (sometimes waistbeads over india)

The sequenced rites of passage for females among the Kalabari, described and analyzed above, relates to dress and stages of maturation as practiced for many years, primarily ending for young and adolescent girls whose families became Christian and for girls when Universal Primary Education became common. Nevertheless, some stages are practiced in the twenty-first century. The *pièce de résistance* is when women dress as iriabo at celebratory events like family funerals, supporting family masquerades, and select gatherings emphasizing Kalabari identity. They are considered the epitome of being a Kalabari woman, representing Kalabari identity.

THE FUNERAL IRIABO

Kalabari funerals continue in the twenty-first century to be an event worthy of emphasizing the importance of a prescribed Kalabari appearance, especially when incorporating the dress of an iriabo. The difference between a birth iriabo and a funeral iriabo is that the event for the birth iriabo is singular for her in celebrating the birth of her child as part of the postnatal practices. In contrast, a funeral iriabo's dress is worn by a female chief mourner and other female kin mourners. As many kin female mourners as possible dress in iria outfits at an elder's funeral to underscore the importance of the deceased, the family, and the lineage. Their iriabo appearance emphasizes the continuity and regeneration of Kalabari culture. An elder's funeral merits an elaborate and costly "high" funeral, incorporating more formal practices than a "regular" funeral does (Daly 1983a). The display extends to the appearance of all participants in the general activities and especially that of female descendants who, like the birth iriabo, follow a sequence of prescribed dress during the total funeral activities. Because the eldest daughter represents the continuity of the lineage, she is expected to dress as an iriabo, especially if she is the chief adult mourner. Additional female children wear iria ensembles that identify their kin relationship to the deceased. Parading multiple iriapu (plural of iriabo) dressed in different stages of iria displays wealth and lineage status.

Female relatives dress in stages of iria for both male and female deceased. When the deceased is male, his wife or wives dress as iriapu. However, there are exceptions. If any wife is physically unable to participate as an iriabo because of illness or infirmity, her daughter or granddaughter will represent her.[8] She in turn dresses in bite sara, the dress of an adult woman. In the rare situations where no female descendants exist, a male dresses as an iriabo. If the deceased is female, appropriate female kin dress as iriapu. The iriabo prototype for female appearance during funerals originates from the last phase of the iria tradition discussed above, with its main function to safeguard, through confinement and fattening, the health of a new mother and her first child throughout the prenatal and postnatal period. Consequently, iriabo appearance serves as a metaphor for female fecundity, health, and maturity and has become incorporated at funerals.[9]

There are also some differences between funerals for men and for women in terms of the dress for the parade and dance displays. If the deceased is a man, items of male dress—typically jewelry, hats, and handheld items like elephant tusks, fans, and canes—are incorporated in the general iriabo ensembles throughout the funeral events. In addition, the chief male mourner dresses in ensembles appropriate for the funeral parade, the evening dance, and church thanksgiving, as discussed in chapters 13 on male dress and 18 and 19 on funerals.

The dress of funeral iriabo derives from that of birth iriabo and includes all aspects of appearance outlined in the composites above. The funeral iriabo's ensemble artifacts come from lineage box room and cloth boxes. Generalizations can be made about birth iriabo appearance that extend to funeral iriabo. Named cloth types as sets or ensembles determine the composite for iriabo dress, the number of wrappers, and the way they are arranged. The kind of jewelry, its amount, and its arrangement correspond to the specific cloth type or ensemble. Symmetry in adornment and regularity in bead size and shape exists within the same composition. Upper-body treatment, headwear, bare feet, and handheld objects are chosen as appropriate for the outer named cloth type.

As discussed in chapters 18 and 19, the funeral follows a pattern from the first wake (*dinkoru*) through the final wake, dance, and thanksgiving. Throughout this period, the Kalabari continuously evaluate all aspects of the funeral activities. Female kin dress, parade, dance, and prepare appropriately for the final festivities. They practice the prescribed proper posture, gait, and dance steps; this may take about three to seven days to learn if they lack familiarity. At the same time, a knowledgeable woman (*birimabo*), from the deceased's lineage, if possible, selects the appropriate dress and items of adornment for all who dress in iria ensembles.[10] She also dresses them for the parade and dance. The number and size of those to be dressed and the range of named cloth types determines the compensation given the birimabo. She is offered only in-kind reimbursement, such as food and drinks, if directly related to the mourners. Otherwise, the family pays for her consultation according to its financial ability.

Ideally, the birimabo incorporates cloth and accessories from the dressed funeral beds (ede), usually adorned with the deceased's personal cloth or property or the lineage corporate property; as a result, a mourner's appearance expresses a collective identity.[11] Some relatives, however, favor using their own property to express personal identity. For example, one woman who preferred not to dress her daughter from the lineage cloth boxes said, "You gain respect by purchasing all these items." Commissioning or buying cloth in the market for this occasion arose when many women became employed, exhibiting their own income. Some of the named cloth types that are part of ensembles, however, may be borrowed to exhibit lineage prestige.[12]

During my fieldwork the Kalabari were judging funeral display and appearance not only by their aesthetic integrity and quality of presentation but also by the number of properly dressed mourners and funeral rooms. According to several informants, "During this period it is nearly a competition of sorts between the wives with their children." The following comments concerning a funeral in Abonnema in 1982 are typical of the Kalabari viewpoint:

> It was a fantastic show of wealth. Everybody (the relatives) wanted to show what they had (cloth and coral). Nobody compared notes (beforehand). Everybody asked for a room to display . . . I will put all that I have (into the occasion). Before we could never afford even one room, when money was not throwing itself all over the place. Before it was more (a) communal show of wealth where now it's an individual (show); brother and brother competing against each other. Just like at funerals. Everybody before would go and ask Aunty for cloth. Now you go and spy and then bring something bigger than that. (Daly 1982)

From the wake on Friday evening through the Saturday afternoon parade (*amabro*) and dance (*din krama ti*), they dress according to the textiles appropriate to the event. In amabro they walk single file through town, visiting and honoring other lineage shrines and the town shrine in the marketplace, then returning to the deceased's family compound shrine. For the final Saturday evening funeral dance, each major female mourner (a wife or eldest daughter)

Fig. 11.5. The chief female mourner (center) seated at her table at the funeral dance (din krama ti). Buguma, 1983.

sets her own table and sits with her relatives, as in figure 11.5. The female mourners then dance separately in a competitive fashion. They sit nearby when waiting to dance, covering their legs modestly with madras pieces, as expected whenever sitting with a short wrapper(shown in fig. 11.6). In presenting a collective appearance, funeral iriapu differ from the birth iriabo, who appears as a singular individual.

Although some people say that even for a funeral an iriabo's "body should be fleshy," like a birth iriabo's, it is more important that she dances well and exhibits the proper demeanor. If dancing well, she receives many compliments and dashes of money. If she dances poorly, her family is abused (criticized) and loses respect for its poor choice of iriabo. According to one woman, someone dressed as a funeral iriabo must be substantial in size and move precisely and properly; otherwise, the whole affair is just a display of wealth.

The ensemble changes according to the time of day as well as position, based on female age in the family and lineage structure. Saturday evening is the most

Fig. 11.6. Three women, front right, modestly using madras to cover their legs at the 1984 Centenary celebration.

formal. As that day progresses, the women change from dressing alike in the parade, wearing the injiri ensembles—the most traditional but least costly named cloth type and adornment—to dressing similarly, wearing the india or loko ensemble—the costliest named cloth types and adornment. Regardless of time of day, typically the eldest or elder females dress in the more expensive ensembles. Even within the injiri composite, a hierarchy exists among the various named injiri cloth types and the accompanying jewelry. The younger female descendants follow their elders, wearing the ensembles that correspond to their kinship status with respect to the deceased.

In Kalabari society, one who lives a long life, produces descendants, and provides social and economic contributions to the community is respected for these traditionally valued achievements. Horton suggests similar sentiments from his Kalabari informants: "The deceased has realized his [sic] full potentialities; he has done what he came for and his life represents a significant addition to the pool of ancestral forces" (Horton 1970, 70). One means of communicating respect for the deceased is through the female descendants dressed as iriabo. The relationship of funeral iriabo appearance to birth iriabo appearance also suggests the cycle of birth, death, and regeneration for both the lineage and the Kalabari people. Those who die having lived a full life must be recognized in a proper manner. According to one of Horton's informants, "If no one dies again, no one will bear children again!" (ibid.). Ancestors bless the women of their lineage with children. Women complete the cycle of life as descendants and perpetuators of the lineage.

M. CATHERINE DALY, research associate, Eoin McKiernan Library, has extensive skills in the textile and dress arts. She completed research in Nigeria for her MA degree at Michigan State University and moved to the University of Minnesota for her PhD on the Kalabari topic of the female maturation process and dress called *iria*. She conducted her fieldwork primarily in Abonnema. After her PhD, she pursued research on Afghan dress, published in the *Encyclopedia of Dress and Fashion* (2010). She currently researches lumberjack wear in North America.

NOTES

Adapted from Daly (1984) and Daly (1987, 58–61, 86).

1. Although there is visual, written, and oral documentation of the stages occurring from the nineteenth century and continuing into the twenty-first, none exists about its origin or prior dating before the nineteenth century.

2. The term *kappa* translates as clothing. Within the context of iria, *kappa* refers to a blouse or upper-body covering.

3. The term *treatment* is used since feet may be either covered or uncovered.

4. Unreferenced quotations refer to informants' comments.

5. A Kalabari woman's undergarments are the foundation of her appearance. If she chooses the traditional underskirt or private cloth (similar to Western briefs), it is usually of Akwete (a handwoven cloth from the Igbo-speaking village of Akwete in southern Nigeria), accraa (handwoven cloth similar to Ghanaian kente), or "some really good material." On ritual occasions such as a funeral, one may even wear a softer and more costly type of raffia cloth (bite okuru). European undergarments are usually briefs and a brassiere.

6. Daly (1984a, 101, 111) describes the injiri ensemble for an iriabo who continues parading in the community as part of her sequestering after the thanksgiving service.

7. Since the advent of Christianity, many women have preferred wearing blouses.

8. In rare cases, if she was visiting relatives abroad and her husband died suddenly, she might not be able to return quickly enough to attend.

9. No written or oral documentation exists about when iriabo began appearing at family funerals.

10. Expertise is key in being knowledgeable, thus a woman may not be from the lineage.

11. Ideally, the mourner's dress draws from family heirloom items; the ensembles are likely to be similar rather than identical, the latter resulting when the same cloth is purchased for all the participants.

12. One woman said: "For those women who don't have it (property), the only way is to borrow from others. They then show others they have it (property) by being photographed as opposed to wearing it for the occasion."

12

Dress and Gender in Women's Societies

Susan O. Michelman and Joanne B. Eicher

ONE OF THE MOST SIGNIFICANT boundaries in any society relates to definitions of gender. Dress, a sensory expression of gender intimately related to the body, is a central component of how women and men define themselves in any society.[1] Eicher and Roach-Higgins (1992) suggest that visual properties of dress outweigh the impact of other sensory stimuli, such as sound, touch, odor, and taste, in establishing identity, including that of gender. The power of visual impact ordinarily means that assessment of an individual's dress precedes verbal communication in establishing an individual's gendered identity.

Douglas (1982) asserts that the body, and by extension dress, represents the social body. The meaning of each gendered appearance symbolizes social structure. In the following example of the Kalabari of Nigeria, political leadership has historically resided in the domain of men, visibly acknowledged through progressive stages of dress. The reproduction of culture resides with women, represented by the tradition of marking the female stages of maturation with changes in dress. As roles for many Kalabari women move in the direction of increased social and economic achievement, their dress reflects and influences this change.

In this chapter we examine how members of Kalabari women's societies, brought together as age-graded female support groups, often providing financial aid to each other, began to renegotiate gender roles. We analyze dress in Nigerian Kalabari women's societies as a form of visual communication that identifies diverse and changing gender roles. Focus is on dress of members of sociocultural dance groups known in the Kalabari language as *eremne-ogbo* (*eremne* = women and *ogbo* = club). In eremne-ogbo women sing and dance in identical dress (called uniforms) at ceremonial events, particularly funerals, chieftaincy installations, and other civic occasions, as seen in figure 9.2. We also discuss comparative data on prescribed dress for Kalabari members in the International Lioness Club (Eagle Island chapter, Port Harcourt, Nigeria) and Better Life for Rural Women, a Nigerian government program. Women increasingly choose more types of dress less associated with the traditional Kalabari female aesthetic as they join women's societies outside Kalabari culture.

After an orientation to the culture and relevant literature, we discuss research methods and historical, economic, and sociocultural events that led up to the expanded development of the women's societies from 1960 until 1990. A section on indigenous cultural expression and importance of Kalabari dress and dance precedes an expanded discussion of the importance of dress and dance within eremne-ogbo and the relevance of dress in International Lioness and Better Life for Rural Women.

BACKGROUND

West Africa is noted for the independence and organization of its women (Leis 1974; Enabulele 1985; March and Taqqu 1986), but we found no specific research on dress in women's associations within African countries or other developing nations. Male colonial administrators, such as Talbot (1932), writing in the early 1900s, and others writing historical accounts (Alagoa 1965; Alagoa 1966; Alagoa 1967a; Alagoa 1967b; Alagoa 1970a; Alagoa 1972; Jones 1965; Jones 1963; Tamuno 1980) have documented and researched the Kalabari. Anthropologist Robin Horton (1962, 1965, 1970) has extensively researched the Kalabari worldview. Unfortunately, little exists about these women and their view of society, a reflection of the androcentrism in anthropological literature (Atkinson 1982). The chapters of this volume cover the hierarchies of dress for both Kalabari males and females. Related research by Michelman (1987, 1992) and Michelman and Erekosima (1992) used visual analysis to analyze the Kalabari female and male aesthetic symbolized through dress, body form, and movement.[2] Analysis revealed that indigenous men's dress reflects political power and social responsibility while women's attire represents achievement through the procreative aspect of social development (Michelman 1992). Our chapter examines changing women's roles and dress worn in women's organizations.

AN OVERVIEW OF NIGERIA: 1960–1990

Historical, economic, and sociocultural events occurring between 1960 and 1990 directly influenced the development of Kalabari women's societies and symbolic importance of dress within these organizations. The process of indigenization, initiated after independence in 1960, was a Nigerian social movement that resulted from prominent Nigerians expressing pride in indigenous cultural practices and criticizing British colonial domination in everyday matters of dress and food practices. Systematic actions by the new Nigerian government attempted to reestablish precolonial cultural patterns or introduce alternatives to conditions imposed on them under British rule. One aspect of this process was a focus on a return to indigenous dress forms.

The news media assumed positions on issues such as expressing contempt for wigs and miniskirts. They exhorted young Nigerian women to wear and style their hair according to indigenous customs and to follow Nigerian habits of dress. The *Nigerian Observer* gave front-page coverage to the Midwest Dance Festival, quoting the federal commissioner of labor who asserted "that the study of traditional dances . . . will be an impetus for a more conscious appreciation and the involvement of the people in our cultural regeneration" (*Anvil* June 1973, cited in Jarmon 1988, 41).

This return to indigenous dress can be compared to the actions of Gandhi in India in the early 1920s when he promoted the wearing of *khadi*, or indigenous handmade cloth, as an easily observable, political affirmation of Indian national identity and resistance to British domination (Bean 1989, 360–365). In both Nigeria and India (each with a multilingual and largely illiterate population), dress has been used as a powerful method of communicating ethnic identity and political resistance. However, in Nigeria this occurred after independence, and in India before.

The Nigerian Civil War occurred in the late 1960s and affected Kalabari women socially and economically. Some women became responsible for family survival and acquired skills they never needed before. For example, one who was fourteen at the time of the war told Michelman (1992), "I went to the mangrove swamps from sunrise to sunset to hunt for periwinkles to feed my family, which I would not otherwise have done." Some practical skills women attained were later used in postwar Nigeria to develop economic autonomy, as in the example of women who became contractors. In such cases, a portion of their substantial income was often spent on items of personal adornment, such as wrappers and jewelry, visually affirming their economic position.

Universal Primary Education, started by the Nigerian government in 1976, also contributed to changes in women's lives by mandating educational opportunities for females. In addition, during the 1970s, women's consciousness, which attained global recognition with the UN Decade of Women, 1975–1985, no doubt contributed to educated Kalabari women's awareness of issues of identity and autonomy.

DEVELOPMENT OF EREMNE-OGBO AND SOCIAL SIGNIFICANCE OF DRESS

Both Universal Primary Education and the Nigerian Civil War stimulated membership in eremne-ogbo, which were reported by respondents to have proliferated in the 1960s and 1970s, as Kalabari women began to identify shared interests and concerns with other women. Although these Kalabari women's societies are not overtly political in nature, the process of forming these organizations helped build an awareness of needs of other members within each organization as well as the larger Kalabari community. Women's societies periodically lend money to needy members or contribute to community development. The proliferation of women's societies in the 1970s indicated that Kalabari women were beginning to identify mutual concerns. In the process of doing this, they were developing the importance of an independent reference group, based on gender, that was extradomestic and outside kinship.[3]

During the 1970s and early 1980s, Nigeria's economic prospects were transformed by the development of petroleum production, the rapid increase in economic rent derived from oil, and the success of the government in appropriating this money. The Nigerian *naira* was strong on the world market and many Nigerians, including Kalabari and other southern ethnic groups also known for their opulent attire, were able to spend large amounts of discretionary income on dress and travel. At the height of the oil boom in the 1970s, eremne-ogbo began to proliferate, and these women's societies became an important arena for women to display their ability to gain social and economic power outside the roles and rituals related to kinship. Dress, always a tangible way for Kalabari to display status (as both Kalabari males and females acknowledged in interviews), took on new meaning for women. A dramatic change was occurring particularly for financially accomplished Kalabari women, who now wanted public acknowledgment of their economic success outside Kalabari society, a recognition previously reserved for men.

Women began to rely less on the storehouse of heirloom textiles kept in the family "cloth box" for needed apparel. Rather, new wrappers were often purchased with money the women had earned themselves as traders and busi-nesswomen. During the 1970s and early 1980s, affluent women commonly spent one thousand naira (then equivalent to $1,500) or more for a silk or embroi-dered-velvet wrapper, with additional outlay for blouse, hat, and jewelry, a requirement of many women's societies for special events such as funerals or chieftaincy installations. Decline in oil revenues in the late 1980s had subse-quent negative effects on Nigeria's economy. The value of the naira dropped in 1990, during the fieldwork period, to around ten naira per dollar, creating economic hardship for Nigerians. What was once affordable became prohibi-tively expensive. The economic downturn affected eremne-ogbo in several ways. First, women had less expendable income for costly items of apparel, as devaluation of the naira was linked to buying cloth from an international rather than local market. Second, many women worked harder to support their families and thus had less time to spend on eremne-ogbo. Third, educated and more affluent women devoted more time to philanthropic organizations like International Lioness and Soroptomist.

KALABARI INDIGENOUS DRESS AND DANCE

Although this chapter analyzes the social meaning of dress in eremne-ogbo, our interpretations are done within the context of the larger research study involving indigenous Kalabari attire and its associated meaning for both men and women. A cultural analysis of Kalabari dress as related to gender has been developed from Michelman's prior research (Michelman 1987; Michelman 1992; Michelman and Erekosima 1992), which examined formal design quali-ties of Kalabari men's and women's dress to discern cultural meaning. At one level, clothing choice represents personal aesthetic expression, but choice is also influenced by knowledge of status distinctions within the social system as represented by age and gender. Both Kalabari men and women progress through stages of dress, each in a distinct, culturally prescribed manner, and achieve status separately. Daly's description in chapter 11 of the last two stages of the female hierarchy, *bite sara* and *iriabo*, relate specifically to the types of dress worn for eremne-ogbo participation. Social status in eremne-ogbo is identified through group conformity. If all items of dress are carefully matched, it is a visible sign that everything, possibly excluding jewelry, was purchased for a specific dance performance.

Kalabari men and women acknowledge dance and dress to be a symbolic expression of Kalabari identity. Movement and dance steps for each gender are distinct and separate in character, just as dress is. Women dance as part of the tradition of iria as well as during women's society performances, while men dance as members of the Ekine Society during masquerade performances.[4] During the 1990 fieldwork in Abonnema and Buguma, Michelman observed many formal and informal dance performances by both men and women. Kalabari girls begin to learn the dance steps at a young age as part of the tradition of iria and participate in dance practice with their mothers at the women's society meetings. Iria dance is not directly related to women's society dance, although the women's society members incorporate some iria steps (Michelman 1990).

Women's dance during funeral celebration or chieftaincy installation includes accompaniment: men beat clay water pot drums and women sing chants. Dancers progress in a slow, snakelike procession, bending forward at the waist. Women rhythmically sway their arms from side to side and move their heads back and forth to coordinate the movement. Periodically, they bend closer to the ground and shake their buttocks, with the rest of their torsos remaining stationary. Women tie wrappers snugly to emphasize the buttocks and inhibit rapid and acrobatic movements of the legs (as contrasted with men's dance). They hold handkerchiefs in each hand that provide a fluttering motion as they dance. Their feet bear the weight of their swaying bodies as they move slowly and methodically forward. If the audience regards a dancer as being particularly good, she can be "dashed" (given money) by anyone. When they perform dance, members of eremne-ogbo appear visually cohesive as a group, because of similar dress, movement, and rounded body form. In addition, they often dance huddled together.

In contrast to women's dance, the men's dance is usually seen as part of a complete masquerade performed by Kalabari men as members of the Ekine Society. *Ada seki* is a slow, graceful dance around the performance area by men dancing in a single line, usually attired in the long gowns of Indian madras or the opulent velvet gown (Madume 1976). In part of the dance known as *Tu-Seki*, the men lower their heads, bend their bodies forward, and slowly move their hips from side to side to the sound of the drums. At intervals, each spreads out his hands to an adjacent dancer to give a short greeting. *Pekele*, an acrobatic display, is reserved for agile dancers (ibid.). A dancer jumps up on his left foot, makes a quick turn in the air, and lands on his right foot. He may do this as an individual turn or several successive turns that move him across the performance area to the drum house.

The large size of the ornate hats requires men to keep the head, neck, and shoulders upright to prevent the hat from falling. Held objects restrict the use of both hands. In the right, the dancer carries a fan, and in the left, a cane or elephant tusk, occasionally with a handkerchief. As the dancer shakes his buttocks, he may jauntily move his arms in rhythm with the drums. Periodically, each dancer turns and gives greeting to an adjacent dancer by touching his left hand to the other's right and his right to the other's left. Dancers repeat this movement in succession down the row of dancers, moving forward in a slow, snakelike manner. There is no random dance; each performs prescribed and similar movements, concentrating on individual skill. Although they dance as a group, individual displays allow each dancer to show his particular ability in contrast to the effect of moving as a group when the women dance.

General style of dance is similar for both Kalabari men and women, emphasizing the relationship of the body to the earth. Dance and dress are a symbolic representation of both cultural and gender identity. Men's dance stresses individual performance to a much greater degree than women's. This is symbolic of and consistent with men's ability to rise socially and politically through individual achievements in a society where they are viewed as competitive individuals. Women's cohesive, often huddling presentation stresses Kalabari female identity, visually represented in activities of iria and eremne-ogbo.

THE KALABARI TEXTILE HIERARCHY

The Kalabari people have a designated textile hierarchy based on cultural importance, tangible value, and aesthetic criteria. When certain cloths are chosen for use by an eremne-ogbo, it reflects both the social knowledge of members coordinating cloth and event as well as their buying power, through their ability to purchase fabrics from the least to most expensive. Wrappers used by eremne-ogbo include pelete bite, *ikaki, accraa, gom, Akwete, krukrubite,* and *blangidi* with *loko* and *india* reserved for the most prestigious occasions.

Group members choose attire for each event by consensus: the entire ensemble is selected in relationship to the cloth hierarchy and must correspond with the significance of the occasion. Thus, for a chieftaincy installation, velvet wrappers with an appropriate blouse and hat would be worn by members of a group such as Asari Tomina Ereme (Prominent Women of Buguma). Even guests who are close to the person being honored with a chieftaincy are expected to dress according to the rules of the Kalabari textile hierarchy. For example, when attending a chieftaincy installation in Buguma with Mrs. A. Bele (affiliated with Asari Tomina Ereme), Michelman wore a silk wrapper and sequined blouse as advised by Mrs. Bele, illustrating Erekosima's observation that inappropriate choice of cloth is considered a social infraction (Erekosima 1989).

DRESS IN EREMNE-OGBO

Dress visually identifies a woman's membership in an eremne-ogbo, as the societies require the women to dress alike in bite sara for ceremonial dance presentations. When wearing bite sara for dance performances, women dance barefoot and hold white handkerchiefs and an *nkro* (a carved stick) in each hand to accentuate movement (Michelman 1990).

Not all Kalabari women are members of eremne-ogbo, although a large percentage are said to belong.[5] Kalabari women interviewed claimed that in 1990 there were over fifty women's societies in the town of Abonnema alone, with many societies having as many as fifty members. Women's societies are voluntary organizations, and membership is not linked to marriage, kinship, or the female tradition of iria.

Eremne-ogbo extends membership to those who have the economic resources to join. Although not strictly age-graded, similarity of age and social status are the strongest criteria for membership. Women are asked to join certain societies according to their ability to pay membership dues, supplement their wardrobe with the required dress, and, on specific occasions, buy drinks and food for other members. To start the process of initiation, one or more existing members present the applicant's photograph to the group. While she is absent, the group raises questions concerning her general appearance, her character, and, if married, her husband's emotional and financial support for his wife's attendance at monthly meetings.[6] The society holds an open discussion, and a new member can be approved or rejected at this point.

Women appear to join eremne-ogbo according to their age, as these groups serve the needs of specific ages. Certain women's societies are more prestigious and influential than others. As an example, economic status of individuals and the collective group dictate membership epitomized the eremne-ogbo named *Asari Tomina Ereme*. Started in 1976 by a small group of influential Kalabari women, the society had over fifty members in 1990. It has made substantial contributions to community development. Each member must maintain good financial standing; otherwise, she may not participate. Outside of performing at social events, members give moral support to each other, as well as financial assistance if necessary. As a group, they present a visual statement of wealth and prestige, frequently attained through their own initiative and skill in business and trade, as indicated by the photograph of Asari Tomina Eremne from the 1984 Buguma Centenary in figure 9.2 and figure 16.1. In this society, members were reported to dance in purchased cloth instead of borrowing it from the family cloth box, indicating their success and financial prowess to purchase, on demand, the outfits needed.

Women interviewed often expressed pride in their purchase of cloth wrappers specifically for society use. One informant said that when she joined *Nyemoni Kengema Iriawo* (Kalabari Ladies from Abonnema) in 1977, members relied on family cloth boxes for attire in dance performances.[7] She remembered cloth merchants coming to their meetings around 1980, at which point the organization began to rely on cloth purchases rather than family holdings. Merchants often display new textiles for sale, but they also borrow cloth from family boxes for members to see. The women's societies examine the cloth samples as a group, vote on their cloth choices, and the Kalabari merchant gives the sample with a large order to the supplier in England or India.

When members of an eremne-ogbo dress alike for a ceremonial event, each woman's affiliation with a specific society is easily identified. Initially, societies require one or two full ensemble uniforms. Collective and individual financial resources of members have bearing on the costliness of items chosen. Quantity and expense of the uniforms vary from group to group according to economic resources of the individuals and expectations of the group. For example, *india* or embroidered-velvet cloth imported from India that was traditionally reserved for men is now purchased and worn by members of more affluent associations, such as Asari Tomina Ereme.

The following is a transcription of an interview done by Susan O. Michelman (SOM) with a member of Asari Tomina Ereme (ATE).

> ATE. India is rare. It has mainly been for men.
>
> SOM. When did women start wearing it?
>
> ATE. Oh, you know time changes things. The more women are getting [financial] independence, they can afford [india]. Maybe you'd like to use it but you can't afford. It is still going on among men. There are certain cloths that only the chiefs use.
>
> SOM. You have to be of a certain status before you can use it [india]?
>
> ATE. The men are now giving us free hand. They don't say, "Why are you using?" Since you can afford, then use it [india].
>
> SOM. So, it has to do with your purchasing power?
>
> ATE. Yes.
>
> SOM. Is it a statement about the purchasing power and strength of women?
>
> ATE. Yes, I think so. Now women are economically independent.

SOM. Is part of the expression in the women's society, women's strength, women's financial ability?

ATE. Even at the national level, now women are coming out [to be more powerful]. Even in the north, women are now commissioners. It wasn't so before. (Michelman 1990)

INTERNATIONAL LIONESS AND SOCIAL SIGNIFICANCE OF DRESS

Women's interest in membership in philanthropic clubs such as the International Lioness in the late 1980s indicates increasing economic hardship. In joining philanthropic organizations, affluent and educated Kalabari women show a sensitivity about their own financial struggles and indicate their exposure to government propaganda about the plight of rural, indigent women. In these programs, women's dress emphasize group affiliation and philanthropic intention, rather than elaborate dress displays.

Dress in the Lioness Club consists of either traditional or Western dress and the addition of the Lioness vest and cap. A club pin is worn on the vest, with additional pins obtained through attendance at other installations, regional meetings, or by trading with other members. For example, Mrs. Bele is vice president of her chapter and had a cursive pin with her office designated on it.

In addition, members have uniforms for international or national conventions, which can be either skirts or wrappers and blouses. Mrs. Bele told Michelman that she had four for the chapter and one for the national body. "Average cost for each outfit was about 150–350 naira for each outfit (approximately $15.00–$35.00). The one [skirt and blouse] we picked for 1989, which I attended was a wax print made in Nigeria, which everybody was meant to have for the convention that was staged in Lagos. In addition we had uniforms for different chapters, too. We had a yellow brocade material with eagle bird appliqued on the front with purple trimmings on the blouse. Then, we have another one, which is a wax print. It has purple and gold in it, too" (Michelman 1992).

BETTER LIFE FOR RURAL WOMEN AND THE SOCIAL SIGNIFICANCE OF DRESS

The Nigerian government has acknowledged that women are the mainstay of agricultural production by supporting women's issues with programs like Better Life for Rural Women, which was established in 1987 as a national program to help improve the lives of the large population of women in rural areas. Economic pressures and government policies of the 1980s limited importation of foreign goods and forced Nigeria to increase rural production, which is in the hands of women working as individual farmers or traders. The Better Life program has urged the formation of cooperatives with the incentive of loans.

A graphic way government officials have chosen to advertise this program is through cloth printed with the national insignia of the Better Life program. Women members can fashion this cloth into varying forms of dress. Throughout 1990, television and newspaper articles showed well-dressed women wearing Better Life cloth to promote the value of this program. The cloth cost 90 naira, comparable to about 135 naira before devaluation. As 90 naira represents a large amount of money for these rural women, the cloth is financially out of reach for most members of the Better Life organization and may be more a form of advertising than affordable dress for many members.

DISCUSSION AND CONCLUSIONS

The development and proliferation of eremne-ogbo from the late 1960s and 1970s can be linked to political and socioeconomic developments within Nigeria. Independence from Great Britain in 1960 and subsequent indigenization influenced Kalabari women's awareness of their ethnic identity. The new skills women learned during the civil war were often independent from their roles of marriage or kinship, making women more financially autonomous. The oil boom in the 1970s created a prosperous economic environment for them to use these skills to become successful traders and businesswomen. Kalabari women, through socioeconomic gain, were able to see themselves as more independent from men than was reported to be Kalabari custom earlier. As roles for many Kalabari women move in the direction of increased social and political achievement, so, too, does their dress indicate this change.[8] This does not imply that Kalabari women are emulating men's dress; rather, it indicates a change in cultural perception of women as they begin to take on roles in the economic and political domain of Kalabari men.

Cultural significance of appearance is associated with gender distinctions in Kalabari culture. As men attain higher status, indigenous dress becomes increasingly elaborate and expensive, epitomized by the velvet cloth embroidered with metallic threads used to make the attigra gown of the chiefs. Men ascend the hierarchy after they have accumulated income and have made tangible and intangible contributions to the community. Few men ascend to chieftaincy, the highest status achievable for men, and none before middle age. The ceremonial process of becoming a chief requires large sums of money to buy dress for oneself and family, food and drinks for invited guests, and invited masquerades and dancing by women's societies. Appearance (at all levels of status) is a reflection of chiefs' social position that helps culturally construct their status through social acknowledgment of their achievements.

Women's status is achieved differently from men's through marriage and the birth of a child, but by purchasing the most expensive textile within the hierarchy of cloth, women's society members display themselves as a prestige group. The velvet wrappers for women's dress emphasize their new economic positions. Kalabari say that women cannot be chiefs, but women have begun to be involved and elected to office at the local government level. In the International Lioness and Better Life for Rural Women, the dress indicates a movement away from the traditional Kalabari women's dress and role and illustrates women's involvement in international and national organizations. As members of these groups, they wear international types of clothing (Eicher 1992) or wrapper outfits.

Within the context of culturally proscribed differences of both the form and meaning of dress for Kalabari men and women, we have examined the social meaning of appearance within eremne-ogbo. While these women's societies are linked to cultural expressions of female dress and dance, they are simultaneously cultural expressions that demonstrate, through dress, social and economic changes for Kalabari women.

Kalabari women's societies have helped to develop group solidarity among members, outside marriage or kinship. This group consciousness has taken on symbolic manifestation through the custom of dressing identically, whether in eremne-ogbo, the indigenous organization; Lioness International, the philanthropic; or Better Life for Rural Women, the Nigerian government program. The phenomenon of uniforms emphasizes that women are working cooperatively and, in doing so, are establishing a female ideology.

Douglas (1982) states that conflict, symbolically represented by the body, is about boundary definition within a social institution, such as gender. The conflict focuses on how to deal with normative behavior that becomes encoded as rules. In the Kalabari case, these rules have been associated with dress. Social control of women, visually defined and reinforced through gender-dichotomized patterns of indigenous dress, has helped protect the cultural, political, and economic domains of Kalabari men.

Analysis of dress in Kalabari women's societies indicates that gender and power are being negotiated at the level of the body. Women in eremne-ogbo and during iriabo rites of passage now wear prestige textiles, like india, previously worn only by male chiefs. Through this practice, women reinforce the social reality of their ability to ascend economically in Kalabari society.

SUSAN O. MICHELMAN received her MA and PhD from University
of Minnesota, conducting research on *Kalabari Male and Female
Aesthetics: A Comparative Visual Analysis* (1987) and *Dress in Kalabari
Women's Organizations* (1992), respectively. Following a BS in
occupational therapy from the Ohio State University, she came into
dress and fashion studies primarily interested in gender roles as well
as textile aesthetics. She coedited *Meanings of Dress* (1999, 2005).

JOANNE B. EICHER is Regents Professor Emerita in the Department
of Design, Housing, and Apparel at the University of Minnesota. She is
coeditor of *The Anthropology of Dress and Fashion: A Reader*; coeditor
of *The Visible Self: Global Perspectives on Dress, Culture, and Society*, 4th
ed.; and editor in chief of the *Encyclopedia of World Dress and Fashion*.

NOTES

Adapted from Michelman and Eicher (1995).

   1. See Hamilton and Hamilton (1989) for a description and analysis of the
Karen of Thailand that illustrates this point.

   2. Research data collected on eremne-ogbo by Michelman included two case
studies of an individual Kalabari woman, Mrs. A. Bele (a pseudonym), and a
woman's society called Asari Tomina Ereme, (translated as "Prominent Women of
Buguma"), an eremne-ogbo to which Mrs. Bele belonged. Michelman met her in
1985 when she was traveling in the United States. Eicher has known her since 1980.
For example, Mbonu Ojike, a prominent Nigerian who died in 1956, came back
from his education in the United States with a cause that emphasized "being Nigerian" and a slogan "Boycott all boycottables" that accompanied his philosophy.
He endorsed dressing in indigenous outfits and eating food with the hands, in the
"traditional" manner (Uwechue 1991).

   3. Erekosima noted that the Kalabari clubs and social groups that flourished
for both men and women cut across class interests and lineage affiliations and promoted social solidarity (Erekosima 1984) and were nonreligious. Michelman made
a similar observation during 1990 fieldwork.

   4. Kalabari men who belong to the Ekine Society must demonstrate their
ability to understand and interpret dance. There are three grades of members of
Ekine Society. The Iwo-Sekiapu, or junior grade, includes new members and old
members who are not very skilled at the Sekiapu dance steps, or dancers who have
not attempted the more difficult masquerades. The second level is Elem-Sekiapu
that comprises mature or highly skilled members who have performed the most
intricate masquerade. At this level men are known as Sekibo, and they must also

have mastery of drum language. The third level, or Omongiapu, are elders of Ekine who possess deep knowledge of the traditions of the cult (Madume 1976, 24). Men in Sekiapu dance to drums that include the following: (1) Ikiriko, or drum of authority, which is a large slit gong carved out of a large piece of wood so that two sides produce different sounds when beaten. (2) The owu-pele or kala-ikiriko is a smaller slit drum. (3) Bobo-Akwa is a skin drum, as is (4) Akwa-Yingi, the master drummer plays all simultaneously. The skill of the dancer is assessed based on his comprehension of the drum language and his sensitive reactions to its messages (Madume 1976, 71–72).

5. One Kalabari informant who does not belong to any women's society said that a category exists identifying such women as Ogbo-so-aa-apu (translated as "people who are not members"). They "are dressed well and look respectable, sit together and socialize at funerals."

6. Fieldwork data suggests that there is no difference between being a wealthy husband/ non-income-producing wife and being an income-producing wife.

7. Eicher (1988a, 1988b) has described both the cloth boxes and strong rooms of the Kalabari. The strong room is a specially designated space for precious valuables, largely textiles, apparel, and accessories, including jewelry. A variety of containers called cloth boxes (such as suitcases, trunks, cartons, and hat boxes) are the responsibility of the eldest woman of the family who knows their contents and allows family members to use them for appropriate occasions. She makes sure of their return, as they are constantly used and revered as treasured items of family history and identity. Cloth is carefully folded and preserved with mothballs or the tiniest red peppers. Cloth garments are usually stored according to textile type or by previous ownership. Beads and jewelry of coral, gold, and other materials as well as hats, canes, ivory tusks, and fans are also stored for safekeeping. The woman designated as guardian and record-keeper knows the names and accomplishments of the original owners of cloth and garments. Genealogies of a family can be reconstructed by jogging the memory of a woman who is extracting a textile or garment from the strong room.

8. Kalabari say that women cannot be chiefs, but women have begun to be involved and elected to office at the local government level.

13

The Aesthetics of Men's Dress

Tonye Victor Erekosima and Joanne B. Eicher

KALABARI DRESS AS ENSEMBLE

Molefi Asante (1993, 54) uses the term *African aesthetics* to mean "the conscious aesthetics of people of African descent who are aware of participating in some African tradition." Chapter 1 regarding Kalabari dress and the social order sets the stage for analyzing Kalabari men's dress and textiles as one example of African aesthetics. Kalabari data provide an in-depth analysis of the aesthetics of one group of Africans who exhibit a rich dress and textile heritage that contradicts much stereotyping of Africans. Ghanaian dress and textiles are seen and used by many African Americans as representing "typical" African dress; the Kalabari, however, illustrate another of many African traditions of dress existing in the large and complex continent of Africa. This chapter focuses on Kalabari men's types of dress (from young adulthood through old age) worn commonly on Kalabari islands and often in Port Harcourt on a daily basis and abroad during special Kalabari events.

The Kalabari case of African aesthetics in men's dress typifies a distinctive clothing tradition of cut-and-sewn fabrics for the upper garments worn with a wrapper or with tailored trousers. Other outstanding examples of distinctive West African dress from cut-and-sewn fabrics for men include the Yoruba hand-woven materials in stylistic varieties of ensembles (Wass 1975) and the Hausa dyed and embroidered ensembles (Perani 1992). Similar Ghanaian handwoven textiles are not made into tailored garments but worn toga style (Picton 1992).

Other men's outfits include those of the Oba of the Benin kingdom's ensembles of heavy coral beading with wrappers and skirts and the Mande hunters' shirts with leather charms (McNaughton 1982). These West African examples have not, however, been studied principally from the aesthetic perspective that we offer of the wearers.

Within Kalabari society both male and female basic styles of dress have been analyzed as indicating respectively sociopolitical and sociophysical placement of individuals. We focus on adult male dress, drawing from our interviews and fieldwork, briefly summarizing the types of dress related to sociopolitical meaning and elaborating on the aesthetics, etiquette, and nuances understood by the Kalabari as necessary for a man's proper appearance in public.[1]

Kalabari men, as traders with Africans and non-Africans for centuries, treasured a variety of imported textiles for their daily and ceremonial lives. A unique aspect was and is their creativity in taking materials from elsewhere and subjecting them to rigorous, indigenous standards to make new ensembles. The art of ensemble for Kalabari men characterizes most of their forms of dress with subtle distinctions and aesthetic elaborations that combine discrete and foreign-made items into a montage. We describe and provide illustrations of the ensembles peculiar to Kalabari men, discuss their use, and analyze the expressive aspects the ensembles convey. An elaborate set of aesthetic rules about cloth and dress among the Kalabari with appropriate local nomenclature provides evidence of their sophisticated taste. Stylistic differentiation plays a key role in communicating men's roles within the social order, and a clear-cut set of aesthetic standards accompanies the practiced style differences.

The conversion of borrowed artifacts to indigenous, cultural usages has been covered. The process of cultural authentication is found throughout Kalabari life, not only in men's dress ensembles, as this chapter elaborates. What Kalabari men regard as traditional dress consists largely of textiles used as wrappers and garments or accessories and ornaments imported from overseas or beyond Kalabari culture. These include familiar Western clothing like shirts (in modified form), trousers, hats, shoes, handkerchiefs, walking sticks, and jewelry like gold and silver chains or studs. Some ensembles include wrappers and gowns of Indian textiles combined with Western garments. Superficially, a man in such attire is not visibly wearing indigenous Nigerian dress. To the Kalabari, however, these dress items represent considerable economic value and aesthetic worth and also indicate the sociopolitical status of males in terms of age and social position.[2]

KALABARI MEN'S TRADITIONAL DRESS

The peculiar ensembles and the characteristic use of the imported items of dress together define Kalabari men's traditional dress. As one informant put it, Kalabari dress for men means "to tie *injiri* cloth, wear a garment over it, put on a hat, and pick up a walking stick" (Erekosima 1989, 337). Two major components make up the classic styles of Kalabari men's traditional dress ensembles. One is the sewn garment that covers the upper torso. The other is the wrapper, a length of cloth tied on the wearer, covering the lower torso from waist to feet. The most frequently used and preferred textile for a man's wrapper is madras, early imported from India through European merchants to West Africa.

VARIETIES OF SEWN DRESS AND THEIR PATTERNS OF USE

The linguist Charles Jenewari (1976) identifies the Kalabari word *kappa*, which stands for sewn garments, as a Portuguese word, meaning dress. Likely a correspondence exists between the emergence of this sewn variant of Kalabari women's and men's dress (in contrast to lengths of cloth used as wrappers). Portuguese influence among the Kalabari started from the early sixteenth century. These Europeans clearly introduced a whole range of items of dress to the Kalabari, both Western and non-Western (Vogt 1975).

A direct reference to the impact of Portuguese fashions on Kalabari society occurs in the following remarks by Amaury Talbot, who surveyed southern Nigeria cultures in the early twentieth century. He described one of the revered deities of Kalabari society as follows: "When one remembers the number of Portuguese mariners who, in old days, made their way to this part of the coast, it is not difficult to understand why the carved figure of *adumu* is here shown with the pointed mustache and beard, the ruff and feather-trimmed hat of a don of the period when these bold seafarers first penetrated to the lower regions of the Santa Barbara [river]" (1932, 38).

The Kalabari were not merely passive recipients of borrowed forms of dress, not just retaining or copying the Portuguese garments. Their response was unlike the unimaginative and almost passive use of Western dress by contemporary Nigerians, with over a century of adoption of modern European dress (Wass 1975), like the men's suit ensemble, worn with little change or modification. In addition, these items are not given local names nor modified in form or function and not used in an indigenous way. In contrast, the Kalabari reacted differently; they introduced their own words for innovations that they made, adjusting the innovations in a practical way to fit their own perspectives of life. The result was a genuine learning situation such as Jean Piaget and Bàrbel Inhelder (1969) stipulate with their emphasis on being engaged in an activity to learn it rather than just being taught; the Kalabari effected a significant adaptation of the received artifact to their deeply challenged and versatile culture. Creatively, they altered and accommodated new inputs, or adjusted their preexisting frame of reference, and brought both to an adaptive equilibrium. Their approach, which we defined as the cultural authentication, applies to Kalabari men's outfits: a series of modified upper garments worn with wrapped cloth for the lower garments, adding a variety of imported accessories for a complete ensemble.

The traditional ensembles worn by Kalabari men in public are indicated by the names of the sewn garment for the upper torso that is knee-length, calf-length, or ankle-length, as shown in figure 13.1. Kalabari traditional dress ensembles representing four ranks of the sociopolitical order are listed below in descending order of importance.

Fig. 13.1. Kalabari men's dress ensembles, upper-body garments from left: etibo, woko, doni, ebu, attigra. Courtesy of M. Catherine Daly, drawn by Sylvia Ruud.

The gown known as *attigra* is outside the ranking system and is described afterward:

Ebu (gown worn by king and paramount chiefs)
Doni (gown worn by chiefs)
Woko (top garment worn by "gentlemen of substance")
Etibo (top garment worn by "young men who matter")

DESCRIBING THE EBU

The *ebu* is an ankle-length gown made of imported madras that is traditionally worn by the king (Amanyanabo) and his paramount chiefs (see fig. 13.1, second figure from right). The style is specifically characterized by a broad "V-shaped" front for the collar that reaches to midchest but is square across the back, reminiscent of a sailor's uniform (see fig. 13.2).

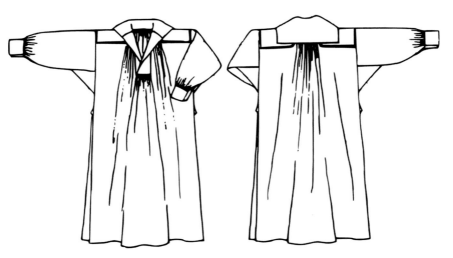

Fig. 13.2. Front and back view of ebu gown. Courtesy of M. Catherine Daly, drawn by Sylvia Ruud.

Kalabari contact with European sailors and traders may have provided this key symbol of new developments in Kalabari society that resulted from stimulation from Western mercantile activity.

The gown is worn only with a matching piece of injiri wrapper (*bite wari*). Its decor is one of simplicity, since no loud or rich accessories normally accompany it. A bowler hat or top hat is appropriate headgear, along with simple jewelry such as one solid piece of coral bead stretched across the stud-fastened minicollar of the white shirt worn underneath. The gown's long sleeves must be folded to slightly above the wrist, exposing the white shirt cuffs underneath, usually secured with gold or silver links. A few gold rings may be worn on one or two fingers of both hands and a simple cane or walking stick held.

The ebu is regarded as most fitting for king and the very elderly chiefs of eminent status, no longer needing to assert high public visibility through ornate habiliment. They project the image of a chief actively exercising power to those who are younger and for whom the *doni* is more appropriate attire than the ebu.

The ebu's simple style matches the elder statesman's status, gracefully staying in the background offering words of wisdom and tactfully guiding the strategies of the active community leaders who serve as public representatives. This perspective led to the unplanned situation of the king (Amanyanabo) of Kalabari appearing as the only one among his Council of Chiefs wearing the ebu at the 1966 cabinet session Eicher visited.

Close discriminations are also made about the quality of Indian madras. The top quality is "Real India" cloth, recognizable by textural qualities as well as perforation markings at the sides of the cloth. "*Mandras*" or "*madras*" is a less refined quality of injiri; *Pinion*, even less durable, is rather cheaply sold with an inferior or rough texture and its colors readily fade after laundering.

DESCRIBING THE DONI

The doni is an ankle-length robe by Kalabari notables who are chiefs (*alapu*). Made like an elongated shirt, from thick and colorful woolen material, its collar is narrow at the back with two flaps at the front, (middle figure, fig. 13.1). Four buttonholes are centered in a front placket for display for good-sized gold or silver studs. A chain connects the studs to a brooch pinned on the left-side pocket. The placket is often fashioned in a pattern called fish gill (*sangolo*), ladder, or such other designs, with a large tab at the bottom (*doni bele*) that apparently enables the wearer to pull down the garment while walking, to straighten it out.

The sleeves of the doni are slightly folded back when worn, to expose the cuffs of the white shirt that must be worn underneath it. The collar band of the shirt is fastened with a big, matching gold or silver stud, and the shirt cuffs fastened with a big, matching gold or silver stud. The doni is ankle-length or sometimes slightly shorter, and it must have an injiri wrapper of good quality tied underneath that shows an appropriate "volume" relative to the "big" fit of the doni on its wearer. The gown should not fit too closely or be too tight around the ankles.

Use of a walking stick is almost always mandatory when wearing the doni; shoes are optional. The hat need not be elaborate except during ceremonial occasions, perhaps a top hat or bowler hat. Wearing gold rings is expected. The doni is slit on each side, from the hem to below the arms, to allow for easy movement.

Informants did not agree on the doni's origin. Some insisted that it initially came from the Portuguese in its present form, claiming that Portuguese merchants wore it and gave away some in token of friendship to their leading trading partners. This item of clothing was argued to be worn by the *dons* in Portugal, the title for a nobleman in Portuguese, as is shown by examples like the legendary Don Juan, Don Quixote of literary fame, and Portuguese and Spanish notables with names like Don Pedro. Some were taken up by Kalabari families. Some suggested that the outstanding Kalabari traders of the period who received this gift of clothing— called doni in their own dialect—were thereby being recognized as members of the league of successful entrepreneurs.

Other informants contended, however, that the word *doni* came into use only during the period of English dominance and presence in the Niger delta, which was sometime in the early eighteenth century. They insisted that the English introduced a knee-length, woolen shirt (somewhat like the later English "boiled" army shirt). The Kalabari chiefs, only then emerging as a force in the internal political scene, needed to be distinguished by adopting some highly visible status symbol. They instructed the Sierra Leone and other repatriated black tailors on the ships at the time to sew these for them by making them reach "down." These tailors were black men who had been repatriated from America to Africa and who had acquired artisan skills. Some became itinerant craftsmen plying the Atlantic coast and sharing their modern ways as missionaries and artisans or tradesman. Communication in any common language at the time was difficult, so the story is told that the chiefs said in a halting English: "doni" for "down." These accounts argue that the ankle-length gown emerged as an elongated shirt that became the doni and the exclusive garb of Kalabari chiefs.

In examining the credibility of the first version, we found that a search through books illustrating European period dress (Evelyn 1968) does not show anything like the doni being worn by the Portuguese, or any European peoples at all, from the sixteenth to the twentieth century. The idea of an indigenous adaptive thrust using dress as a symbol of the new order, therefore, becomes more plausible or reinforced.

Whether the garment was adopted or adapted, however, the doni remains a Kalabari dress on account of the ensemble that forms it and the etiquette rules associated with wearing it. Apparently, such an ensemble never existed in Europe, and it even differs markedly from a similar outfit worn by neighbors of the Kalabari in terms of its association aesthetics (Erekosima 1989).

DESCRIBING THE WOKO

This garment, worn by Kalabari men in the rank of Opu Asawo, or the Gentlemen of Substance, also differs from similar garments called the *jompa* that are worn by other Niger delta neighbors in the riverine city-states and other areas outside the delta (as among the hinterland Igbos). This word derives from the English "jumper" but does not designate clothing that fits the same description. Among the Kalabari, however, it is called *woko* and is made of plain-colored fabric in contrast to the figured cloths members of the other Eastern Nigerian communities use. This form of dress probably originated from other communities, possibly Bonny, but Kalabari informants remained quite vague when discussing its origin. The Kalabari may have, again, simply devised their unique version of the existing outfit in order to serve some pressing internal need of status demarcation.

The Kalabari make the woko out of white or khaki sturdy cotton fabrics known as drill, plain wool, serge, or Terylene, a synthetic fabric. The colors used are yellow or beige, off-brown, or a neutral hue. This contrasts with the bright red, black, green, or crimson background colors with animal or bird motifs that characterize the *blangidi* or woolen material from which non-Kalabari peoples make an equivalent garment. With the Kalabari, it is generally boorish and an anathema to wear this latter type of designed textile. A general sense of disdain for use of the supposedly garish blangidi therefore sets the Kalabari apart, even though this disdain is an insular appraisal by the Kalabari about others.

The woko is simply cut and hangs from the shoulders of the wearer, with a front placket and no collar band (second figure from left, fig. 13.1). The front placket of the Kalabari woko or jompa is plain in contrast to the elaborate gill-pattern or ladder-design motif on the plackets of the non-Kalabari jompa and the Kalabari doni. The sleeves are wide and elbow-length; the garment itself is knee-length. A band of the same cloth is sewn full-length at the back center of the Kalabari woko "to give it character," according to informants. The bottom hem is straight with side slits, which are largely only stylistic. The earlier version of the woko had two front pockets and was not as long as later ones. The term *woko*, apparently from the Kalabari word *wokoro*, meaning "loose-fitting," seems an apt description.

The woko placket has buttonholes for three studs of gold or silver, attached to each other by a chain. A wide pocket on the left usually sports a fluffy matching handkerchief. A walking stick is considered a necessary accessory, and a straw hat or other informal headgear like the embroidered one, called "smoking cap," will be worn. This cap is an embroidered round hat, flat on the top but decorated with tassels or metallic thread trimmings.

The woko is frequently worn with an injiri wrapper but can also be worn with trousers, as it has been for many years. A photograph of Chief Ikiriko of Buguma, said to be taken in 1917, shows him dressed with woko and trousers. Wearing trousers supposedly reflects a need for convenience, as when the wearer is bustling about at the beachfront handling commerce and does not want to worry about the breeze lifting up his wrapper.

The Kalabari do not sew their woko with blangidi like their neighbors use for the jompa. They agree in their judgment that the use of this fabric for woko shows poor taste. Nearer to the truth, however, may be the fact that heavily patterned and brightly colored fabrics had generally been assigned to the sewing of doni, to add to the full-view colorfulness and commanding presence of chiefs. By sticking to only the blandly colored fabrics for their woko, a clear-cut and highly distinguishable collective identity was also established for the Kalabari.

DESCRIBING THE ETIBO

The name *etibo* is an elision of the words *eight bob*, or eight shillings, which represented the cost of such a shirt brought for sale during the English period of dominance. Etibo is at the bottom of the hierarchy of Kalabari men's dress in the valuation of traditional dress and is associated with the lowest rank, the sociopolitical status of *Asawo* or the Young Men That Matter. The garment, simply a large, white long-sleeved shirt, is made of cotton. The bottom of the etibo has a rounded shirttail (far left, fig. 13.1), in contrast to the straight hem of the woko. The cotton material is comparatively much lighter and cheaper than the heavier woolen cloth of earlier versions. Respondents said the early examples were not usually white but colored, thick flannel material, and shorter than the current style called etibo. The version of the 1980s and 1990s reaches to about midcalf, whereas the original etibo was knee-length. The original imported etibo appears to have simply disappeared from the market, just like several other European imported dresses that were formerly popular. One was the "Bush shirt," which had fur-padded parts on the shoulders and back and was made of thick wool so that it served well in keeping the cold away. Another was the formal dinner shirt, with the buttonholes inserted in the wide front placket (called *ekpe kuro*).

The contemporary etibo appears to have emerged from being the undershirt (*sheti*) that chiefs wore beneath their doni and ebu. Some Kalabari chiefs of the past were very big and tall people for whom the European shirt was ill-fitting. These men, such as Chiefs Jim George (died 1943), Inko-Tariah (died 1943), and Graham Douglas (died in the 1950s), locally ordered their own shirts to be sewn to size. Before long, such "trendy" shirts went on to become the single outside garb of the lower status young men and took on the name etibo. Its use specifically enjoyed a boost after the Nigerian Civil War of 1967–1970.

The sheti worn underneath other garments by chiefs had a detached collar as well as one buttonhole for a stud and sleeves with buttonholes for cuff links;

it was not the regular European shirt. Some informants called it the imported English "Crown Shirt," for which the local terminology "Krama Sheti" appears to have been substituted. The new etibo looked much like its forerunner, with no collar and a cloth loop at the center of the back yoke. Its sleeves have buttons, not linked buttonholes; this change accommodated the decreased concern for prestige among younger men, although a shirt pocket was added to permit display of colorful handkerchiefs. Etibo is worn only with a single stud at shirt front, as opposed to three worn with the woko and four with the doni. Etibo can also be worn with any pair of trousers, although an injiri wrapper is the only correct accompaniment to the garment when one is dressing formally as Kalabari.

The etibo has become the focus of connoisseurship of injiri-tying styles because it allows more of the wrapper to be seen. Skill is required to manipulate the slim gingham piece (*injiri ikiba*), two yards long and one yard wide. Tying the cloth around the waist must be carefully done in order that the wrapper does not appear to be tied carelessly and too loosely, thus inviting a comment about the careless appearance (*biri ayi sima*). Normally the bottom edge of the injiri wrapper should be at least two inches above the instep. However, this general rule is offset by the opportunity to display a variety of cloth-tying styles that modify the rule, indicating the wearer as one thoroughly at home with cultural knowledge and etiquette of men's dress, as discussed later.

DESCRIBING THE ATTIGRA

The attigra ensemble does not fit into the set of four previously mentioned but instead derives its great importance simply as the foremost ceremonial or dancing garb of men (far right, fig. 13.1). The attigra also attests to the primacy the Kalabari give to culture over politics, for cultural events have continued to be important and resilient in Kalabari life even as their political structure has become subordinated to that of the larger polity of Nigeria. The contrived dazzle of an attigra outfit is, therefore, another Kalabari original, along with its companion *ajibulu* hat that produces a bulky effect that balances the gown. One informant described the wearer of this hat as holding forth like a masquerade and amply filling the vista with his dazzle on appearing (Erekosima 1989, 339).

Attigra is the Kalabari designation for a northern Nigerian, handwoven cotton robe with Arab-influenced embellishments of embroidery that came into Kalabari hands before Nigeria came into being as a nation. The Kalabari word *attigra* is formed as an elision of "Atta Igarra," derived from the words *Attah of Igalla*. This king of an ancient kingdom at the northern limits of the Niger delta (Miles 1936) with whom the Kalabari chiefs carried on their early trade was described by informants as the donor of the outfit to his contemporary Kalabari nobility, and the dress was then named after him. A more fashionable version is made from embroidered velvet from India. The attigra is primarily distinguished by having open sleeves that are about one-third the length of the garment. The rich fabrics are cut amply to give the wearer bulk and to provide an image of the wearer as munificent. Matching velvet material is tied as a wrapper beneath the velvet attigra and shows below its hem (reaching to the lower calf or ankle). If the homespun variety of attigra from northern Nigeria is chosen, then a matching wrapper of injiri is worn.

Underneath either gown type, the man must wear a European-style long-sleeved shirt and beneath that a singlet (cotton u-neck, knit undershirt). It is normal to wear heavy gold rings on several fingers with this outfit. To wear the early form of attigra, for instance, a man must have either an English top hat or the imposing indigenous creation of the ajibulu hat. A circlet of tiger's teeth (*siri aka*) or of cowry shells around the neck is a required accessory to accentuate the ajibulu hat. The velvet version is usually worn with an ajibulu and layers of coral beads bedecking the neck.

Because shoes are viewed as restrictive of dance steps, being barefoot is preferred, but if shoes are worn, socks are generally not worn. To complete this outfit, a decorated fan (*ye biri efenge*) should be held in the right hand, and an elephant tusk (*oworowo*) or other material of tusk shape, made of glass or cowry shells, should be held in the left hand. Walking sticks and canes are not used when wearing attigra.

CLOTH-TYING TECHNIQUES

Each of the above ensembles includes a wrapper as part of the outfit. The Kalabari recognize two distinct classifications of cloth-tying methods for men's wrappers. One is *biri oki* or *biri olo*, which means to hold the cloth on to the waist, and within which such techniques as *akinda, ikpukpu kpo, pele suka,* and *tingili* are practiced. Akinda involves placing the middle of the cloth at one's back, then looping the ends over the private parts and tying its tips around the waist. This is generally practiced today to prepare corpses for burial. Wrestlers would also resort to a variant of this form in a bid to secure themselves adequately from exposure. Injiri or any other domestic cloth can be used to tie ikpukpu kpo, which entails making a firm knot so that the rest of the cloth can be gathered, especially around the knees, to permit strenuous work or vigorous movements. A picture of the war party of Chief Will Braide of Bakana, presumably taken in 1879, shows some soldiers in this style, a common injiri-tying method for young people at the time.

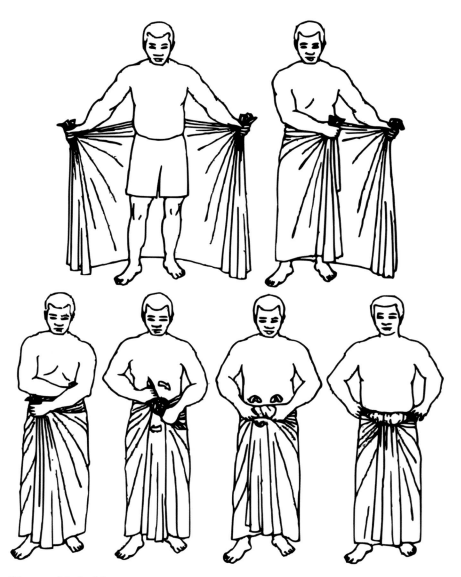

Fig. 13.3. Method for tying a wrapper in tingili style, most often used with tawulu or wax print cloth. Courtesy of M. Catherine Daly, drawn by Sylvia Ruud.

Fig. 13.4.
Method for tying a wrapper
in inturu style (left) and
eremoni style (right).
Courtesy of M. Catherine
Daly, drawn by Sylvia Ruud.

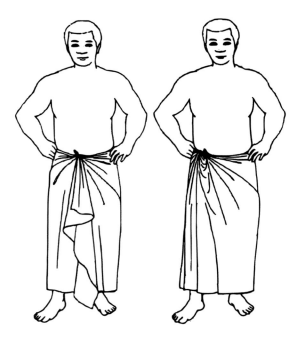

Pele suka entails laying one side of the upper end of a cloth on the other and tucking it in, without actually tying either tip. The thick *tawulu*, or beach towel, is normally worn this way for situations like going to the river for an early morning dip. Tingili is another way of wearing the tawulu but is better suited to the lighter and more voluminous wax prints. It entails rolling the crossed-over tips of the cloth's upper section over and over on itself at about the level of the navel till the length of the cloth comes to just above the feet. This firmly secures the cloth on the waist through the multiple rolling turns, as shown in figure 13.3.

The second main method of cloth tying for Kalabari men is that of actually wrapping the cloth (*inwain*) around the waist. A variety of styles or techniques have been developed (see Table 13.1) including *eremoni* or *kiri pele, alaate* or *amatubonye, inturu,* and *otobiri* and are described below. Figure 13.4 illustrates eremoni and inturu.

Men's cloth is always tied to the right of the waist, while women always tie theirs to the left. Any man who consistently ties his cloth to the left risks being accused of wizardry for so audaciously flouting a key rule or practice involving gender differentiation.

The Kalabari invested much creative energy in tying wrappers as one aspect of the man's complete ensemble. So elaborate has this become that clearly more

Table 13.1. Styles of Cloth Tying (*Bite Inwain*) in Kalabari Men's Traditional Dress

Style Name	Description
Eremoni or *Kiri pele*	The cloth is wrapped fully to the ankle; the bottom tips are even, with one overlapping the other. This is tied like Kalabari women tie their cloth (except women tie to the left, not the right), hence the name eremoni or "fit for women's envy." This method of tying assumes slow, dignified movements in walking, because the manner of wrapping around the body does not allow a long stride. The name kiri pele depicts the precision of "roundedness" at the bottom of the wrapper in encircling the body from waist to feet.
Alaate or *Amatubonye*	One tip of the cloth points down in front on the right side, with this tip longer than the rest of the bottom of the cloth. The names alaate (meaning, "I have made good") and amatubonye (meaning, "Who owns the town anyway?") are suggestive of its "dare me" casualness.
Inturu	The cloth is wrapped so that the hem is parallel to the ground, with the two ends open on the left side. As the wearer strides along, the wrapper opening shows off white underpants (knickers) trimmed with lace at the knee (*buo sua kappa*). The cotton plaid textile called *injiri*, usually selected for this style, often has a pair of white shirting strips sewn at the waist for ease of tying the style.
Obobiri	The wrapper length is tied shorter than the inturu; the hem is equal and round, with the tying occurring at both ends of the waist. The word *otobiri* is suggestive of "sweet experience." This is a relatively new style, which a leading men's club in Buguma is teaching all its members to tie as a presumably proprietary discovery.

than just the use of dress in basic or ordinary socialization is involved. These style options for men, their range of skill, the particular occasions of use, verbal designations, and specific shared meanings constitute an important dimension of Kalabari aesthetics in dress for men.

Additional evidence gives us further insight into the subtleties and the mystique built around the cloth-tying style called inturu that enthralls members of the Kalabari public. One middle-aged informant told Erekosima during fieldwork interviews that when a man ties inturu:

O bu ke bu sin te,
(He has laid hold of his dignity)

O Kalabari bo bara sime te
(He has taken on the true image of being Kalabari).
(Erekosima 1989)

To convey the way most informants felt about tying inturu, we might say that it gives a Kalabari man the feeling that is as luxurious as getting to tool around town in a prestigious car, even if for only an evening. For among the array of styles that Kalabari men may display in cloth manipulations, the inturu is the "Mercedes Benz" of them all.

Another informant, forty-two years old, a "Young Man" by Kalabari classification (*Asawo*), rhapsodized as follows on the pleasures of tying inturu: "When the wind blows, the injiri has to open up and the underpant(s) (*drosi*) just shines forth, the white underpant(s) is just beaming (*saniari*). The dancer or wearer is mounting an underpant(s) display declaring that he is neat down to the pin, for it [the underpants] is just as immaculate as the etibo [outer garment] is immaculate."

An elderly informant explained that "for the Kalabari man, the style of tying injiri which exposes his long underpants is treasured" (Erekosima 1989, 376).

One man went so far as to point out that the original name of this style was intuku (which relates to uprightness) but has colloquially become inturu. Thus, the ensemble is linked to the portrayal of moral integrity and character as the Kalabari define these. This reference to character is one that reflects an apparent demeanor of nonchalant leisureliness (*asa-ti*) while remaining fully alert to one's responsibilities (*bu nimi*). Robin Horton (1966) has given similar depictions of the ideal Kalabari man in masquerade portrayals.

The wearer of the inturu wrapper exudes subtlety of character, or sophistication. He is "surprised" by the breeze lifting his wrapper (but actually his gait does it) to expose, ever-so-inadvertently, his immaculate underpants to onlookers, until he adjusts his wrapper once more to feign modesty by covering it. Indeed, because of its one-upmanship intricacies, the inturu was initially a style of wrapper tying reserved exclusively for chiefs.

THE RULES AND ETIQUETTE OF KALABARI MEN'S DRESS

In expressions such as *orattigrabulo warari* (he is donning an attigra), *osime barabu gbem* (his turnout is befitting), or *orokapa ogbeaa* (his dress does not fit him), Kalabari people convey an evaluation of man's attire, which combines items on various parts of the body in forming a single unit of accoutrement. The assessment of a Kalabari man's appearance does not end simply with the mix of appropriate items on the head, neck, body, and waist or in the hands, pockets, and plackets that make up each of the ensembles of the attigra, ebu, doni, woko, and etibo. It also extends to details of color, fit, and proper accessorizing.

A stringent adherence to aesthetic standards demands that white material must retain its whiteness; that cloth be tied so that its tip is only about one and a half inches above the ankle and not way up away from it (*fekepu*) or awkwardly below it; that allowances for body fit be made in the design and sewing of clothing, so that it neither appears too short nor too long, too loose nor too tight; that rich and heavy material for sewn garments not be worn with lightweight or cheap cloth for the wrapper; that studs be worn in specific ways when dressing is casual or formal; and that ornaments like gold or silver match the colors of dress and shoes that are worn. Therefore, silver is matched to black and blue shades; gold goes with beige or brown colors of dress.

These examples illustrate subtler attributes and standards of Kalabari men's dress than does the mere ensembling process of specific items put together from different parts of the world. Instead, explicitly recognized lengths, textures, amount of bulk, positioning, and color choices all contribute to a configuration that only the practiced eye will catch, and on which the Kalabari instruct their youth. The fact that each Kalabari ensemble combines materials from different cultures and not from a single source, and that the Kalabari also apply their own indigenous aesthetic standards of proper dress, indicates that they have not copied another society's styles or aesthetics.

Among the rules of dress, tradition decrees that no man should wear the ensemble of a rank higher than his on an everyday basis. An Asawo or Young Man that Matters, for instance, is not supposed to wear a woko or jompa, for they belong to the Opu Asawo or Gentleman of Substance category. Nor should anyone who is not a chief put on the doni, for he invites being fined, beaten, and stripped. Exceptions apply for dressing for funerals as a chief mourner, as indicated in chapters 18 and 19.

Through observation of these regulations, all members of the social system maintain orderly relations; aspiration to the next functional level is sustained for all who still may climb higher; and authority operates undiminished from the higher levels to the lower without recourse to sanctions.

"STEPPING DOWN," "STEPPING UP," AND "STEPPING OUT" PRACTICES IN KALABARI MEN'S DRESSING

Among the understood rules, however, there is a generally permitted pattern that a member of a higher rank may wear the outfit of any of the ranks below him, in a context of dressing informally. For example, a chief wears black woko for attending the funeral of a person who is not a chief but will wear only a black doni to the funeral of a fellow chief. A chief could also wear the etibo to receive visitors at home, but he must wear at least the woko in going out for a meeting of his War-Canoe House and not a formal state affair, where he can only wear doni or ebu. He may also informally walk about town by "stepping out" only in the innovative *kala doni* or woko, but not in a straight etibo.

A chief who informally wears the woko that is allocated to "Gentlemen" and strolls out on the street, however, may show his actual status by wearing his woko with only one stud. This is different from the three that an Opu Asawo, or Gentleman, would need, all in place, while wearing this outfit of his rank. The Opu Asawo may show informality by wearing the etibo on the street, ensuring that he wears a felt hat and carries his walking stick. The Asawo, in turn, dresses informally by wearing his etibo without buttoning the single stud and, if possible, wearing a pair of trousers with it instead of tying a madras wrapper. In either case, he does not need a hat or a walking stick.

The above practice of "stepping down" from one's proper outfit has its "stepping up" counterpart also. Funeral obsequies, which mark a transition in families, provide for temporary suspension of the strict code of dressing by one's rank only. At this time, events are introduced, like the funeral parade and final funeral dance, with younger men of the family allowed to wear the woko and even the doni or ebu in public, temporarily advancing their status.

If the death were of a chief or very old person, there is even a complete loosening of clothing regulations, in the accompanying evening of *igira sara* (storming out with a stomp). Here women join in too, with the youth of the affected community, trotting about in martial and other uncomely or sexually explicit gait.

A return to normal dress marks the end of the disequilibrating episode of death on which attention has been briefly lavished. Thereafter, only persons close to the deceased may enter into a period of seclusion and of mourning dressed in black, which somehow takes them out of the mainstream of the visual communication setting for public conduct.

POLITICAL CHANGE AND ITS INFLUENCE
ON KALABARI MEN'S DRESS

As the power of the king and the chiefs as Heads of the Canoe Houses began to wane under the impact of British colonialism, their control over those under them lessened. Following an administrative change in the 1920s, subordinates of the Heads of War-Canoe Houses were appointed by the British administrator to exercise power over everyone in certain cases. The move spelled a death-knell to Kalabari traditional authority and initiated a marked era of individualism. The rule of the previous indigenous political regime collapsed accordingly, and along with it went strict adherence to some of the practices it had sustained, including those related to dress as a visible expression of sociopolitical rank. Then in 1960, not only were Kalabari men generally relieved of their previous allegiance, but they also had an opportunity to pursue broader identities and affinities in the new framework of an independent Nigerian state. Consequently, changes, not only in aspects of the clothing that constitute Kalabari men's dress ensembles but also in their patterns of use, have occurred. The old order has changed and its significant symbols have been diminished. We have identified six changes in the aesthetic standards, as follows:

1. The attigra has been shown to have changed from a traditional handwoven cotton material with stitched-on designs to richly embroidered, factory-produced velvets worn with heavy coral beads. This style, introduced about 1914, also came with a distinctive Indian Sikh-type of headgear with a streamer running down the back. This form of dress may not be strictly considered contemporary given the time of its introduction by people like Chief Charles Inko-Tariah, but it is not traditional. It may be labeled simply as a modern response to current industrial life in contrast to the life of the trader during the mercantile era. It particularly reflected personal style as a result of pronounced individuation in Kalabari society.

2. The chiefs' choice to wear ebu in the twenty-first century shows the impact of modern trends, partly because its cotton material is lighter than that of the woolen doni and is more suited to the tropical conditions of the delta climate. Also it is less demanding to wear in terms of required accompanying accessories. Virtually any chief may choose to wear it today with little adherence to established protocol.

3. The doni, too, is more regularly worn with shoes, as all chiefs are not expected to be expert dancers as they were in the past, and showing off the feet for dancing has not retained its importance. The several long gold chains that were frequently found worn with the doni in pictures of earlier

chiefs seem to have, in turn, disappeared. There is a greater orientation toward economy and practical personal considerations and less involvement with group norms and display.

A new form of dress called kala doni (the mini-doni) is appearing on Kalabari men. It is virtually like the doni, or sometimes the contemporary etibo, except that it is often made of light woolen material instead of white cotton. It has the characteristic Kalabari decorations for a doni. These are, in particular, the chest decorations in the form of *sangolo* (fish gill) or *lada* (ladder) frills on both sides of the strip marking the buttonholes. Then there is the flap (*bele*) sewn on underneath the strip. This outfit dispenses, however, with requirements like being worn with a shirt underneath it. Kalabari chiefs are increasingly found wearing this dress as semiformal outdoor gear instead of the woko. A few chiefs, of course, condemn the use of the "newfangled" kala doni that they think is inappropriate.

4. The woko is innovatively worn today with trousers that are made of the same material as the top garment. Previously a white or khaki woko or one made with some plain woolen material would be worn with injiri, or else trousers of serge or wool that only color-matched the upper apparel.

    Kalabari young men also wear the woko now (rather than it being seen as the outfit suitable only for their elders) with a lace inner shirt (similar to the Yoruba men's buba that is topped by an *agbada* upper garment). This innovation is apparently reflective of fairly comfortable financial standing and may be a contemporary Nigerian fashion. The neighboring Ikwerre people appear to be the ones introducing this fashion.

    Another aspect of this trend toward greater fancifulness among Kalabari young men is the increasing introduction of decorative chest designs on their woko. This was clearly unacceptable earlier to the Kalabari and was more characteristic of their neighbors like the Okrika.

    An even more forbidden practice that middle-class Kalabari young men are beginning to adopt is the wearing of woko sewn with the textiles popularized by men in the Bonny, Opobo, and Nembe societies. The Kalabari men adopting this form of dress still wear it only in the townships, because it is more expensive (showing them to be well-off) and colorful, unlike the generally drab type preferred by traditional Kalabari etiquette.

5. The contemporary etibo, as shown earlier, is a rather recent innovation starting around the 1950s, which got its latest boost beginning in the 1970s. In addition to its adoption, the younger generation of Kalabari males who are about the age of new secondary-school graduates are avid consumers of this etibo as well as other fashions that are emerging as Nigerian forms.

6. Adoptions have arisen from other Nigerian traditional forms of dress, such as those of the Yoruba or Hausa. One case is the *danshiki*, the short

embroidered or tie-dyed garment that is worn with trousers. Other examples are loose-fitting buba or bariga gowns derived from Yoruba and Hausa sources respectively worn with tight trousers that hug the legs closely, usually made of the same material as the upper garment. New fashionable versions of such male dress, which appear in silk or other modern fabrics, cut to contemporary taste by Nigerian fashion designers, are quite frequently worn by Kalabari young men on the streets of Buguma.

Thus, Kalabari young men have rapidly adopted some of the styles and current fashions from their various neighbors. Male members of Kalabari society appear committed to explore new options of identity as represented through dress, no doubt as a continuation of their willingness to combine cultural development with a political focus.

In contemporary Nigeria, however, it is not only the Kalabari who are responding to change and adopting the forms of dress of their neighbors. Kalabari men's dress is also being widely adopted by new users outside its traditional cultural circles. Many young men from various Rivers State communities, such as Ahoada, Abua, Engenni, and Ikwerre, have been seen wearing the etibo in the 1980s and 1990s to go to work in government offices or to stroll about on the streets of Port Harcourt, the state capital. Similarly, the "traditional dress" claimed by the bulk of hinterland Igbos today, of a woko (jompa) made from figured textile designs and worn with regular European trousers, comes from the societies of the Niger delta city-states. Contemporary Igbo chiefs have also shown a penchant for adornment in the doni, worn especially with Benin- or Yoruba-derived headgear and beads, when dressed in their royal garb.

Through their exposure to members of Western society and interactions with members of other African cultures, the Kalabari developed systematic, aesthetic rules of dress. These were clearly understood and practiced within Kalabari society, for the dress codes paralleled the social order. There has been a recent loosening of attachment, however, to the protocols of Kalabari appearance. As our data suggest, even the chiefs or community leaders have not been conservative custodians of the "good, old ways," but there is no suggestion that the Kalabari, as purveyors of an African aesthetic in men's dress, have diminished interest. Vigorous interest and animated discussion continue among them concerning the "rights" and "wrongs" of dress and the appropriateness of new styles and fashions.

We have added another dimension of the aesthetic knowledge relating to dress as cultural heritage in the diverse African continent. We caution against oversimplified or glib references to and descriptions about "Africa" through profiles that are too limited and narrow. In addition, with the concept of the cultural authentication, we have demonstrated that the use of materials and artifacts from other cultures is a dynamic and creative process that indicates strong aesthetic commitments and choices.

CHAPTER ADDENDUM: AESTHETICS OF THE
COLOR WHITE IN KALABARI MEN'S DRESS

Tonye Victor Erekosima

The following addendum further expands Kalabari dress aesthetics, following general observations by John Barbot (1746a) and paraphrasing those made by the Dutch traveler Dapper, the knight, in 1676: "The principal thing that passes in Calabari as current money among the natives, is brass rings, for the arms or legs, weights they call *bochie* . . . the English and Dutch import there a great deal of copper in the small bars round in equal about three feet long, which the black Calabari work with much art, splitting the bar into three parts, from one end to the other, which they probably should as fine as gold, and twisted three pieces together like cords to make what sorts of armoring they please."

The same meticulous involvement with the aesthetics of dress similarly characterizes contemporary Kalabari, now mainly professionals and businesspeople in modern society, with others continuing in free trade and some fishing. With a high concentration of them working in the metropolis of Port Harcourt, which is an oil port and large industrial city, a majority return to the Kalabari indigenous towns of Buguma, Abonnema, Bakana, Tombia, and Obuama during weekends to relax. And here they turn to wearing traditional outfits, either lounging about at home or attending community meetings or family funerals.

I focus on Kalabari aesthetics of the color white in men's dress. It is important to know from the outset that Kalabari aesthetics of dress encumbrances such matching of colors; matching of clothing items with regard to quality of materials, related to the series of men and women's ensembles; matching of accessories for two types of clothing; and matching the gait of one's movement to dress worn for the occasion, requiring a particular kind of outfit for women's ceremonial outings or men's masquerading. Various other forms of aesthetics include "fit," such that proper dressing must be seen to be not too long, too loose, too short, or too loud by well-established standards. Dressing must also conform to a variety of style requirements as concerning which particular way of tying the wrapper is applied or how correct folding is of the sleeves of men's shirts, relative to given aesthetic standards. All of these, therefore, are not dealt with here, only the Kalabari interest in the color white and their focus on expectations regarding men's appearance.

The abstract concept of whiteness has been a subject of considerable intellectual exploration and practical application for the Kalabari. The color white, adapted as a symbol of the sacred among them since antiquity, is demonstrated primarily through the use of kaolin. This white, chalky clay substance is applied around the eyes of traditional priests and prophetesses in association with their proclaimed foreknowledge of affairs, an analog to Western man's peering into microscopic and telescopic lenses to view very tiny and very distant realities, respectively. For the Kalabari specialists, the kaolin signifies their perceptions and spiritual or abstract realm outside their capability of seeing literally in the mundane sphere. White cloth, when it became available in this society, also came to be tied on the shrine structures of the various Kalabari deities as their main insignia. White cloth transferred to the unique headpiece (*ogborigbo*) of the founding Kalabari king, Amachree I (died about 1900), as his personal gear for ritual and ceremonial occasions. An instance of personal gear is the occasion of the burial of one of Kalabari's kings, His Royal Highness Cotton Charlie (Kieni) in 1975, with his first son described as leading the obsequies so clad. White cloth, therefore, has application in religion and politics, appears in rituals and ceremonies, and shows family solidarity.

White has also passed under the social psyche of the Kalabari, not just as a color but as an attribute, a quality against which human character is measured. Perhaps the sheer plainness of white, in contrast to the patterned form of all other types of cloth, gave white a special aura. But the handy material of white cloth became, of all these, the manipulable elements that the Kalabari could lay hold of to measure human character. For the innocent man, Kalabari declared that his hands were clean or white (*obra fia-fia warari*). A linguistic connection provides further interest. The ingenious Kalabari terminology for white, *pina* or *bia*, can only be expressed in superlatives or verbal retakes, with the actual expressions of usage being "*pina-pina*," "*bia-bia*," or "*fia-fia*." The last of these words means clean, but it is also used synonymously with being spotless, something without color or any stain, also holy or blameless. The abstract quality of purity and the superlative syntax just described have been assimilated into the Kalabari term for white cloth or a plain white sheet, as is the term *abila-la*, also used as the name for paper.

The verbal applications regarding the concept of white cloth (abila-la) have been further extended into mythological history, which the Kalabari narrate.

For example, the great sea goddess (*Owu-Iyingi*) was purportedly mother to the female tutelary deities of the Bonny and Kalabari. She was said to have once given her daughters a piece of abila-la, either a cloth or a book. But while the younger of them, called Owamekaso, who led the Kalabari, held the object in her hands, the elder daughter, Ikuba, tore away the larger portion from her sister. This myth apparently accounts for how Bonny, which was once in the ascendancy in the European trade of the Nigerian eastern delta, later lost preeminence to the Kalabari newcomer, at least in the area of the cultural and political arts.

The fact is that whiteness (concretized as cloth or book, a metaphor for the trade of the political entities) further came to encapsulate an idealized account of Kalabari history. In addition, it upheld the postulate of a fictional kinship between the Kalabari and their Bonny archrivals who were so recognized, once one came down to the level of mundane reality. In this anecdote, the make-believe that only characterizes true literature was probably the key, and served, besides the myth's value, in perhaps attenuating the sharp edge of clashes that occurred between the polities. People that I once interviewed in Buguma talked about this Kalabari romance with whiteness and explained the significance of its embodiment in their white clothing, which on appearance every eye inspects for immaculateness. The reductionism concerning the concept of whiteness from its abstract level to application in a variety of structural milieu ranged through such areas as religion, politics, ritual, social organization, linguistics, history, literature, and morality, as well as education. The latter was in respect of its influence on selections of the color of Kalabari men's dress. The foundation or base dress was the man's etibo.

TONYE VICTOR EREKOSIMA (1940–2008), PhD, native-born Kalabari, lived in the Igbo towns of Owerri and Umuahia, because his father was an educator and secondary-school principal, until Erekosima's university years in the United States. He was steeped in Kalabari cultural tradition, however, thanks to his family's routine travel to Buguma, his parents' birthplace, for holidays and significant events like funerals. Following his PhD, he served as Director, General Studies, Rivers State College of Education, and Director, Instructional Resources Center, University of Port Harcourt. He coedited *A Hundred Years of Buguma History in Kalabari Culture* (1984) and *Buguma 1984 Centenary Symposia on Kalabari* (1991).

JOANNE B. EICHER, PhD, is Regents Professor Emerita in the Department of Design, Housing, and Apparel at the University of Minnesota. She is coeditor of *The Anthropology of Dress and Fashion: A Reader*; coeditor of *The Visible Self: Global Perspectives on Dress, Culture, and Society*, 4th ed.; and editor in chief of the *Encyclopedia of World Dress and Fashion*.

NOTES

Adapted from Erekosima and Eicher (1994) and Erekosima (n.d.).

1. We collected data during eight field trips by Eicher, three overlapping with Erekosima, who is Kalabari. He collected data as participant observer over a number of years. In addition, his dissertation research included an eight-week, detailed pedestrian survey, twenty formally structured interviews, ten informal interviews as well as conversation and discussion about men's dress. Eicher's research included taped interviews, informal discussion recorded in written field notes, and slides documenting daily and ceremonial dress for all eight trips.

2. Elsewhere in the context of African cultural continuity and change with the Nigerian Kalabari as a case study (Eicher and Erekosima 1993), we analyzed Kalabari use of textiles and dress to communicate social order in four main dimensions: (1) the order of sociopolitical ranks as assigned to a predominantly male gender; (2) the reproduction and socialization order that is predominantly female; (3) the ritual order of funerals; and (4) the ceremonial order of masquerades and dance.

14

Dress as Symbol of Identity of
Sir (Chief) O. K. Isokariari

Joanne B. Eicher

IN THIS CHAPTER, I provide sartorial details about the successful life of businessman Sir (Chief) O. K. Isokariari, an indigenous contractor in Port Harcourt, a Buguma "son of the soil" (a favorite Kalabari phrase). Through his dress practices, he communicates his identity and roles. I dispel stereotypes about Africans by showing how dress as an aspect of material culture both passively reflects values and actively perpetuates them. Early in my research, Erekosima introduced me to Isokariari in Buguma, and the chief and I kept in contact during my research trips. In one visit, he showed me his chieftaincy installation photographs, graciously answering my questions about it and providing me information about his company and travels. This opportunity allowed me to highlight the following example of one Kalabari man who balances his professional life with his Kalabari heritage, privileges, and obligations.

Isokariari exemplifies a Kalabari living both in Port Harcourt and Buguma, his birthplace. When installed as chief, he was in his fifties. He graduated from Kalabari National College (KNC), a secondary institution at Buguma's edge where he was a student in a five-year program from 1952 to 1956. In his final year, he was appointed as a prefect in Lincoln House, one of the four Houses at KNC. His homes are comfortable "Western-style." One is two stories on a large compound in Port Harcourt, the city of his contracting firm; the other is a three-story in Buguma. He is the retired chair, managing director, and chief executive of O. K. Isokariari and Sons (Nigeria) Ltd, (called O.K.I.); chair of O.K.C. (Nigeria) Ltd; and fellow of the indigenous Nigerian companies in

Fig. 14.1.
Sir (Chief) Isokariari in a custom-
tailored suit with accessories,
1987. Courtesy of Sir (Chief)
O. K. Isokariari.

the field of "high quality engineering services."[1] O.K.C., an O.K.I. subsidiary, began in 1979 to specialize in the building of roads and bridges.[2] He gave me a brochure, "Building for the Future," which describes the services of both firms, emphasizing their expertise and modern technology in his "Message from the Chairman."

Isokariari's brochure portrait in figure 14.1 shows him holding a walking stick and wearing a tasteful Western-style suit, shirt, and tie with pocket handkerchief, gold rings, and a Rolex watch—a ensemble most appropriate for the Western values of efficiency and modernity expressed by his message. He told me that he had his suits tailored in Paris and London.

Isokariari plays an important role in Buguma. For the 1984 Buguma Centenary, in which the Elem-Ama migration was reenacted and celebrated, Isokariari chaired the executive committee that organized all activities. The construction of King Amachree Hall and the statue of King Abbi (Amachree IV) in the town square were completed for the centenary, with the contract awarded to O. K. Isokariari & Sons Nig. Ltd with Isokariari as managing director. The

Fig. 14.2. Sir (Chief) Isokariari wearing a top hat, woko, and injiri wrapper with the Amanyanabo (center), other Kalabari notables, and two honored guests from Benin City in white gowns, flanking the Amanyanabo, 1984.

entire Buguma population contributed funding for the project, and he was one of the major sponsors.

In his capacity, Isokariari appeared throughout the centenary festivities wearing an ensemble of *woko* and *madras* wrapper, appropriate as one of the *opu asawo* (gentlemen). True to his station, when dressed formally, he wore a hat and carried a cane, umbrella, or walking stick. A variety of hats are appropriate for the woko, such as homburg, fedora, or top hat. Isokariari has chosen the top hat as his personal symbol and is most always seen wearing one with an ensemble that requires a hat. In figure 14.2, Isokariari sports a top hat with his woko and madras wrapper, posing with the Amanyanabo, other Kalabari notables, and two honored guests from Benin City wearing white gowns, who flank the Amanyanabo.

In 1984, Isokariari was not a chief; his chieftaincy installation was held in January 1987. It is a privileged position in Kalabari society, available to a select number of men when a chieftaincy position opens within a lineage and an appropriate lineage male has attained a level of prominence (meaning sufficient wealth and social standing) for the Amanyanabo to invite him. Isokariari

Fig. 14.3. Sir (Chief) Isokariari and wife in matching ensembles consisting of his velvet, gold-embroidered chieftaincy gown and her wrapper set. He holds an elephant tusk, a symbol of power, 1987. Courtesy of Sir (Chief) O. K. Isokariari.

planned well in advance for his installation, purchasing the items for his wardrobe several years ahead. Isokariari told Eicher he selected brown velvet "india" embroidered with gold peacocks for his *attigra*, with a matching fan and *ajibulu* headwear, the latter specially designed by Buguma's premier ajibulu maker. He selected matching velvet for his wife's wrapper on that day, as figure 14.3 shows. Both wore necklaces of fabulously large pieces of coral; his ladder-type necklace is typical of chiefs and men of high standing. The necklaces; embroidered-velvet garments; and other accessories, such as the ivory tusk held in Isokariari's right hand, symbolize the affluence needed to assume chieftaincy. In addition, his attention to detail in the motif selected for their matching textiles, his fan, and his hat indicate the sophisticated taste and elegance expected of a prominent Kalabari.

Becoming a chief is a major event in a Kalabari man's life—an accomplishment achievable by only a few men. This position gives him power, privilege, and responsibility within his lineage and the larger community. He becomes a major voice in the decisions of his immediate family, extended kinship group, and the town as a member of the Council of Chiefs. After becoming a chief, he is allowed to wear not only the attigra but also the gown called *ebu*. Isokariari wore doni and top hat for the June 1988 ceremony celebrating the then Amanyanabo's tenth-anniversary installation, figuring prominently with his wife as the Amanyanabo's daughter.

In 1995, Isokariari was elected as Knight of St. Christopher for the Niger Delta Diocese, comprised of Port Harcourt City, Buguma City, Abonnema Town, Bakana Town, Andoni Clan, Ikwerre Clan, Okirika Clan, and later the entire Bayelsa State. He was elected as president of Knight of St. Christopher for the Diocese for 1999–2005.

His dress illustrates his position within several social systems. His well-tailored business suit shows him to be a man conversant with, and part of, the industrial and global corporate world. The outfits worn for special events such as the Centenary of 1984, his chieftaincy installation, and the tenth-anniversary Amanyanabo celebration indicate his being a man of taste. His woko was hand-tailored by the outstanding tailor of Port Harcourt.[3] His chieftaincy outfit had been systematically purchased and prepared.[4] The way he dresses exemplifies Kalabari values placed on displaying one's position in a cool manner. Colors within an outfit match; accessory colors complement his chosen apparel (generally gold with brown, silver with gray or blue). Holding his walking stick in his business portrait subtly indicates a Kalabari gentleman whose ensemble must include his walking stick, cane, or umbrella. Similarly, the fabrics selected for the chieftaincy outfit express Kalabari values. In each outfit worn by Isokariari, the imported fabrics visibly exhibit Kalabari global trade since the late 1400s; these symbolize the successful commercial ventures of the Kalabari past, results of good fortune brought by the water people. The glitter of gold embroidery on velvet and the ajibulu hat ornaments similarly reflect the milieu of the water people's kingdom. The ability to buy and display coral and gold similarly relate to family success—including the ancestors who encouraged personal enterprise and accomplishments. Traditions are said to be the province of the community deities—those who guard the culture, guaranteeing that Kalabari people know the right way to behave and the correct things to wear. Thus, traditional dress itself relates to community beliefs and behavior.

Sir (Chief) O. K. Isokariari's ensembles reflect his value system and that of Kalabari society; he wears Western dress in his brochure portrait, which demonstrates business success and participation in the international economy. His chieftaincy dress conveys Kalabari values to children, adolescents, and young adults who also participate in community rituals. His gown and hat, as well his wife's ensemble, also display cultural authentication. His dress provides insight into contemporary Africa.

JOANNE B. EICHER, PhD, is Regents Professor Emerita in the Department of Design, Housing, and Apparel at the University of Minnesota. She is coeditor of *The Anthropology of Dress and Fashion: A Reader*; coeditor of *The Visible Self: Global Perspectives on Dress, Culture, and Society*, 4th ed.; and editor in chief of the *Encyclopedia of World Dress and Fashion*.

NOTES

Adapted from Eicher (1989).

1. "Building for the Future," undated brochure from O. K. Isokariari and Sons (Nigeria) Ltd., p. 1.

2. Ibid.

3. Field notes, May 1988.

4. Field notes, May 1988.

15

Beaded and Bedecked

Joanne B. Eicher

INTRODUCTION

This chapter continues to document the Kalabari importing items of dress, overland and by sea. Along with the variety of imported fabrics and accessories, such as canes, hats, and various kinds of jewelry, beads are one of the most frequently worn accessories, especially Italian coral.

Because of the interrelation of cloth and beads to Kalabari gender and age hierarchies for dress, I discuss the hierarchies of imported textiles and beads used with their dress ensembles, turning to the story of a specific glass bead that is the exclusive property of only one lineage. I analyze how this bead, said to come from Venice, relates to gender.

THE HIERARCHY OF BEADS

Along with the hierarchies of dress and textiles discussed in earlier chapters, there is a hierarchy of beads. Females wear a larger variety of beads than do men, and women's dress ensembles include beads at all stages of life. Boys do not wear beads on an everyday basis. Tiny girls often wear a string of beads around their waists.[1] *Ikuta de*, the "bead display" stage, usually involves several varieties of beads, but they are small in size whether agate, glass, or coral. They hang as necklaces and circle a girl's waist and hips, and are they are worn symmetrically on wrists, ankles, and knees. As she matures to wear ensembles that include more cloth, she continues to don the same type of beads, but with increasing size and number.

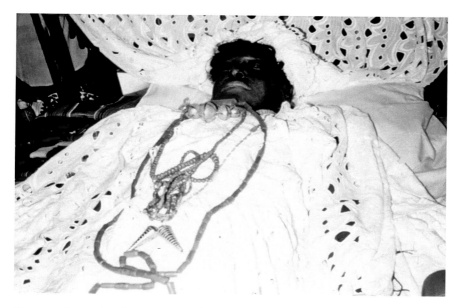

Fig. 15.1. Corpse in white gown, in Christian room with coral beads. Buguma, 1981.

Beads are an optional item for a woman wearing a full-length wrapper; when worn for dressing for church or parties, they are not usually a focus of attention. The notable exceptions occur when a woman wears a velvet full-length wrapper to accompany her husband during his chieftaincy installation or a silk or velvet wrapper to attend a thanksgiving service as chief mourner or new mother, and when members of a women's society dress to attend and dance for the community, discussed in chapter 12, illustrated in figure 9.2 and figure 15.1. At that time, they wear large coral beads. When a new mother completes being sequestered, her ultimate outfit includes big chunks of coral around the neck worn with a beaded hat, a coral-beaded walking stick, coral upper armlets, and a special coral bead necklace with matching pendants (usually heart shaped) that hang in the middle of her chest and upper back. Women's hats worn for ceremonial purposes exhibit a wider variety of beads than do men's, as seen in the ensembles for an *iyi iriabo* (a new mother), *aseki iriabo* (masquerade dancer), or *ede iriabo* (chief mourner).

As with textiles and garments, both Kalabari men and women during their lifetimes individually own beads, purchased or received as gifts. At death, socially significant and prestigious strings of beads and other important jewelry

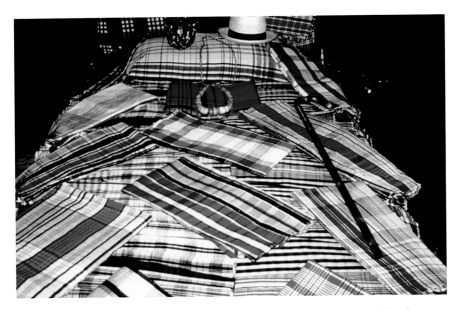

Fig. 15.2. Funeral bed decorated with madras textiles, two hats and coral beads placed where the corpse has lain, 1983.

and accessories of the deceased pass into the lineage holdings to be kept as joint or shared family property. As heirlooms, beads are stored in the "strong room" (usually an inner, locked room) in containers called "cloth boxes" along with the prized family textile inheritance. The eldest woman in each lineage supervises the care and lending of these treasures to lineage members for specified occasions. She is knowledgeable about the items as part of extended family genealogy and identity.

Beads worn by Kalabari men and women have some similarities. Both men and women cherish coral strings and accessories. Red-orange coral is used most often, although deeper red and white are also selected to wear depending on the colors found in the total ensemble. Both men and women display strands of coral beads when dressed as chief mourners. As well, a corpse may wear coral before burial, seen in figure 15.1. After the burial, coral is often laid on the funeral bed, which is decorated with textiles and other accessories, as seen in figure 15.2 (positioned as if the corpse were on the bed).

Prominent men and women frequently wear necklaces of huge coral beads to complement the prestige of embroidered-velvet gowns and wrappers as worn by Sir Isokariari and his wife for his chieftaincy installation, as seen in figure

14.3. He selected an impressive array of coral to underscore the significance of the position.

In addition to coral, adults wear gold beads. Many beads, especially those used by young girls, are of agate and glass. A wide range of beads decorate ceremonial hats for both men and women. Bead use differs for men and women when they dress for special occasions. As with hats, women's dress generally allows for more variations of beads than does men's dress, with the exception of the men's velvet ceremonial gown for chieftaincy and funeral events that encourage extensive personal display of textiles and strings of massive coral beads. As with dress and textiles, beads reinforce the hierarchical patterns of Kalabari life.

THE SELEYE FUBARA OR JACKREECE BEAD

Generally, the wearing of coral indicates individual wealth and prestige, but one Kalabari lineage distinguishes itself further by its ownership and display of a clear, fragile glass bead, about four inches in length. The hollow bead is hand-blown with spiral stripes of color. Because the glass is clear, the spirals appear as a lattice design, shown in figure 15.3.

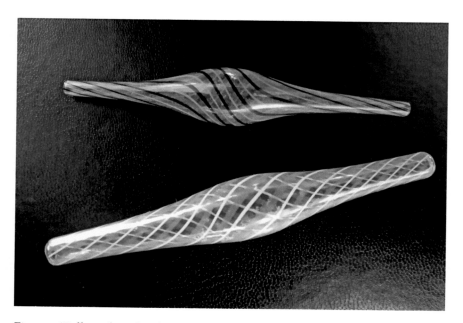

Fig. 15.3. Hollow, clear glass beads, possibly Venetian, about 4.5 inches (11 centimeters) long. Photo: Kate Leibfried, 2015.

Seleye Fubara, the founder of a prominent Kalabari lineage, is credited with making the bead exclusive to his lineage. He is also known as Seleye Jackreece or Seleye Jack Rich. English traders, generally unwilling to learn the pronunciation of indigenous names, gave him the name of "Jack Rich" because he was a wealthy and prosperous trader. The Kalabari changed Jack Rich to Jackreece, and Seleye Fubara is referred to by all three names.

The story shared among community members about his bead begins shortly after his birth. As a baby, Seleye was given one of the glass beads described above, called *ila*, to wear when his first tooth appeared. However, the bead fell into a crabhole and was lost. My source continued the story:

> Because he had no ila, his family was going to have to give him away to another family. The day he was to go to the other family, the crab threw up the mud from his hole and the ila showed a little and was finally seen. The ila bead was given to Seleye, and the other family couldn't take him. When he grew up and was the richest man (among the Kalabari), he went where the ila were made and brought many, many, many back to Kalabari land. He brought so many he stamped on them and crushed them and when they were used, more were crushed. He [still] showed he had many and that ila belong only to the Jackreece compound. (Eicher 1983)

The bead's connection to the Fubara lineage is reinforced by Data Ine Akobo's (1985, 52–53) description of how the female descendants of Seleye Fubara dress as *iriabo*: "There is another type of [body] painting, which is done only by the chieftaincy house of Seleye Fubara in Buguma. They paint red camwood on the hair. Also after wearing the Iriabo with the big coral beads, they have to add another bead called 'ila.' No other family in Buguma can add 'ila' except the Seleye Fubara family. Any Iriabo from Seleye Fubara house will be identified by these special features." (See fig. 15.4 for girdle of Jackreece beads.)

Why is this story about the bead and the founder of the Jackreece lineage significant? Seleye Fubara was wealthy by both English and Kalabari standards. The importance of wealth in Kalabari society is established by Kalabari author Alate Fubara-Manuel (n.d., 38–39), who reports that the word for "chief" in Kalabari "can be broken into two parts: 'ala' means riches or wealth in terms of money, property, manpower and character, 'bo' means a person. An 'alabo' in Kalabari in the past was, therefore, a person who possessed riches or wealth."

Fubara-Manuel (n.d., 41) stresses the importance of wealth by declaring that "wealth, it must be pointed out, never hides," for a chief must be wealthy to fulfill his obligations to himself, his people, his town, and his national deity. To become a chief, an individual must go through an *alate* or installation

Fig. 15.4. A Jackreece new mother parades after sequestering, wearing girdle of Jackreece beads with beaded hat, coral necklaces, and pendants. Courtesy: Mrs. Dumo Jackreece, n.d.

ceremony, which includes an exhibition of followers and, most notably, his possessions, along with feasting, singing, dancing, and the swearing in. "And so it is
equally clear that if a man is not wealthy, he has not the means to make himself
and his premises attractive and cannot, therefore, have a large following" (45).

Among his duties to himself, a chief must take care to be clean and tidy in
body and character and look dignified and respectable. Furthermore, "the man
history extols is he who, by dint of hard work, rises from obscurity to fame"
(Fubara-Manuel n.d., vii). In Kalabari terms, this obviously includes not only
the achievement of great wealth but also the display of possessions. In the example of Seleye Fubara, he flaunted his wealth through exclusive ownership of
the glass bead and by his boast that he would obtain so many that he could literally smash many of them and still have more to display to the community. His
exclusive possession of this bead epitomizes the ideal chief in Kalabari terms.

Alfred Gell (1986, 110) claims that "consumption is a form of symbolic action," with consumption goods being "objects made more or less desirable by
the role they play in a symbolic system." Thus, consumption of a precious item
by the lineage founder furthers the entire lineage's prestige and prominence. As
his descendants continue to display the bead through several generations, the
reputation that the founder established for himself and his War-Canoe House
in earlier days is constantly reaffirmed. Within Kalabari society, the competition of the War-Canoe Houses continues to flourish, and ostentatious display
of luxury goods reflects pride of family achievements both from the past and
into the present, as exemplified by a fragile glass bead.

The story of the Seleye Fubara bead was recounted during my fieldwork.
At a final funeral dance in 1983, for a venerated elder of a prominent family
in Buguma, one woman, a chief mourner, wore a striped silk wrapper and a
distinctive pillbox-style hat decorated with the lattice-design glass beads. Several days later, I observed a younger woman preparing to support her lineage
masquerade in the town square dressed in a short silk wrapper with large coral
beads around her neck, wearing the same hat as seen in figure 15.5. My friend,
Mrs. Nume Taiwo West, a prominent businesswoman, had invited me to photograph her and the young woman. I expressed surprise at seeing the same hat
on another person. Mrs. West explained that she owned the hat and loaned it to
relatives of her mother's lineage at appropriate times. She originally made the
hat with glass beads for her mother's funeral in 1978. The woman at the funeral
previously wearing the hat was Mrs. West's sister, born of the same mother but
a different father. She had displayed her Seleye Fubara—that is, Jackreece affiliation, their mother's lineage—by wearing the hat of distinctive glass beads
at a funeral of her father's lineage.

Fig. 15.5.
Young woman wearing
Jackreece bead hat and coral
to dance at time of Jackreece
masquerade, 1983.

Mrs. West said that the distinctive beads on the hat were called ila and could only be worn by members of the Jackreece family. She then related the story of the baby, the bead, the crabhole, and Seleye Fubara's pledge to show his wealth by obtaining a seemingly unlimited number of the beads, which became so important in bonding him with his lineage.

At the time, my research centered on textiles, not beads, and I assessed the information as supplementary to data collected on named textiles used to underscore the importance of lineage distinction and rivalry in Kalabari life. Later, when analyzing beads, I focused on their place in the hierarchy of dress and gender, emphasizing the frequent use and prestige of coral. In revising that paper (Eicher 1996), I discovered a photograph of beads identical to those worn by members of the Fubara family in two general books on beads (Francis 1994, 6; Liu 1995, 31). Peter Francis (1994) stated that the beads are "apparently Venetian, late 1800s." Robert Liu (1995, 3) provided additional data: "Venetian blown glass beads, probably from Nigeria . . . thin white and blue cane are twisted;

the thin cylinders are blown in the center, 9.3–10.0 cm long . . . It is remarkable that these survive both transit to Africa and being worn." This information added to our data about world trade into the Niger delta and supports Seleye Fubara's claim that his beads came from afar.[2] Liu's claim about a Venetian origin seemed reasonable. Consequently, I conducted research in Venice in 1997 but could find no trace of the beads when interviewing beadmakers in Murano, the Venetian island of glassblowing. One Venetian bead dealer said one of his collectors had seen one in a specific bead store in Washington, DC. I later visited there and purchased one and was given a shard. I sent the shard to the Experimental Station for Glass laboratory; chemical analysis showed no connection to glass produced in Murano (Report, Stazione Sperimentale del Vetro 1998). Further conversations with bead experts, such as Jamey Allen (2006), suggested Czechoslovakian or German origins, but to date, I have not been able to document the bead's origin any further.

My field observations, photographs, and field notes from 1980 to 1991 identify hats and girdles decorated with these glass beads as an exclusive possession of the Fubara family, worn primarily by women at funeral celebrations, dancing at a masquerade, or dressing in the ensemble of a new mother. I was fortunate to later connect with a Seleye Fubara descendant, Telemate Jackreece, who reported, "The ila was very common in our household when I was growing up" (Eicher 2006). He knew it as his family symbol; his grandfather used it as a signature on items he made, but he does not have any additional information about where it came from.

Seleye Fubara, as founding male of the lineage, provided the prominence and reputation for himself and his heirs through obtaining and displaying an exotic trade bead that continues to reinforce this lineage image, particularly through the dress of family members in celebratory occasions.

These data reinforce the importance of world trade in Kalabari life and expand our knowledge about global sources for material goods entering the Kalabari world. Evidence about imported beads supplements the documentation on Indian madras and velvets discussed in earlier chapters. Beads are an integral part of the hierarchy of dress and textiles among the Kalabari. The hierarchies of beads and textiles are intertwined in the age and gender dress hierarchies. All signify importance of occasion as well as the prestige and reputation of individuals and lineage.

JOANNE B. EICHER, PhD, is Regents Professor Emerita in the Department of Design, Housing, and Apparel at the University of Minnesota. She is coeditor of *The Anthropology of Dress and Fashion: A Reader*; coeditor of *The Visible Self: Global Perspectives on Dress, Culture, and Society*, 4th ed.; and editor in chief of the *Encyclopedia of World Dress and Fashion*.

NOTES

Adapted from Eicher (1998).

1. Kalabari friends said that many women continue wearing these into adulthood under their clothing, for beads are considered sexually enticing and attractive to their male partners.

2. Skimpy evidence exists on the bead trade into the Niger delta. Only descriptions, particularly about coral in Kalabari life, were noted by observers such as Talbot (1926, 395) who stated that coral was a principal ornament among the Edo and Ijaw (*sic*) and is "now imported, but apparently in the old days was found in some of the rivers, particularly those in the neighborhood of Benin and was polished by Bini artisans."

16

Coral Use and Meaning

Susan J. Torntore

MY CHAPTER SURVEYS and documents, in general, the Italian coral bead industry and its relationship to Kalabari coral use, providing an illustration of the global world of the Kalabari dress. For four and a half months in 2000, I studied the coral industry in Torre del Greco, Italy, the major production center of Italian coral and the center of luxury coral production in the global marketplace.

CORAL BEADS

Dressing the body is a process of negotiating the intensely personal and the constructed layers of social and cultural meaning. Coral beads begin with intrinsic value based on material and physical factors. They gather market or economic value as objects made from precious material and associative cultural value in terms of meaning as such materials are exchanged through trade. Coral beads are ideal, then, for analyzing the construction and appropriation of value and meaning across cultural borders globally. Contemporary functions related to the symbolic significance of coral beads could be seen as new translations due to long-term, complex trade relationships. This negotiation occurs within specific contexts or within what Arjun Appadurai (1986) calls a "social web of relationships." The value of coral beads as used by the Kalabari particularly illustrates the category of negotiated exchange value from a global marketplace perspective.

Coral beads have a long history of trade and use as luxury goods. Coral was an important product in the wide-ranging and centuries-long Mediterranean luxury trade between Europe, India, and the Middle East. Economic values of coral beads as dress are seen in their use, for instance, by two groups of long-term traders in West Africa. The value and rarity of coral beads as luxury items of dress in these settings arise in part from the fact that the materials are all acquired through long-distance trade and are manufactured far away. Ceremonial garments and objects made from thousands of coral beads are worn as the most important regalia for the Oba, king of Benin, and his court (Ben-Amos 1980; Pokornowsky 1974) and the Kalabari Ijo ethnic group of Nigeria, who have incorporated coral beads into their dress. Early Portuguese traders gave luxury items like coral beads to important Africans and high officials along the coast, like the Oba of Benin, to help open trade; after trade was established, gifts of coral continued in an effort to maintain exclusive trading monopolies in the face of fierce European competition (Pokornowsky 1974; Ryder 1969).

The precious corals used to make beads are deepwater corals, of the genus *Corallium*, geographically distributed in the Mediterranean and the Pacific (Campbell 1976; Silverberg 1965). The three most prevalent Corallium species are *C. rubrum* from the Mediterranean, called "Sardegna" in Italy and Taiwan; *C. elatius* from the Pacific, called "Cerasuolo" in Italy; and *C. japonicum* from the Pacific, called "Moro" in Italy. Mediterranean and Pacific varieties of coral have physical characteristics that limit or predetermine the final product. The Mediterranean Sea has been a major source of the prized red coral (*C. rubrum*) valued for millennia. Uniformly red through diameter and length of branches, various shades of red are found in different locations, such as Spain, Morocco, Tunisia, and Sardinia.

Newer species from the Pacific come in a wide spectrum of colors, from pure white through shades of pink, salmon, and orange to a very dark ox-blood red. In comparison, Pacific corals are larger in size and dimension, more compact in structure, and thus easier to handle. They can be more highly polished and more perfectly shaped, but without uniform coloration in either surface or interior. Because Mediterranean coral became scarce and expensive, Pacific corals rose in demand and importation to Italy (Liverino 2000, Balletta and Ascione 1992). This direct international commercial trade kept the Italian coral industry alive. In the twenty-first century, Torre del Greco is one of three coral bead industries; Taiwan and Mumbai, India, are the other two production centers. Taiwan is the largest production and trade center, superseding Torre del Greco (Liverino 2000).

KALABARI CORAL BEADS

For several hundred years, the Kalabari, as traders, imported coral beads among a host of other textiles and dress items from Europe and India. Women wear

Fig. 16.1. Members of Asari Tomina Ereme with red-orange coral beads (Sardegna frange and spezzati) on hats, canes, heart-shaped pendants and arm bands, and canes, seated at 1984 Buguma Centenary event. They also wear large, pink Cerasuolo strands of cannette and barilotti.

them as jewelry in multiple ways, and men wear them as necklaces and studs. Coral beads cover walking sticks and women's hats and decorate Kalabari funerary beds of state. Coral beads symbolize Kalabari identity and cultural survival as an important vehicle through which the Kalabari store, exchange, display, and transmit wealth, status, and prestige.

I used a series of photographs of the Kalabari wearing coral beads to collect data in Torre del Greco on the kinds and market value of their beads. I also observed, photographed, and discussed similar beads at the Iacobelli and Liverino workshops and discussed the beads in the Kalabari photographs with Italian coral jeweler Salvatore Russo (Iacobelli 2000; Liverino 2000; Russo 2000). According to all three sources, the large pinkish tubular beads worn by the Kalabari are made from Pacific coral. The Kalabari also wear large dark orange or dark red beads, also identified as Pacific. Women from Asari Tomina Ereme are shown in figure 16.1 and figure 16.2 wearing their coral beads.

The large beads worn as necklaces and some bracelets are primarily two types—the tubular canister-shaped beads called *cannette*, and the shorter,

Fig. 16.2. Women at 1984 Buguma Centenary celebration. Necklaces and brace-lets are mottled pink Cerasuolo cannette and barilotti beads. Each woman wears different earring styles, illustrating individual identity, contrasting with matched ensembles.

more rounded barrel-shaped beads called *barilotti*. In addition, the women at the 1984 Centenary are wearing the smaller, lighter red-orange coral beads in textured profusion—on hats, walking sticks, heart-shaped armbands, flat pen-dant necklaces, and some bracelets—identified as *C. rubrum*. These beads are the small tips and broken waste pieces of coral branches called *frange* ("fringe") in Italian. The magnificent necklaces worn by Sir and Madam Isokariari in figure 14.3 are made of the large barrel- and tubular-shaped beads. An unusu-ally large, round center bead accents Madam Isokariari's pale pink and white graduated strands.

In the twentieth and early twenty-first centuries, traders and individuals from West Africa, including the Kalabari, traveled to locations in Italy annu-ally or semiannually to purchase large quantities of coral beads (Eicher 1999; Liverino 2000). Two of the three largest and most prominent Torre del Greco manufacturers, Liverino and Iacobelli, shared stories with me about beads similar to those used and purchased by the Kalabari. Basilio Liverino had sto-ries about and snapshots of Nigerians coming to purchase large quantities of coral from him in the 1970s. He told one story about Nigerian women living in London who returned periodically to purchase coral and return to London with it, eventually distributing it among family members in London and Nigeria. I was shown several fading Polaroid photographs from the 1970s that depicted individuals or small groups of Nigerians, men and women in Western- and Nigerian-style dress, posing with Signore Liverino in his workshop, with large piles of coral beads on the table in front of them. One of these was dated 1973 and showed a briefcase open on the table, full of coral beads. Another photograph of a woman dancing, dressed in what appeared to be a Kalabari new mother's ceremonial ensemble, was sent to him from Nigeria to show him how the coral was used; "Bonny, Nigeria" was written on the reverse. Liverino also included other photographs and anecdotes in his books (1989a, 1989b, 1998) about Nigerians buying coral from him.

Cerasuolo is the largest in diameter of the Corallium corals but is marked by large expanses of openings resembling wormholes and appears in shades of color ranging from deep red to the pale pink, colors preferred by the Kalabari.

According to Liverino: "This is certainly not a coral of great value, although with the present lack of traditional (i.e., Mediterranean) coral it is well on the way to becoming so. The raw material is suitable for every type of working and finished product, although for personal ornaments it is almost exclusively used nowadays in Nigeria and, to a lesser extent, in India and in the Arab countries" (Liverino 1989a, 99).

Although the pink coral beads worn by the Kalabari were not highly valued as beads in Torre del Greco by the manufacturer and exporters because of their quality or style, their economic value subsequently rose a great deal in the ten or twelve years after Liverino's prediction in his comment above. The price of pink coral rose because, in the late twentieth century, like Mediterranean coral a century before, it had become scarcer. Iacobelli, for instance, no longer produced beads like those worn by the Kalabari, and Liverino made them in such small quantities that it was insignificant, then only on a custom order basis because there was no longer a demand for them. They could no longer afford the raw coral without specific orders to fill. Liverino had at least three large strands of similar Cerasuolo cannette beads in his showroom at the time of my research. He left some in stock and said he tried to purchase it whenever he could get a good price on the raw coral. He also had some large jars of unstrung smaller-sized pink beads in the workroom (Liverino 2000). Paolo Iacobelli showed me a box of coral beads he began purchasing back from Nigerian sources. He said that in the 1970s, when the sale of these beads to Nigerians was at their height, he sold his entire stock of the corals preferred by the Nigerian market, and he wanted to add some back to his collection because this type of coral was becoming very rare and difficult to obtain in raw form to make these large beads (Iacobelli 2000).

CHARACTERIZING THE VALUE OF KALABARI
CORAL BEADS FOR THE KALABARI

Coral beads are seen in a variety of sizes, shapes, and styles, including many large and heavy cylinders of coral worn in many different configurations by both Kalabari men and women. However, a great deal more coral is used by Kalabari women than men, in a wider variety of configurations and styles of beads. Coral as a precious ornament displays wealth and relates to the link with the water people or spirits who aid in control of activities that make wealth possible.

Kalabari custom celebrating the transitions of the female life course prescribes specific ensembles; the monetary value of the ornament worn by the women is consistent with the costliness of the fabric in the ensemble. Jewelry for the formal *iria* ceremonial activities in terms of style, number, singular versus multiple arrangement, and placement is based on the life course stage that is being celebrated. Coral-beaded hats in an elliptical or crown shape are worn in one stage of the ritual sequence; canes or walking sticks made of coral beads may also be carried.

Funerals are one of the most important Kalabari arenas to display the symbols of the family's social status, aesthetic taste, and accumulated wealth. Heavy coral beads, personal accessories like coral hats and canes, and other "highly valued traditional ornaments" from the extended family storehouse are laid out on the elaborately decorated funeral beds, sometimes adorning the corpse itself (as described in chap. 18), and are worn by the male and female family members, chief mourners, and a parade of sympathizers and dancers. This type of display is very visible; prestige and esteem are conferred on the family as a whole by the observations and comments of onlookers.

According to Eicher and Erekosima in chapter 18, exposure to foreign objects and competition between families in some towns has resulted in the introduction of new items and "decorative innovations in the form of accessories like imported coral beads" into the funeral ceremony. Daly (1987) also says that the transitional stages of womanhood represented in the iria is "one ritual area of life that distinguished individuals by items of trade."

The longtime internal and external trade relationships and exposure to European influences and commerce have contributed to the interchange and acquisition of expensive material goods like coral. In the case of the Kalabari, the coral was clearly introduced and acquired through trade, and its symbolic value matched its high economic or trade value in that it was an exotic or foreign commodity used to convey wealth, rank, status, and prestige. This is in direct contrast to other Middle Eastern, European, or American cultural settings in which coral is valued for its protective value as an amulet against the evil eye.

According to Daly's 1980s field notes, the Kalabari refer to the coral as white, light or pink, and dark or red; they consider the darker color, which is more expensive, to be more beautiful and "truly Kalabari." This information directly contradicts the interpretation from the Torre del Greco coral manufacturers in 2000 who observed and stated that the Nigerians preferred the pink coral over that of the darker reds. There are several factors that could play into this inconsistency. It could be related to the shift in availability of the two types of corals and thereby an assumed economic value shift of the two different types of coral. In the 1970s, the peak of coral production and use by the manufacturers, the darker reds would have been the coral most available in large quantities, and this factor could be reflected by preferences for color in Daly's research. While pink was observed in photographs of the Kalabari during Daly's research, photographs dating to the late 1980s and 1990s show a much wider use of the pink and dark orange Pacific corals in larger sizes than Mediterranean coral. As pink Pacific coral became the predominant coral available, aesthetics could also have shifted as the trade values of demand and availability changed.

The red Mediterranean coral in research photographs of the Kalabari can be easily identified by its smaller dimensions and softer light red-orange color. Larger dark red and orange beads would be Pacific. The Mediterranean coral was primarily used for embellishing the women's elliptical or crown-shaped hats shown in figure 16.2 as part of the iria rituals and worn by women as bracelets, kneebands, earrings, necklaces, flat pendants, and armband plaques. Another characteristic of the Kalabari use of Mediterranean frange beads in these objects is the creation of a dimensional surface texture that is a strong contrast to the smoothness of the Pacific coral bead surface. This jewelry for the formal iria ceremonial activities is based on the stage of the life course that is being celebrated, the passage of a girl into womanhood, a process of becoming a real Kalabari woman. The preferred use of red coral in this context is possibly indicative of its association to the color of blood. In this sense, the red coral becomes an emblematic symbol of a women's passage, as women wear the armbands, kneebands, bracelets, and hats throughout their lives as dress and as important elements in ceremonial, ritual, and community observances. Coral beads of either color are an important part of ritualized, hierarchical ensembles worn by both Kalabari men and women when their identity as Kalabari is on display.

Both Kalabari men and women favor strong color contrast in dress, and the pink coral provides this aesthetic quality immediately in terms of color and form. As it is worn next to their dark skin color, this coral provides a strong contrast by strength of hue and value in contrast to the darker reds. The coral jewelry also provides contrast in creating a more complex visual display, as it is added to rich elements with the patterned and brightly colored cloth to create a complex figure-to-ground relationship that accents the rounded torso and horizontal orientation. In the contrast between the coral and the body, two different kinds of value are communicated based on both types of coral: (1) for the individual Kalabari, conformity to the ideal, maintaining the integrity of the gendered social order and the Kalabari cultural system; and (2) for the outsider (and Kalabari as a group within a global community), the intentional display of wealth and status is foremost.

The cylindrical shape of the big pink coral beads, used in the necklaces, aesthetically and symbolically emphasizes and accents the rounded and horizontal form of the woman. Heavy in their size and thickness, with definite surfaces and clear, rounded, and tubular or cylindrical shapes, the beads relate to and emphasize the desired form of the Kalabari woman's body and the purpose of fecundity. The beads are self-contained as worn and are a closed form around the neck or around the limbs with well-defined contrasts of color, value, line, texture, and shape. They refer to and accentuate the display of the woman's body and the Kalabari ideals of beauty based on fecundity, becoming a micro-version of the Kalabari ideal. This ideal and display of femaleness is readily accented and symbolized by the large singular or double horizontal beads worn in a prominent location on the upper chest of the women. The graduated strands of pink coral beads worn by Madam Isokariari are smaller overall than those worn by her husband, but they are massed together to frame her face and draw attention to her upper torso. Many of these beads are the softer-looking, more rounded barrel shapes; one is a very large spherical-shaped bead worn in a very prominent position in the overall necklace composition. In contrast, there is a certain sense of maleness displayed by the use of the heavy, ladder-shaped coral necklace and the coral and tusk-toothed necklace, both made with large and more tubular pink coral beads, worn by Sir Isokariari.

Coral necklaces for both men and women seem to serve a key function of framing the face and adding a level of emphasis to the head and facial features, providing a visual and metaphorical relationship to an individual's identity while it also encircles Kalabari cultural ideals. These pink coral beads are extremely heavy to wear and carry around the neck, especially in the quantities

Fig. 16.3. In 2018, Mrs. Ibitubo Ukwu (sitting) and her mother, Mrs. Ibifuro Tom-George, wear jewelry blending Kalabari and fashion aesthetics; left, cannette coral strand worn with a coral and gold fashion necklace; right, wide collar-style fashion necklace of multiple frange strands. Photo: Courtesy of Kalabari National Association, USA, Asikhia Rodney, Photographer, 2018.

worn by the Kalabari. Coral is heavy, and Pacific coral is dense and compact and heavier than Mediterranean. I wore one large graduated strand of pink tubular beads like the Kalabari ones for perhaps ten minutes at Liverino's workshop. It weighed 1,134 grams; I felt a definite drag of weight around my neck and shoulders. I could only imagine wearing several strands of them while dancing or participating in a funeral procession. This very physical commitment to the significance of these beads speaks strongly of their high associative value and deep meaning for the Kalabari.

Interesting aesthetic shifts in more recent Kalabari coral use in dress occur in both Nigeria and in an American diaspora context. An online search by Eicher (Nairaland Forum 2018) brought up a Nigerian Kalabari website with photographs that featured both red and pink corals, but primarily pink from the Pacific. It was used for new styles of women's hats worn by young women, with lavish use of large graduated pink beads as multiple necklaces for weddings.

Fig. 16.4. Women's coral jewelry reflects a fashion aesthetic, 2018. Left, a branch coral and gold-bead collar-style necklace worn by Dr. Comfort Briggs Anigboh; right, necklace of tiny beads twisted into strands with beaded earrings worn by Mrs. Obelebra Briggs. Photo: Courtesy of Kalabari National Association, USA, Asikhia Rodney, Photographer, 2018.

Another photograph featured young girls dressed for a ceremony in multiple long strands of red Mediterranean coral beads wrapped around their heads and draped around their necks; they also carried a small, shallow vessel covered with red coral beads.

Eicher and Daly attended the Inaugural Kalabari World Congress and Heritage Celebration in May 2018 in Baltimore, Maryland. Their photographs showed some women and men wearing single strands of red and pink beads and women wearing fashion jewelry of coral in predominantly red and red-orange colors. The fashion pieces consist of coral cabochons set into silver or gold or beads strung with silver and gold for necklaces, bracelets, and earrings, as in figures 16.3 and 16.4.

Two Kalabari women wear complex fashion necklaces of small, smooth spherical beads, earrings made of tiny beads, and a textured collar-type necklace of Mediterranean coral. The use of coral in this diaspora context gives a strong individual identity and style within recognizable Kalabari patterns of practice, possibly reflecting fashion and resource changes. These exciting examples characterize the changing negotiations of meaning and the value of Kalabari coral use in a diaspora context and a global marketplace, as new generations of Kalabari make their way into their world.

CORAL BEAD MARKETS

Different coral beads are made for different markets. Particular destinations and target markets were identified by coral producers in Torre del Greco for specific types of coral beads and bead products. I have categorized these specific markets under the larger headings of fashion, ethnic, and tourist markets (Torntore 2002). These categories are based on differing characteristics of beads and jewelry, as well as the terms used by manufacturers, jewelers, exporters, and retailers, and they are also based on the differing values of coral and coral beads.

The fashion market category is based on current, constantly changing fashions and styles. In this market category, which is primarily related to a Euro-American or Western consumer aesthetic, beads are strung in carefully graduated sets. This market prefers highly refined beads that require a great deal of handwork to shape, polish, and match. Imperfections in coral are not tolerated, unless the "ethnic look" is fashionable and then slight variations may add character to a piece. The more expensive corals for this market are made into high-quality beads that are also mounted and combined with other high-quality, expensive materials like eighteen- to twenty-four-karat gold, platinum, diamonds, pearls, and other precious stones. Beads in this category are only purchased by consumers as finished jewelry from jewelry retailers in Europe and the US. Mediterranean coral is the preferred color and type within this market, although pink and red Pacific corals are also sold. In Italian and European fashion markets, these styles of coral beads are synonymous with classic style, made and purchased in the same way that pearl necklaces are made and purchased—small details like size of beads, length or number of strands, or material and style of clasp may change each season or every couple of years. They are easily read as a cliché in the Italian fashion market, as something that is expensive and classy, worn by a certain level of society, just as gold and genuine diamonds and expensive pearls are worn and understood in the United States.

The ethnic market relates to all the uses outside the fashion market and excludes the tourist market. Beads for ethnic markets differ from the fashion market beads in shape, size, and texture—often larger and less refined in shape and texture. Rough-textured beads and different sizes and shapes, such as the barilotti and cannette beads, are the most common. The branch coral frange beads are also sometimes sold as part of this market. The ethnic market category encompasses diverse cultural settings around much of the world, including Asia, the Middle East, and West Africa along with beads made for Italian, European, and American Southwest ethnic markets. (Beads for these other markets include specific regional uses for traditional or folk purposes based on historical uses).

The tourist market caters to producing and selling less expensive souvenir types of items for a global audience of visitors to Italy. One of the coral items most described in Torre del Greco as part of the American tourist market, for example, was inexpensive, simple costume jewelry necklaces made with Mediterranean coral branch ends and waste pieces. Although these types of beads are all produced from coral pieces that would otherwise be thrown out as unworkable, they represent a significant amount of time to cut, polish, drill, and string. Italian or European tourists may buy something in this market category that looks more fashionable, like a multistrand necklace, instead of a more inexpensive single-strand souvenir-type of necklace like many Americans purchase. However, in all cases, their purpose is to purchase a coral necklace as a sentimental souvenir of their vacation or trip rather than purchase the coral as an investment or classic fashion accessory.

There was a definite bias on the part of bead manufacturers in Torre del Greco toward the red coral from the Mediterranean, on several levels—as a material, as a color, as the traditional coral, as Italian, as being the highest-quality material producing the finest-quality product—all these intrinsic and associative values factor into this attitude. In this sense, the larger pink beads worn by the Kalabari are placed in the ethnic market category by manufacturers. They do not hold the same high value overall as the beads intended for the fashion market, even though they held quite a high monetary value, based on diminishing resources of precious corals in the early twenty-first century when this research was conducted. Associative factors that kept these beads from being more highly valued relate to various biases on the part of the Italian coral industry, part of the luxury product sector. They continued to hold an interest for manufacturers and exporters like Liverino, one of the elder generation of Torre del Greco corallari (coral manufacturers) who worked long and hard to share coral's full value with others in order to continue its rich and complex legacy.

For producers, as a product, the coral beads purchased and worn by the Kalabari also certainly hold an economic value in the sense that Nigeria has been a very lucrative market in the past, although this had changed somewhat by the end of the twentieth century, nonetheless representing a market that provided a way to sell enormous quantities of then-less valuable coral like the Kalabari's pink coral beads. Photographs of Liverino's Nigerian consumers in the 1970s showed enormous quantities of the large pink beads on the tables. I contend that they own and wear more coral than any other group in the world today, perhaps rivaled only by the coral regalia of the Oba of Benin.

Coral bead manufacturers in Torre del Greco understand and explain the associative value of coral beads worn in Nigeria as "a distinctive emblem of society . . . not just a personal decoration but also a way of classifying, or identifying a person, expressing something of great importance and significance" (Liverino 1989a, 122). At least four producers and exporters (Mazza 2000; Liverino 2000; Ascione 2000; Iacobelli 2000) told me that the coral in Nigeria is worn to show their power, or *potere* in Italian. However, Liverino (1989a, 125) related only to the coral worn in Nigeria as that by the Oba of Benin or those in the Benin political and royal hierarchy when he says that "the quantity of coral worn indicates both the social level and the wealth of the wearer." He was very excited by the photographs I showed him of the Kalabari wearing a variety of coral beads. It was the first time he had seen such use, in comparison to his familiarity within the Kingdom of Benin, where red Mediterranean is preferred, not the larger pink Pacific beads that the Kalabari seem to favor.

As documented by earlier research, the Kalabari wear coral beads in numerous ways as dress and as important elements in ceremonial, ritual, and community observances. Coral beads are a significant part of ritualized, hierarchical ensembles worn by both Kalabari men and women. As in many cultures, coral beads are worn as personal adornment, not simply as a matter of individual taste but also as a display of wealth and as a mark of a person's social status, rank, and identity on particular ritual occasions. Rather than make their own textiles and other basic materials out of which dress items are constructed, the Kalabari culturally authenticate foreign materials and elsewhere manufactured items into their own sociocultural use. Thus, coral beads have been completely embedded into the Kalabari worldview and transformed into Kalabari artifacts through stories and mythology. As a material from the sea, coming to them from *across* the sea, coral therefore carries many associations and meanings related to water for them. Coral beads have become an important vehicle through which the Kalabari store, exchange, display, and transmit wealth, status, and prestige, becoming a symbol of Kalabari identity and cultural survival.

We do not know when the Kalabari came to use such large quantities of coral beads or began to purchase the large pink coral beads. As I discovered, this type of coral was not available for production or sale in any market until after the end of the nineteenth century and into early twentieth century. Certainly, the red coral might have been available to West Africa through trade overland with North Africa, East Africa, and India from the time of ancient Rome. India has been one of the largest ethnic global markets for coral and coral beads from the time of ancient Rome; a possible route to the Kalabari would be that of coral beads coming first through their overland Saharan trade contact with India. When the pink coral beads were "discovered" and chosen by the Kalabari, they may have had a long knowledge of and relationship with the red Mediterranean coral. However, the use of the pink coral for beads like those preferred by the Kalabari is unusual in West Africa, or anywhere else in the world, and provides an excellent example of Kalabari cultural authentication for a precious accessory, often serving ceremonial purposes.

The value and rarity of luxury items of dress like coral beads to the Kalabari arises in part from the fact that the materials are all acquired through trade and are manufactured in faraway places. Indeed, all the above factors create much higher intrinsic, market, and associative values of coral for the Kalabari than found in other ethnic or fashion contexts where coral beads are worn or cultural settings where it is used as amuletic protection. The coral beads purchased by the Kalabari have continued to increase in value economically, and as they do, their increase in associative value becomes even more important as symbols of status and wealth. Through time, as the supply of pink coral diminishes, its economic value increases. The Kalabari coral beads also begin to accrue an important history and patina and take on higher market value as investments and as family collection artifacts, which are more and more rare and prized.[1]

These coral beads gain economic and associative value again as they are sold and passed from hand to hand across new cultural lines for various reasons. Some of the Pacific coral beads used by Nigerians also represent a large secondary resale market in the US (Torntore 2002). In the early 2000s, tough economic times in Nigeria resulted in many of these family beads flooding the global market, being sold from Nigerian family collections to itinerant West African traders. The beads were then purchased from these traders by American bead dealers, who sometimes reshaped them for other markets such as Buddhist Tibetan monk refugees or folk jewelry collectors in the US. Four dealers in May 2001, at the International Bead Expo and Symposium in Miami, told me that coral beads were coming out of Nigeria, Yemen, Nepal, and Tibet in great quantities with various estimates of age, as shown in figure 16.5. One dealer, reputed to be the largest coral bead dealer in the US., was honest and knowledgeable about the Pacific (Japanese and Chinese) origin of the coral and estimated that some beads may be approximately one hundred years old (Leung 2000; Nilson 2000; Salter 2000). The dealers mentioned that they do

Fig. 16.5. Strands of "Nigerian" Cerasuolo beads in a large US resale market. The dealer reported that the large pink and red cannette (right) were purchased in Nigeria; Tibetan and Mongolian markets preferred the rounded beads (left), but numerous images show the Kalabari wearing similar Cerasuolo rounded beads. International Bead Expo and Symposium, Miami, Florida, 2001. Photo: S. J. Torntore.

alter the beads to sell to other specific markets—the beads are ground down and polished in the US, Jaipur, or Thailand and then made into high-end, ethnic-style necklaces, which became more fashionable in the early twenty-first century. The larger beads, like many of those Cerasuolo tubular cannette beads worn by the Kalabari, are sliced crosswise and the edges are rounded off into the barilotti shape so that they may be sold to Tibetan and Mongolian markets, where a flatter, more rounded barrel or spherical shape is preferred (Torntore 2002).

All of these coral beads were being sold in Miami at varied prices per gram, depending on the type of bead and the customer (retail or wholesale, dealer, jeweler, etc.). Dealers told me they had purchased the beads for an advantageous price per gram or less, based on at least a 100 percent markup return when sold. Considering that one strand of the large pink tubular and barrel-shaped beads, similar to those worn by the Kalabari, was marked as weighing 440 grams, one can get a sense that the possibility of making a larger number of beads from each strand could be quite lucrative.

CONCLUSION

As a natural resource, we can easily understand why coral beads come with a high value in terms of their preciousness as an organic material. As they move through time and space and through various cultural settings, coral beads are examples of complex global networks and relationships and illustrate varied players or actors. Coral, as a natural material, holds value through intrinsic physical or aesthetic qualities such as color, hardness, size, shape, and the amount of skill required to work it, as well as its relative or comparative rarity and scarcity coming from the natural world. This rarity is a source of value in and of itself and is compounded by the degree of difficulty to obtain the material or objects made from it and the distance they must travel as well as the sense of how exotic they are. Wearing coral beads and jewelry of a certain value and design can indicate power and status in terms of wealth. Coral's form and workmanship, along with perception of taste, are also important. Material wealth is often measured in terms of prestige goods like coral beads destined for conspicuous display.

Certainly, the availability of coral and coral beads is intertwined with price and value, with scarcity, rarity, and supply. The cost of coral beads relates to labor, production processes, and, at the time of my research, a specific Italian model of business and production. The value of this global product so beloved by the Kalabari is determined not only by supply and demand but also by perceptions of rarity and ideas of place and is shaped by manufacturers, merchants, and consumers—more specifically, by and for the Kalabari themselves as merchants and consumers. Coral beads hold multiple meanings in multiple contexts, and clearly consumers take an active part in the creation of meanings, in the construction of their value. The coral beads sold to the Kalabari are viewed very differently in the coral industry by the producers and exporters than they are in the Kalabari cultural context in which they are purchased and used. Additionally, coral beads, from a purely commercial perspective, are merely a commodity, but producers, dealers, and consumers of coral beads are all profoundly aware of the cultural significance and positive associations that are attached to them because they are from Italy or, in the case of the secondary market, Nigeria or Tibet. Christopher Steiner recognizes this role within the marketplace: "Traders are not only moving a set of objects through the world economic system, they are also exchanging information—mediating, modifying, commenting on a broad spectrum of cultural information" (Steiner 1994, 2).

In their awareness of and production of specific beads to sell to specific markets, producers and dealers become what Tommy Dahlén calls "interculturists" (Hannerz 1998, Dahlén 1997). In these occupations that involve contacts and mobility across translocal and transcultural borders, this "emergent profession" in the marketplace shares some of the concerns of anthropologists in trying to understand and interpret an awareness of cultural differences.

In many ways, the Kalabari coral beads are a quintessential consumer commodity—representing clearly in all stages of the Kalabari life course, in all links of the chain within a global marketplace, the relationships that can be constructed and exploited among raw material, objects, makers, buyers, and users within broad and diverse historical and cultural contexts. We can understand more fully the global world of the Kalabari in this deeply meaningful cultural relationship and interaction between human beings and material goods. As consumers of goods within a wide range of behaviors, institutions, and ideas, Kalabari find and make meaning through cross-cultural exchange and cultural authentication.

SUSAN J. TORNTORE, PhD, investigated Italian American use of coral jewelry for her MA, *The Italian Coral Horn as an Object of Intimate Cultural Expression and Meaning* (1999) with fieldwork in Torre del Greco, Italy, for her PhD, *Italian Coral Beads: Characterizing Their Value and Role in Global Trade and Cross-Cultural Exchange* (2002). Subsequently in Taiwan and Italy, she provided consulting expertise for international marine biologists and coedited *Guide to the Identification of Precious and Semi-Precious Corals in Commercial Trade* (2011) and *Fashion Foundations* (2003).

NOTES

Adapted from Torntore (2002).

1. Neither Eicher nor I have purchase price data by any Kalabari. Eicher was told in 1991, however, that some coral in Buguma had been reported stolen, but no details were forthcoming.

17

Headwear

Joanne B. Eicher and Tonye Victor Erekosima

WE ANALYZE HEADWEAR worn by Kalabari males and females as symbols of power, both individual and communal, as an aspect of a total Kalabari ensemble. We elaborate on earlier chapters that focused on men's and women's total ensembles with reference to hats as part of the ensemble, analyzing examples as a concept of cultural authentication.

Erekosima declares that for the Kalabari the head is taken to be the location of personal will: "Just as Westerners locate human sentiment in the heart of a man. Thus, it is forbidden to casually touch the head of an older person and hence demean his person . . . it was also by knocking on the head of a younger person in need of correction that discipline was usually instilled in Kalabari society" (Erekosima 1988, 36).

Furthermore, doffing one's hat to another man is seen as a sign of submission to the other, and a younger man is not allowed to wear a hat in the presence of elders. When the Amanyanabo sits in council with his chiefs, only the king wears his hat, for he "does not doff his hat for anyone, except God" (Erekosima 1988, 36). Similarly, when the Amanyanabo installs a chief, the individual removes his hat and faces the king to receive his title. Thus, Erekosima (1988, 37) posits that "the hat had been adopted as a symbol for personal will in Kalabari society," pointing out that the figures in Kalabari ancestor screens almost always wear hats or headgear to depict personality and not merely to mark status, as Horton suggested.[1]

In *The Power of Headdresses*, Daniel Biebuyck proposes that headgear may have multilevel purposes (Biebuyck and Abbeele 1984). So it is with the hats of the Kalabari. On one level, any one hat has an individual's choice attached to it—the color, the snap of the brim, how tilted on the head, representing what Erekosima calls "personal will" or persona. In addition, the communal aspect of a hat is also visible, for a hat is chosen to complement and complete an ensemble, which is distinctly seen as a Kalabari outfit. The crescent-shaped hat, known as the *ajibulu*, has a particularly distinctive set of requirements and is not duplicated elsewhere on the African continent. According to Kalabari informants, the ajibulu has a basic shape and three items must be found on it: first, the *aji*, the ram's beard (a symbol of power); second, feathers; and third, *biaba*, the Kalabari symbol of concentric circles that looks like a target. Women can never wear this hat, although they can wear other hats for specific occasions—particularly those related to the coming-out celebration after the birth of a baby. Men and women wear a variety of hats called *sun* with some variations. Erekosima suggested that what those women wear are more like crowns, whereas the ajibulu of men represents power, signified by the beard of a powerful animal—the ram.

We begin with male headwear; generally, European explorers, traders, and missionaries observed and wrote about Kalabari males as traders and fishermen, who had more contact with the Europeans than women who remained within the household. Similarly, the ancestral screens (*duein fubara*)—the visual data about nineteenth-century Kalabari life, kept in the family meeting house—center on males. These wooden sculptures ordinarily feature three male figures. Two smaller figures flank a central, large figure wearing a sizable headdress, often European, always prominent. Nigel Barley (1987) pointed out that hats for ancestral screen figures add to the total effect of their appearance.

The hats we describe include top hats, fedoras, and bowlers—variations of European hats of the 1800s on—and large and profusely decorated hats of crescent shape, such as the ajibulu seen in figure 17.1, which exemplifies the concept of cultural authentication. In the twenty-first century, as in the past, men wear hats with their ensembles as required and expected, whether for everyday or for rituals. Barley (1987, 374) states, "The giving of hats to local rulers was a well-established procedure in the Delta . . . used as a dumping ground for outmoded headgear." Indeed, a hat was part of the duty a ruler received in exchange for permission to open trade (ibid.). In response to Barley, Erekosima expands on the reasons for the interest the delta merchants had for eagerly acquiring the hats. Erekosima declares, "They became a symbol of the new social-benefit line of endeavor that Kalabari men undertook toward the advancement of their society—by which they fulfilled the Ancestor-principle

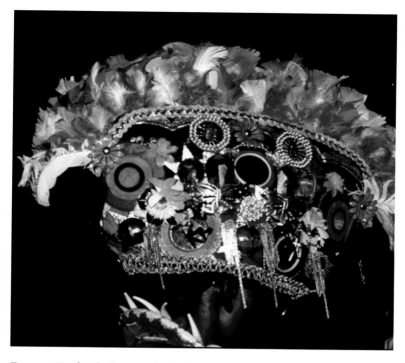

Fig. 17.1. Profusely decorated ajibulu hat. Worn with the attigra gown, 1983.

of goodwill in their personal disposition of life-energies. They represented a form of status-elevation function" (Erekosima 1988, 41). Furthermore, Erekosima argues that the biggest hat for the most central of the ancestor-figures of the Kalabari screens represented that trader's achievement in the domain of trade with Europeans, and he adds, "a symbol for the wills that exploited this opportunity maximally." Such hats (and the manillas on the clay mounds of ancestral sculpture) "represented the society-benefitting endeavor of trade that was then the dominant thing for a man to engage in who harbored goodwill toward his community and descendants" (Erekosima 1988, 42). Thus, the hat not only symbolizes an individual's personal will but also his connectedness and integration into a communal system.

Specific examples of hats exemplify the ideas proffered above, beginning with examples of men's hats and comparing them with women's. Men's status levels of ensembles include hats, differentiated largely by the upper garment,

Fig. 17.2. Kalabari men wearing, from left to right, suit, figured doni, brown doni, and woko and trousers. A fedora, bowler hats, and canes complement the outfits. Buguma Centenary, 1984.

whether worn with wrapper or trousers. For each outfit, the fabrics come from global trading sources, both far (English cotton shirtings, Indian madras, silks, and velvets) and near (Yoruba and Ewe handwoven textiles). The hats also came from past trading contacts, often European: fedoras, bowlers, and top hats, the ones referred to by Barley as outmoded, yet bowlers and a fedora are seen in figure 17.2. Some headgear worn with the *ebu* and *attigra* gowns has other origins, such as a turban from India or a fez from the Middle East, as in figure 17.3 and figure 17.4. The ajibulu crescent hat, with embellishments characterizing it as Kalabari, is often requisite for the attrigra gown.

For everyday wear, women don variations of head ties as commonly found throughout West Africa, but these are not our focus, as they are not singularly Kalabari. Instead, we analyze the hats worn by Kalabari, especially when celebrating being an *iriabo*. Their hats fall into two categories, with the first

Top, Fig. 17.3. Men wearing beaded cap, turban, and pith helmet at Buguma Centenary, 1984.

Bottom, Fig. 17.4. A fez, pith helmet, and top hat adorn men's heads at Buguma Centenary, 1984.

Fig. 17.5. Girls dressed as iriabo, wearing Indian madras with bowler and fedora hats for a funeral. Buguma, 1988.

category including men's fedoras, bowlers, and sometimes straw hats, when worn with the iriabo madras ensemble as in figure 17.5. The second are an elongated shape, called sun, similar to that shape worn by men, sometimes exact duplicates of velvet embroidered with metallic thread. Sometimes only the shape is the same; the decorations and embellishments are made for females, as seen in figures 16.1 and 16.2. Two hats seem never to be worn by females—the top hat and the ajibulu.

In analyzing the similarities and differences of the men's and women's hats, we see that imported fedoras and bowlers are worn with madras, whether men's Indian madras ensembles or women dressed in madras as iriabo. Furthermore, men wear the same hat with the outfits called woko and doni but may choose a top hat if they have attained a sufficiently high status level. The embroidered sun may be worn by men wearing the ebu and the iriabo wearing wrappers of imported Indian silk. Only men, however, wearing an attigra gown, wear ajibulu, and only women as iriabo wear the embroidered-velvet, gold-fringed hat.

What do these similarities and differences mean? In relating dress to symbols within Kalabari society, Kalabari aesthetics demand that certain hats must be combined with certain fabrics. These hats and their associated ensembles represent aspects of Kalabari belief systems. Therefore, felt hats are combined with Indian madras plaids known as *injiri*, whereas embroidered and embellished hats are worn with shiny, more expensive fabrics such as silk and embroidered velvet.

The madras and felt hat ensembles represent the trading accomplishments of the lineage—the prowess of those individuals past (the ancestors) and those living now who have "made it" in the arena prized in Kalabari society. The hat known as sun with silk or India ensembles represents the lineage association with the "water people," symbolizing the flowing river as the physical condition of their lives; the water people abstractly conceptualize the Kalabari experience of their island and water environment. Their dress represents the items the water people prize and are said to wear themselves—fabrics and items that shine and reflect light, just like their watery world.

Michelman analyzed the proportions of males and females in relation to the way they dressed in Kalabari society. Kalabari male ensembles emphasize the head; a variety of hats allows the wearer to emphasize the proportion of the head in relation to the rest of the body. In contrast, Kalabari females emphasize the body's horizontal lines; as discussed earlier, the head is not as much a center of focus or as large a proportion of the dressed body. Thus, the male-female differentiation is reinforced in hats, especially regarding the concept of power with the ram's beard on the men's ajibulu contrasting with gold fringe and tinsel balls on women's smaller hats. Additionally, Kalabari embellished hats illustrate cultural authentication—items combined from global origins becoming distinctively Kalabari.

JOANNE B. EICHER, PhD, is Regents Professor Emerita in the Department of Design, Housing, and Apparel at the University of Minnesota. She is coeditor of *The Anthropology of Dress and Fashion: A Reader*; coeditor of *The Visible Self: Global Perspectives on Dress, Culture, and Society*, 4th ed.; and editor in chief of the *Encyclopedia of World Dress and Fashion*.

TONYE VICTOR EREKOSIMA (1940–2008), PhD, native-born Kalabari, lived in the Igbo towns of Owerri and Umuahia, because his father was an educator and secondary-school principal, until Erekosima's university years in the United States. He was steeped in Kalabari cultural tradition, however, thanks to his family's routine travel to Buguma, his parents' birthplace, for holidays and significant events like funerals. Following his PhD, he served as Director, General Studies, Rivers State College of Education, and Director, Instructional Resources Center, University of Port Harcourt. He coedited *A Hundred Years of Buguma History in Kalabari Culture* (1984) and *Buguma 1984 Centenary Symposia on Kalabari* (1991).

NOTES

Adapted from Eicher and Erekosima (1988)

1. The main lineage meeting house of a Kalabari family contains a wooden screen called duein fubara (meaning forehead of the dead, as the forehead is the location of one's fate). These screens honor and venerate lineage ancestors. Examples exist in some museums in the US and UK, such as the Minneapolis Institute of Art and the British Museum. See https://www.imodara.com/discover/nigeria-kalabari -duein-fubara-ancestor-memorial-screen/.

III

Kalabari Rituals

Kalabari rituals feature dress and textiles as pivotal in birth through death celebrations; families bond when a child is born or a family member dies, as revealed in chapters 18 and 19 about funerals. Our formal documentation began when I first observed a funeral in 1980 on the island of Abonnema. I witnessed or participated in more than twenty funerals during eight field trips. Erekosima participated in a countless number both as a child and as an adult.

Communities also bond at public festivities, such as a centenary occasion or masquerades, as analyzed in chapter 20. I observed several masquerades at the 1984 Buguma Centenary celebration, making only brief notes. In 1991 I attended *Owuarusun*, the masquerade extravaganza held after several yearly presentations, wanting to assess textile use in the costuming. Masquerades provided a special research challenge, however, for a woman. Men only are the masqueraders, and they keep masquerade information secret. Fuller descriptions and analyses of some of the ritual masquerades can be found in Robin Horton (1960a, 1963), Victor Madume (1976), and Danate Tariah (1982). For comprehensive coverage of the Owuarusun masquerade festival, see Charles E. W. Jenewari (1973) and Enefaa JohnBull (2012).

18

Celebration and Display

Joanne B. Eicher and Tonye Victor Erekosima

WE DOCUMENT THE SEQUENCE of a Kalabari funeral and analyze the display of cloth and accessories—key symbols in decorating the "state" bed, called *ede*, and in dressing the chief mourners. Every adult who dies under normal circumstances is generally accorded the honor of an ede funeral, along with a wake held throughout the night after the corpse is brought home from the mortuary, followed by burial the next day, and in the case of elders, an additional week of ceremonial mourning. The exceptions are those whose deaths are categorized as abominable: associated with witchcraft, infectious diseases, or taboo conditions such as death in childbirth and death by drowning. Rituals for infants and adolescents do not involve funerals or lying in state on an ede bed.

There are four types of funerals: (1) the funeral of a young adult, defined as someone between fifteen and fifty, who may not have lived long enough for the person's potential to be realized (particularly "bitter" is the death of a "graduate," a person with a university education, in whom the family had invested its resources); (2) the funeral of an elder widely recognized as successful; (3) the funeral of a chief; and (4) the funeral of the king (*Amanyanabo*).[1] We focus on the second category of elder that represents a central activity in life, dealing with the reality of the death of adult members of society and acknowledging the inevitability of life going on without them.

For people everywhere, death is a disruptive force, threatening the collapse of their socially constructed world. It emphasizes the "precarious unstable quality of our lives" (Danforth 1982). When an elder has lived well in Kalabari terms, life's "precarious unstable quality" is mitigated, and the family celebrates this accomplishment by giving the person a proper funeral. What does it mean to have "lived well in Kalabari terms" so that one's life is celebrated at death? First, one must have honored the *wari* (the smallest lineage unit of the War-Canoe House, which represents both family members and those who are not blood relations) by having married and had offspring. If one had no children naturally, one adopted them. Second, one must have achieved occupational success, accompanied by financial success. In earlier times, a man would have met this requirement as a trader, fisherman, or warrior; a woman would have met it as a wife, meaning not only a sexual companion and bearer of children but also an efficient manager of domestic affairs. The Kalabari in the late twentieth and early twenty-first centuries, adept at incorporating change into their lives, acknowledge contemporary occupations but still regard a firm financial base as mandatory. Third, one had to achieve respectability through correct comportment: good taste and upbringing were reflected in one's speech, conduct, and appearance. A funeral, then, is more important than a marriage ceremony, for being married is only one element of success.

To celebrate these achievements, the family stages for the community as elaborate a funeral as possible. The degree of elaborateness provides a measure of the success of the deceased and his or her wari, and of the intentions of the family to provide a fitting send-off from this life to the next. The Kalabari want those who are to become ancestors to think well of those they left behind. Robin Horton discusses two components in the Kalabari view of death. It is seen as "something profoundly fearful and disturbing," and also "as a fortunate occasion" (Horton 1970, 67). Death, he continues, presents the opportunity for one's transition from mortality to immortality as an ancestor: "The ancestors underpin the strength of the lineages and punish those who contravene lineage norms. They and their actions account for many of the fortunes and misfortunes both of lineages and of their individual members. Now it is only through death that new ancestors can emerge. Hence the funeral rite is not just a way of coping with anxiety and grief. It is equally a means of recruiting and transferring new entities to the pool of life forces" (Horton 1970, 68).

The funeral, therefore, not only celebrates the successful life of an elder but also enhances the power of those elders becoming ancestors.[2] The events that make up a funeral ceremony for an elder constitute an intense, complex social and aesthetic experience. The dress of chief mourners and sympathizers, decorated rooms, dancing, drumming, praise singing, and parading display the symbols of the family's prestige, socioeconomic status, and aesthetic taste.

When an elder dies, family members immediately hold several meetings to decide the critical details of the funeral. Formerly, the body was treated internally and externally with native gin, salts, and leaves and was buried within a day or two. Contemporary mortuary practices allow preserving a corpse by freezing for up to eight weeks, possibly much longer. Family members from afar in Nigeria and even from abroad are expected to return. The initial wake is usually held on a Friday and burial on a Saturday, with the final wake and the funeral dance the following Friday and Saturday, respectively. This practice allows maximum preparation time. The following timetable is typical for the funeral events Eicher (1983) attended in Buguma:

> Death, December 5, 1982
> Four family meetings, December 5, 1982–January 2, 1983
> Preparation of rooms, January 26–27
> Body brought from mortuary, Friday, January 28
> Wake (*dinkoru*), January 28
> Church service and burial, Saturday, January 29
> Final wake, Friday, February 4
> Parade (*amabro*), Saturday, February 5
> Funeral dance (*din krama ti*), February 5.

Events are carefully orchestrated. Rooms and beds are decorated to receive the corpse; tarpaulins are erected in the family compound to designate areas for eating, drinking, and dancing; drummers are engaged to accompany the dancers and praise singers; and elderly women, known for their expertise, sometimes family members and sometimes not, are appointed to select cloth and appropriately dress the rooms, bed, and family mourners.

Those attending the wake are often extravagantly entertained. Some mourners, especially those less well-off and children, may skip their meals for the evening in expectation of a full treat of food and drinks. Assessments of the entertainment, loudly and freely declared, constitute a significant aspect that brings many people to the wake. Their participation in the funeral events gives moral support to the family. In return, they enjoy the family's hospitality. Itinerant urban dwellers and village residents exchange news about members of the community as they comment on the funeral display. The entertainment includes not only food and drink (served for seven days or more to relatives from far and near) but also performances by local song clubs and the record of praise sayings pronounced in regard to past accomplishments of the deceased's family members.

Lavishly decorated funeral rooms and beds are prominent features. Traditionally the corpse lies in state, respectively, in three decorated rooms—called *kalabio*, *biokiri*, and *wariku*—but at least one, the kalabio (bedroom), must be prepared, because it is the most personal room. Sometimes, when the family has the resources to honor the deceased by displaying great quantities of cloth, there will be more than three rooms. For example, seven rooms were decorated for a member of a wealthy family in Abonnema in May 1982, and eight rooms for another family in Buguma in January 1980.

The primary location of the beds is in the home of the deceased. Where possible, for both men and women, one room in the compound of birth is also decorated. Only for a woman, if important as reflected by the status of her husband and family of birth, are several rooms decorated in both her husband's compound and that of her birth. Her body lies in state first in the former, then in the latter residence. Following this, another aspect of display is added to the funeral ceremony: a mock battle is usually staged between members of both families in which the family of birth eventually wins to carry off the daughter's body for the actual burial. According to a Kalabari saying, "He (the husband) who acquires the living flesh (of the wife) has no claim on the bones."

The art of dressing the beds, called *ede de* (see fig. 18.1) is practiced by elderly women called *ededapu* ("those who decorate the bed"), who are known for this skill. They choose the cloth not only for the four-poster bed with canopy but also the walls and ceiling. Designated rooms are stripped of their usual furnishings and a bed is placed in the center. The actual nailing of the cloth to the walls and ceiling is done by men using bits of paper to protect the fabric from the nail head, as seen in figure 18.2. At least two women fold and arrange cloth and accessories on the bed under the direction of the ededapu. Arguments often ensue over the choice of cloth. Its color and design are important focuses in the total aesthetic composition of the room. The first stop for the corpse when it is brought from the mortuary is the kalabio, the traditional bedroom or inner chamber—the most personal room in the residence of the deceased. All four walls and the ceiling are usually decorated only in red madras. Plain madras that has not been cut to be *pelete bite* is ordinarily used. Called *torusimayi* (literally, "things to make the face unattractive"), this textile indicates intimacy just like the one that traditionally serves to cover the body of a woman who has just given birth and is going through the sequestering afterward as noted by Petgrave in chapter 7.

If there are three decorated rooms, the body is transferred later the same day to the second room, biokiri, and placed on the big funerary bed. (If there are only two rooms, the second will be the wariku.) In this "family room," cloths are folded and placed layer upon layer over the whole bed as well as nailed to the walls and ceiling. They include richly colored decorative fabrics also preferred by the Kalabari, such as handwoven cloth from Ghana and elsewhere in Nigeria.

Above, Fig. 18.1.
Ededapu (bed dressers) in the first funeral room (kalabio) decorated with injiri walls. Buguma, 1983.

Right, Fig. 18.2.
Male mourner preparing to nail the textile called accraa to inside walls of a funeral room. Buguma, 1980.

At about midnight of the first day, as the wake progresses, the corpse is moved into the third room (the reception room or parlor) and placed on the final bed for public viewing. In it, the most opulent fabrics of brightly colored silk (*loko bite*) and embroidered velvet (*india*), usually in deep red or deep blue, are laid out in rows on the bed. Photographs of the deceased may also be placed by the bed or on top of it near the pillow. The bed is further dressed with heavy coral beads, gold necklaces and rings, ivory elephant tusks, velvet fans, and other highly valued traditional ornaments. Sometimes the corpse itself is also adorned with these ornaments, removed before burial, which are placed on the elaborate, tasteful, and expensive traditional attire or on the white gown that identifies the deceased as Christian. The influence of Christianity is also seen in rooms whose bed, walls, and ceiling are dressed primarily in white, as shown in figure 18.3. A "Christian room" may replace the traditional third room, in which case the elaborate fabrics are used in the second room, or it may be added as additional room.

The combinations of cloth are the same as those in dress, especially women's dress. The first room always has madras walls and ceilings, frequently madras on the bed, or possibly Akwete. The second may use pelete bite, *accraa* with *blangidi*, or accraa with Akwete. The outermost room, if traditionally decorated as the third room, is reserved for the costliest combinations of india (embroidered velvet), *sinini* (lightweight velvet), and loko bite. Accraa and blangidi may also be chosen.

If the third room is a Christian room, it displays combinations of commercially produced white fabric—lace, eyelet, marquisette, brocade, damask, all referred to generally as "lace." Frequently, small bows of ribbon in pastel colors are pinned on this cloth. Silver tinsel and colored electric lights, used on Christmas trees in Europe and America, may be used to decorate the head and foot of the bed.

The use of funeral room dressing to show distinctions of status is subtle to outsiders but obvious to insiders. To make a good impression, the immediate family of the deceased borrows cloth for the event from the cloth boxes of each family in the extended family. Assessing family status involves appraising the quality, number, type, and age of the cloths. For example, old india, embroidered by hand rather than by machine, is especially prized. The prestige of older versions is easily recognized, and families who own them are noted and praised.

Renting decorative fabrics is censured if discovered. Families regularly buy good-quality cloths, whenever affordable, to have on hand for special occasions. Income differences between families are therefore symbolized by funeral room display.

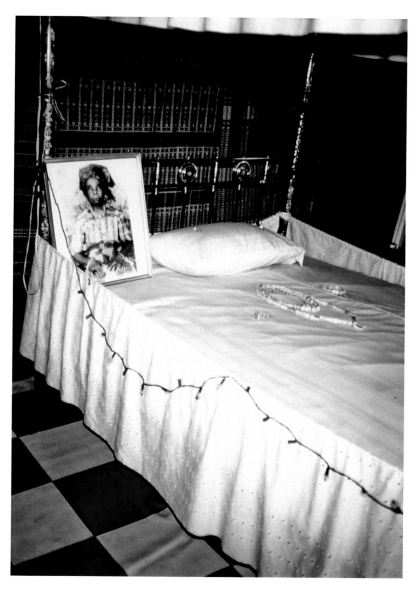

Fig. 18.3. A Christian bed decorated with white fabric, deceased's portrait, and coral beads. Buguma, 1983.

Fig. 18.4. Pelete bite arranged as a head tie on pelete bite funeral bed for postburial decoration. Buguma, 1983.

The cloths loaned by relatives to adorn the beds are women's wrappers. Initially, these are folded in strips ten centimeters wide and placed across the width of the bed in rows. Folding the cloth allows a family's extensive textile inventory to be displayed. The corpse, or the coffin with the corpse in it, is then placed on the decorated bed. In the Christian room, one white lace or brocade cloth, not folded, covers the mattress. It does not come from the traditional cloth box but indicates the family's ability to purchase an appropriate textile for the funeral to identify Christian affiliation.

Two or three days following the burial, the women who initially dressed the beds return to refold the wrappers and redesign the decoration of the beds (the walls and ceiling fabrics are not changed, and the fabric combinations are retained). For this display the simple design of rows of folded cloth is abandoned. Instead, the textiles may be twisted or folded in complex and flamboyant shapes, showing the creativity and ingenuity of the ededapu, as shown in figures 18.4–18.6. Different cloth or the same cloth in different juxtapositions may be used. The result is a giant fabric sculpture placed on the bed for mourners to view in passing through the rooms to express their sympathy. Many designs are used repeatedly and are easily identifiable by names, like *alapa*

Top, Fig. 18.5. Many varieties of cloth folded in alapa (jellyfish) style in third funeral room (wariku). Buguma, 1983.

Bottom, Fig. 18.6. Akwete folded as a hat on blangidi bed. Buguma, 1983.

(jelly fish), *owu sibi* (masquerade triangles), or *odum ikelekele* (sinuous python). Others the ededapu originate on the spot.

Personal accessories ordinarily are laid on the pillow and bed as they would have appeared on the body lying there, hats on the pillow, earrings below. Necklaces are put below the pillow, and bracelets, watches, and rings are placed further down on the bed. Coral and gold jewelry are used in the traditional rooms, often white and silver jewelry in the Christian rooms. Canes, fans, walking sticks, or purses appear to the side as if being handheld. These items also come from the storehouse of the extended family. Family members, ordinarily women, keep vigil over the decorated funeral rooms.

The ededapu are said to change the cloth daily for mourners to return to view, which is common. In twelve funerals Eicher observed in 1983, the norm seemed to be every two days for changing designs. The most elaborate designs usually are saved for the last day of display, which immediately precedes the final wake, parade, and funeral play. To the mourners, the events build to an aesthetic crescendo of color, texture, and sound.

The clothing and accessories of the mourners, particularly the chief mourners, follow a sequence also building in effect. On the day before the burial, when the corpse is carried from the mortuary to the residence for lying in state, it is accompanied by female friends and relatives dressed in madras or *krukrubite* ("black" cloth) wrappers with white blouses and by males dressed in injiri wrappers with white shirts. Pelete bite is particularly appropriate for the mourners' madras or krukrubite wrapper when the deceased is a well-respected, wellknown elder. Renne (1985) reported that an informant declared that only the relatives of the deceased had the right to wear pelete bite during this stage of mourning. T-shirts imprinted with the deceased's portrait and name may be distributed by the family for mourners to wear instead of blouses and shirts, as shown in figure 18.7. Frequently, members of the family hand out small photos of the person for mourners to pin to their garments.

On the day of the burial, the closest female family members dress in expensive white lace blouses and wrapper combinations of accraa and blangidi fabrics. The chief male mourner (eldest son or grandson) wears a white *etibo*, madras wrapper, Akwete or accraa sash, and matching head covering wrapped in the style of a loose turban, as in figure 18.11. Young grandchildren of the deceased often dress like miniature versions of their mother or father. The various men's or women's societies that come to praise, sing, and dance distinguish themselves from other groups by selecting identical cloth for their members' wrappers. Those in the church choir wear choir gowns, and ministers wear clerical robes. Several male relatives carry the coffin from the compound to the church, and then to the burial site, followed by the choir, clergy, other relatives,

Fig. 18.7. Female relatives wearing pelete bite wrappers and deceased's portrait on T-shirts and escorting the coffin from the mortuary to house for corpse lying in state. Buguma, 1983.

and other mourners. The first son of the deceased has the privilege and duty of holding the head of the coffin as the procession moves.

After the burial, usually at high noon, formal activities subside until Monday morning, when final preparations begin. Male and female descendants who will participate in the final wake and funeral dance start dance rehearsals. If the family is wealthy, the rehearsals are held nightly as minor events of the wake. The female relatives dressed as *iriabo* are presented as the essence of femininity, and their appearance and dancing must be elegant. Women and men dance at separate times, except for the final dance on the last night, when the women, on the signal of drumbeats, choose fortunate male relatives as partners, reinforcing the importance of the bond between male and female. The complementarity of male and female in Kalabari life is seen both in dress and dance, but interestingly enough, only the women are coached in their dancing. For these practice sessions, the females who dress as iriabo dress as they

Fig. 18.8.
Family mourners on the morning of the
burial. Chief female mourner wearing bite
sara wrapper of embroidered velvet (india).
Buguma, 1987.

do when they first come out of seclusion,
wearing madras wrappers.

On the final day of display, both for
the parade, called *amabro* ("going around
the town"), led by the chief mourner and
other family members, illustrated in
figure 18.9, and for the funeral dance at
night, called *din krama ti*, the males and
females of the lineage dress in appropriate garments. The chief male mourners
wear gowns, usually heirlooms from the
family cloth boxes, that are generally reserved for chiefs, with a variety of appropriate hats and accessories. Depending
on family circumstances, the outfits may
be different for the parade and the final
dance, with a change of dress displaying another set of the family's heirlooms,
enhancing its prestige. While parading, the mourners visit each lineage compound of the town, with the males in the lead, followed by the female relatives
dressed as iriabo in madras, and finally townswomen who praise-sing as they
parade. Prestige is bestowed on the family by onlookers who observe and comment on the finery worn by the relatives as a whole, and particularly on the
number of females dressed as iriabo, as in figure 18.10. One commonly hears
onlookers counting the iriabo as they pass through each compound or *polo*.
To dance in the evening event, the chief female mourners select embroidered
velvet and striped silk.

When the next day is a Sunday, there may be either a quiet interlude or a
religious "thanksgiving" held during the regular church service in the town.
Sometimes the thanksgiving takes place the Sunday after the last amabro and
dance, sometimes on a Sunday much later. For these occasions female family
members dress in traditional wrappers with lace blouses; men wear the woko
ensemble, a somber-colored upper garment with matching trousers or madras
wrapper. Chiefs, however, wear doni or ebu gowns, depending on their position. The contrast between dress chosen for parading and final night dancing

Above, Fig. 18.9.
Male mourners wearing chiefs'
dress examples for funeral parade
around the town (amabro).
Buguma, 1983.

Right, Fig. 18.10.
Female relatives dressed as iriabo
in madras with hats and canes. The
saucer holds gifts of money from
well-wishers in showing approval
of iriabo appearance and charm.
Buguma, 1983.

Fig. 18.11. Family mourners dressed for the thanksgiving church service. Chief female mourner wears velvet bite sara and male mourner wears madras gown. Buguma, 1988.

and those for Sunday service emphasizes how the former reinforce the image of male and female complementarity: each close male relative, especially the chief mourner, dresses as a chief, symbolizing power, and each close female relative, also especially as chief mourner, dresses in velvet bite sara, symbolizing creativity (see fig. 18.8), themes presented in earlier chapters. Male and female dress during the funeral displays also emphasizes the focus on the family or expanded lineage as the communal agency countering the intractability of death.

Funerals of elders are central social events in Kalabari communities, occupying large portions of time and representing large expenditures of individual and family resources. The elaborate celebration displays the socioeconomic standing and the aesthetic taste of the deceased's family to the community. One 1980s funeral was said to have cost 80,000 naira ($120,000 in 1980), because much cloth had to be purchased to outfit the relatives and bedeck the beds. Another report indicated that a family was completing a house in order to host a proper event, spending even more. In still another case, all the personal property of a poor woman was sold to finance her mother's funeral.

Although costly, these funeral celebrations serve several functions. First, they incorporate visible symbols that document the economic and social standing of the extended as well as the immediate family of the deceased. Economic status is easily noted, whereas social standing involves an understanding and assessment of taste. There can be differences in the funerals depending on the social status of the family, but families "do their best" to stage an appropriate funeral, often borrowing as they can from their extended kin groups. Second, they result in an extensive reunion of relatives and a renewal of family ties; in some cases people may not have met together in years. Third, they allow itinerant urban dwellers to affirm social and economic links with indigenous residents of the towns, as the former usually bear most of the expenses and transfer money into the rural communities. In return, the rural residents exchange information and provide services. The result is social cohesion between these two groups. Fourth, representation of all parts of the family in the funeral ceremonies shows the continued salience of the wari in Kalabari society. The presence of the female relatives who dress as iriabo signifies procreation, birth, and renewal of the lineage. The wearing of outfits for chiefs by all males of the lineage reinforces political identity within the lineage and its preservation.

Thus, among the features of the funeral ceremony for an elder, textiles, dress, and accessories, all costly items, are key ingredients. The funeral room decoration and the family's dress at the parade and dance ceremony are assessed publicly as indicators of socioeconomic status. Those indirect mourners check for appropriate matching of colors and materials as they inspect the bed, funeral room, and dress of chief mourners and extended family. Opinions are freely expressed, including comments about innovations or sloppiness. Only families of long standing are considered adept at effecting a subtle integration of the aesthetic elements. The nouveau riche are often dismissed as lacking finesse, in spite of a large and impressive array of expensive materials.

In view of their durability, ease of storage, transferability, and functional quality, the cost-effectiveness of apparel, accessories, and cloth must be rated highly. Dress and cloth display are highly visible and give a family esteem. In towns like Buguma and Abonnema, great competition seems to have ensued by way of families introducing decorative innovations in the form of accessories like imported coral beads, unusual cloth for the dress of the corpse, or a coffin ordered from overseas. Generally, exposure to foreign artifacts has allowed the incorporation of new items into the funeral ceremony.[3] Christians respond to church requirements as well as to the elaborate demands of Kalabari tradition. Use of deceased elders' dress, preserved in family cloth boxes, maintains a link to history and introduces the authority of the past into present structures. Although cloth has durable qualities (some families, through oral history and recitation of genealogy, can document that wrappers in their cloth boxes are over one hundred years old), it is generally thought of as delicate and perishable.

These fabrics symbolize relationships that are equally delicate and perishable, such as are found in the institution of the family and the wari, which constantly need reaffirmation.

The surrogate picturing of the deceased by laying decorations on the ede bed after the corpse has been buried suggests a ritual gesture of withdrawal of the deceased from the family circle when it was first removed as a corpse, because Kalabari tradition insists that the legs of the corpse be placed toward the door, indicating an exit position. The living are, by convention, averse to sleeping or lying down in this way. The subsequent decorations on the bed after the corpse has left represent a person who "goes out" in various changes of dress and accessories. Cloth becomes a concrete, symbolic expression of what remains a very significant social and psychological fact for the mourners. They experience the reality of the death of a family member in transition from life to the hereafter. The material manifestation of the event allows a catharsis for all those close to the deceased. They then relate to the symbolism of the decoration on the bed, which marks the final point of departure. Even the movement of the corpse from the kalabio through the biokiri to the wariku is an orchestrated ritual paralleling "the outings" marked by the ede decorations executed after the burial. Each outing of the corpse, from the inner chamber of the house to the public parlor, is also symbolized by cloth in the progression from the intimate injiri to the West African handwoven Akwete or accraa to the manufactured and handwoven cloth of more exotic origin. Injiri holds a special place in Kalabari life as a symbol of a person's journey from the womb to the vault of family and community, then out into the embrace of the world beyond this life—which the Kalabari usually consider to be benign, if not inviting, and certainly not a void or unknown. The opening scene in the drama of life includes a piece of injiri that is ceremoniously delivered to the mother by the father of a newborn child, "for carrying it." This personal emblem of entry into society for that child also becomes the cloth marking departure the moment of arrival at the house as a corpse. The trappings of funeral ceremonies and ritual may seem excessive to onlookers unfamiliar with Kalabari culture and even, at times, to some Kalabari. However, this life event is central in the ethos of the people and supports Mary Douglas's proposition: "More effective rituals use material things. The more costly the trappings, the stronger we can assume the intention to fix the meanings to be. Goods, in this perspective, are ritual adjuncts; consumption is a ritual process whose primary function is to make sense of the inchoate flux of events" (Douglas and Isherwood 1979, 65).

Anthropological literature emphasizes that death is the extreme crisis because it threatens the collapse of our socially constructed world. Those left behind must face living on without the deceased. Thinking of those yet un-born and newly born helps the mourners accept the idea that the death of an individual is not terminal for the lineage. The female relatives dressed as iriabo symbolize the bringing of new life to the Kalabari; their presence at the funeral ceremony highlights the contribution of women to the continuity of the lineage and community. The male relatives dressed as chiefs in imported cloth represent the power of the wari and the successful enterprises and lives of forebears. The display of cloth to honor the life of the deceased and mark the strength of the wari reminds us of Horton's observation of the Ekine Society as a borderland between art and religion. He concluded that "*Ekine* is essentially a society dedicated to the production of art" (Horton 1963, 111), referring to the secularization of religious notions, with the activity of the dance taking precedence by focusing on aesthetics and display. Similarly, in Kalabari funer-als, the art of dressing the bed and the mourners is a salient feature dedicated to the production of the art in the celebration. However, in the Ekine Society, equality is emphasized, and the ancestors are not invoked so as not to promote competition. In the case of Kalabari funerals, the art of dressing the beds and the mourners promotes competition among the War-Canoe Houses by saluting the wari as well as easing the way for the dead to enter the world of the ances-tors. Many facets of Kalabari life are integrated into the funeral ceremony—male and female complementarity; power, prestige, and the competition among War-Canoe Houses and the importance of the lineages within them; and the innovative incorporation of material objects into daily life, coupled with firm adherence to a traditional belief system. Annette Weiner (1976, 61) observed that Trobriand Island mortuary ceremonies in Kiriwina "are moments of spec-tacular visual communication . . . through the use of such visual qualities as style, color, and space, they frame the oppositional nature of relationships." Similarly, the funerals of the Kalabari provide spectacular visual communica-tion, frame the complementarity of male and female and life and death, and epitomize cultural authentication in the use of globally traded textiles.

JOANNE B. EICHER, PhD, is Regents Professor Emerita in the Department of Design, Housing, and Apparel at the University of Minnesota. She is coeditor of *The Anthropology of Dress and Fashion: A Reader*; coeditor of *The Visible Self: Global Perspectives on Dress, Culture, and Society*, 4th ed.; and editor in chief of the *Encyclopedia of World Dress and Fashion*.

TONYE VICTOR EREKOSIMA (1940–2008), PhD, native-born Kalabari, lived in the Igbo towns of Owerri and Umuahia, because his father was an educator and secondary-school principal, until Erekosima's university years in the United States. He was steeped in Kalabari cultural tradition, however, thanks to his family's routine travel to Buguma, his parents' birthplace, for holidays and significant events like funerals. Following his PhD, he served as Director, General Studies, Rivers State College of Education, and Director, Instructional Resources Center, University of Port Harcourt. He coedited *A Hundred Years of Buguma History in Kalabari Culture* (1984) and *Buguma 1984 Centenary Symposia on Kalabari* (1991).

NOTES

Adapted from Eicher and Erekosima (1987).

1. An elderly person who was not particularly successful or outstanding and who had no financially strong children or relations is accorded as much honor in a funeral as the family is able to muster. The first category (a funeral for a young adult) allows family and community to recognize that an individual's death has occurred, but there is no reason to celebrate. The third and fourth categories (respectively, a funeral for a chief and a king) allow celebration at death but have different requirements because of the special status of these individuals in life.

2. See Horton (1970) for a discussion of the power of the elders as ancestors. Horton describes a funeral rite, witnessed in the small village of Soku, in which the spirit of the deceased manifests itself. He focuses on three aspects of the rite: its drama, its role in relation to death, and its divination power, but he does not mention ede. Professor Horton died in December 2019 (Douglas Camp 2019; Ogbonnaya 2020) in Nigeria and, significantly, was given a Kalabari funeral in Buguma. Images were taken and uploaded to the internet for family and friends.

3. The funeral of a chief has the added dimension of poku doku (an elaborate canoe regatta), the shooting of cannons, and okuru fari (the beating of a special drum). The burial of a king features special rituals. He is not laid on an ede, consisting of an imported iron bed, but rather on a raffia mat on the floor with appropriate injiri and other cloth placed on it. Then a special masquerade, kala ekpesiaba, is staged at his burial accompanied by various animal sacrifices (Erekosima 1984).

19

Fitting Farewells

Joanne B. Eicher and Tonye Victor Erekosima

*Among most Southern Nigerian tribes the proper carrying out of
the burial ceremonies is the most important duty in life . . . especially
the case in those parts where worship of ancestors is most strongly
developed. . . . Families often impoverish themselves for years in
order to give a fitting farewell to an important member.*
(TALBOT 1926, 469)

THE INFLUENCE OF TRADE continues to be key in funeral celebrations and
is important to understanding Kalabari funerals, with the textiles and personal
accessories, such as jewelry, hats, and canes, coming from global sources. The
family mourners, particularly the chief mourners, display an art of dress by
wearing a specified array of fine textiles throughout the week in appropriate
ensembles for escorting the body to the family compound, the burial, the parade through the town, and the final dance, as delineated in chapter 18. The funeral rooms with decorated beds first display the corpse (see fig. 7.3 and 14.3)
and afterward allow community members to admire the display of ephemeral
art, pay their respects to the family of the deceased, and admire the family's
wealth. The imported textiles, jewelry of coral, silver, and gold, along with
impressive hats, canes, and other accessories add to the fanciful arts that the
women create to honor the deceased and family.

In this chapter, we place the funerals described in chapter 18 against the
backdrop of early twentieth-century practices documented by P. Amaury Talbot (1926), a respected chronicler of Kalabari life. We analyze the place that
funerals hold in Kalabari life and how they emphasize Kalabari beliefs and cultural values, focusing on the honor accorded the deceased by funeral practices,

on the affirmation and reintegration of kinship through celebratory measures, and on the display of family wealth and prestige through dress and textiles provided by the extensive trade of the Kalabari overland and by sea.

HISTORICAL COMPARISON

How did funerals of the late twentieth century compare to the reports by Talbot? He reports generally on the funeral practices related to a Kalabari male that involved the preparation of the corpse by immediate relatives and the expected behavior of the "lawful" and "secondary" wives (Talbot 1926, 487). He also provides information about the procedure for preparation of the deceased by "full brothers, sisters and adult sons" who wash the corpse in the backyard after the lawful and secondary wives leave. He declares that after being painted with camwood and black dyes, the body is wrapped with a raffia cloth (*okuru*) that is "passed round the loins by his sister" (ibid.). Only after this do the lawful wives return and wrap a cloth (unnamed type) around the corpse "while some of the dead man's most valuable cloths are laid over all" (ibid.). His comment illustrates the significance of the funeral in two ways: how cognatic lineage reintegration is generated and how Kalabari cultural values are emphasized.

Rubbing the corpse with the red camwood (*awu*) and other dyes (*buruma*) serves an aesthetic function of making the skin glisten. However, it also gives the deceased the dignity of being claimed by kin. As the sister of the deceased covers a male's private parts with fabric, she participates in a prescribed ritual. This assertive community act symbolically countermands the vulnerability of death. The presence of females representing fecundity in proximity to a naked male implies sexuality, but this ritual is not about reproduction. Wives are not a part of this crucial rite. Instead, only close relatives with whom the man could never have had intercourse are admitted.[1]

Kalabari view of death indicates that physical demise is only a transition into another postmortal state of being, an existence of a disembodied energy in the realm of the soul and spirits. There are four categories of the self (Erekosima 1973): the corpse (*duein*); fate and fortune (*so*); vital body or flesh (*oju*); and spirit, personality, or the soul (*teme*). When a person dies and becomes a corpse (duein), he or she leaves the body (oju) behind, but merely shifts from one realm to another, essentially remaining the same in spirit or soul (teme). The spirit realm, for the Kalabari, is not strictly mundane to the extent that it does not refer to causative or quantitative phenomena, nor is it related to embodied, time-bound phenomena. However, these spirits can be motivated to yield good or render damage; they can be placated, assuaged, deflected, or directed. Acknowledging their existence in Kalabari cosmology is parallel to acknowledging the existence of airwave bands in an invisible spectrum within which our contemporary culture projects and transmits radio messages and television images.

The categories of the self also relate to three Kalabari classes of free spirits within the spirit realm: the societal forces (*oru*), the good dead or ancestors (*duein*) and the water people (*owuame*) of the rivers and the creeks of the Kalabari environment. The state heroes (oru) such as Owamekaso, the tutelary deity responsible for prosperity and wealth, intermediate between the ancestral dead and the water people, for only through the beneficence of and control by the water people could the wealth and position of the family occur.

Yet the spirit realm does not address the realm of the divine and ultimate power or the supernatural. Another realm, that of the sacred, is set off from the reverential realm of the spirits, deities, and gods and is specifically delineated only by the dual and complementary forces of Tamuno and So, the Creative and Directive matrices, respectively, of the entire Kalabari ordered universe. An exuberant fecundity of femaleness and an organizing male modality couple to become the quintessence of the Kalabari worldview. However, the genders of maleness and femaleness reflect and sustain these clearly demarcated yet complementary roles. The heightened focus of attention that funerals place on the occasion of death underscores these fundamental values of the cultural system, which heavily involve dress and textiles. Such poignant messages, generally couched in the rituals of Niger delta funeral rites, led Talbot to observe that "the proper carrying out of the burial ceremonies is the most important duty in life . . . especially in those parts where worship of ancestors is most developed" (Talbot 1926, 469).

The practice of having only the closest female and male relatives admitted into the intimacy of dressing the deceased's body was still carried out at the end of the twentieth century. Only those who would not divulge family secrets (such as whether any blemishes were apparent on the corpse) could share in this most intimate moment of exposure when kinship solidarity receives its firmest seal. However, in the period that we researched the funerals, contrary to Talbot's time, a sister undertaking the act of tying the cloth over the man's loins (*amana*) occurs infrequently. Instead, the responsibility has passed to the first son in the case of men and to the eldest daughter for women.

Talbot's description of how the body is dressed for lying in state offers a glaring contrast with our research when only traditionalists (never church members), priests to the deities, and royalty retained the basic form. Talbot observed, "For those who had visited the Aro Chuku oracle or were members of the Peri Club, chalk is rubbed up the right arm and a manilla placed round the right wrist, on which feathers and blood from sacrificial fowls are smeared, while an eagle's feather is fixed in the hair" (Talbot 1926, 488).

Short of adding that the corpse must be laid out on a mat on the floor, while a peculiar masquerade dances in attendance, Talbot portrays Kalabari's most revered form of burial (called *emine*). It eclipses that of regular chiefs, which demands use of the colorful canoe regatta and cannon volley salutes as highlights. Although rarely practiced, the emine funeral was enacted for the late Chief Wokoma Horsfall and the late King (Amanyanabo) Charlie Kieni "Cane" Amachree.[2]

A brief analysis follows, describing the elements of the traditional funeral for Kalabari's eminent sons, which contrasts so significantly from our descriptions. We discuss those practices or elements, which continued and have become even more elaborate. The most important shift is from a focus on virtuosity in earlier times, while the material achievement at the end of the twentieth century and the twenty-first now looms more prominently. The former stressed the moral dimension of living by qualitative values that qualifies one to become an ancestor and to make a successful transition into the nether land.

For example, applying white chalk (*toru*) to the body at once elevated the corpse to a representation of the Body-Life ideal, signifying issues of the soul or qualitative living and marking off one's existence from the physical and material realm. The chalk mark up the right arm and the manilla armlet on the right wrist indicated both the character and accomplishments of living as a mature man. The manilla (trade currency of the period) portrayed the strength of bringing prosperity to the family through entrepreneurial leadership. It meant sustenance as well as protection of one's own.

The references to visiting the Aro Chukwu oracle or joining the Peri Club related to demonstrations of moral uprightness and of valorous courage in the spheres of community engagement and service. A Peri Club member produced an enemy skull as a warfare accolade and, to his credit, showed the member as ably arising to the defense of the community. To have survived an Aro Chukwu oracle's verdict was to have assumed a mantle of innocence and rectitude in public matters. This oracle emerged during the slave export era in an Igbo enclave, from among the hundreds of local Nigerian deities that arbitrated an endless variety of criminal allegations in the various societies.[3] The Aro were able to elevate their own oracle to imperial rank with scores of societies. This oracle helped to contain the internal conflicts and mediate the external relations of these diverse clans and cultures. European merchant adventurers often instigated intertribal warfare with their gifts of guns and alcohol to neighboring community leaders. The oracle also served to mitigate the complete social chaos that could have resulted from the inexorable demand for slaves by these merchants. Other countermanding mechanisms of cohesion among the coastal delta communities included the mythology of an underwater goddess (*Oruyingi*) who was mother to the tutelary gods and goddesses of societies like Nembe, Kalabari, Bonny, and Okrika (Alagoa 1972, 141).

The Aro deity's verdicts were generally summary and not open to further appeal. In practice, this was a key channel by which people were conscripted or extracted out of the diverse Nigerian societies, to be smuggled out and handed to the Europeans, who required healthy, able-bodied adults as slaves. The community that awaited the Aro deity's verdict on disputes only knew that the accused had one option, to be cleared of wrongdoing and return to society as an innocent and decent person. Otherwise, the person was truly a wizard who deservedly had lost his life for his crime and consequently missed the honor of receiving a fit burial.[4] When a Kalabari elder died, therefore, without being trapped in an Aro oracle's verdict, it meant passing the muster of integrity after scrutiny in the realms of esoteric testing.

The eagle feather that was stuck to the hair of the deceased or in the region of the head marked the ultimate of excellence, or the best of human aspirations. The deceased accomplished the full ideal positive human activism. The rarity of eagles and the lofty heights at which they soared, along with the rarefied symbol of a white eagle feather, converged in communicating this message.

The blood of innocent animals, like the slaughtered fowl smeared on the corpse, stood for a different level of intervention or memorializing. Briefly, it forged the link to the sacred realm of the Creator Spirit, the Ultimate Creative/Directive Center of human destiny where vitality and its nemesis abut. Asking for mediation from these creatures shorn of the human motivation toward negativity and malevolence commended the energy or spirit of the departed to the same course and cause of the Creator Spirit. With such sacrifice, the spirit of the departed thus remained in the soul domain and within the scope of its positive potential, able to continue on the same distinguished trajectory of providing succor to the living. Hence the Kalabari were little concerned with the soul's or life-energy's verdict from a divine perspective. Everything was measured by its impact on the living and how the departed's vital-energy was itself oriented or disposed.

The machinations to provide these spirits with sufficient comfort to not want to return among the living or to exert any negative sanctions (especially since disembodied life-energy is always more potent) explained a good part of the additional funeral rites that follow.

After ritual preparation of a male corpse, Talbot states that generally a cannon goes off and the sons and brothers lift the body and carry it into the *Wari Kubu* (*sic*) hall to lie in state on a bed. The lawful wives stand behind the head of the bed with lawful daughters and sisters in two rows on each side, "fanning the body with a heavily scented handkerchief" (Talbot 1926, 488). The women wail through the night as the town chiefs come to "take farewell of the dead man and bring gifts" (ibid.). If the deceased was a member of the Sekiapu Club, "the members come and sing a farewell song, and in the case of a rich free-born woman, give an Owu play" (ibid.). Soon after dawn the next day, the body was buried, first enclosed in mats, then sprinkled with the blood of sacrificial fowls and goats, and finally wrapped with more mats and interred under the innermost bedroom amid the sounds of cannon shots. Talbot specifically mentions precious trade goods being buried with the deceased: coral beads, gold and silver ornaments, yards of silk and other cloths "together with tobacco, snuff, a plate, knife and bottle of gin" (ibid.). These were symbols of wishing the departed to continue in the opulence that he had experienced on earth.

Talbot indicates that these practices are not undertaken for "those who are not members of the great societies" (Talbot 1926, 489). Instead, the sound of a cannon went off to announce the death and then, for the next six days, at morning and evening, to proclaim the steps of the funeral. Other details that Talbot provides relate to the expectations for the widow during and after a funeral, describing a series of practices involving isolation along with deprivation. These practices related to daily cycles of eating and toileting to show the widows' bereavement and loyalty. For instance, the hardship of sleeping only on a plank of wood might have been intended to punish and inflict pain on the wives or to implicate them in the crime of causing the husband's death. These explanations, however, are unlikely, because this was prescribed conduct for all deaths of a male spouse. Clearly death was generally expected. In contrast, this society placed a premium on the psychological aspect of living. Hence, the society focused on expunging or draining the widows' grief through parallel exertion. The pain of physically sharp discomfort would by its distraction neutralize and displace the ache of fond memories. Many non-Western societies include such acts as a critical essence of mourning rituals, whereas the West keeps remnants of these acts only in church services. In his account of Kalabari funerals, Talbot generally refers to customs related to the death of males and chiefs. Occasionally he includes comments about women: "The bodies of free-born women are borne back to their father's house, while the aged ones receive burial like chiefs" (Talbot 1926, 490).

Many of Talbot's descriptions of funeral practices were still carried out at the turn of the twentieth century and into the twenty-first. One exception is that respondents indicated that precious personal items are rarely, almost never, buried with the deceased.

DESCRIPTION OF MATERIAL ARTIFACTS
USED IN FUNERALS

What part do the material artifacts play in the funerals in giving homage to the distinguished departed who will become one of the esteemed ancestors? To answer the question, we compare Talbot's descriptions of funerals at the beginning of the 1900s with those we observed. He lists textiles and objects of personal adornment: coral beads, gold and silver ornaments, silk "and the finest of cloths" as well as "tobacco, snuff, a plate, knife and bottle of gin" (Talbot 1926, 488). While our list of textiles and jewelry coincides with Talbot's, the practice of burying the precious commodities with the corpse has stopped, apparently sometime after Talbot's observations. However, during the days following the burial, by the waterside at full tide, a practice continues of burning some precious items owned by the deceased. Some women family members assemble and burn the cloth and other material not directly touched by the corpse. They also identify, to be burned at the same time, any specific objects to which the deceased was particularly attached or that represented very personal mementos. These may be an item of dress, a favorite chair, a briefcase that person always carried, or a cherished watch. Although claimed to be personal objects the deceased person will use in the netherworld, they serve as a ritualized acknowledgment of the personal identity of the deceased.

Other items that the individual privately owned or used, such as clothing, slippers, perfumes, shoes, hats, albums, or other form of self-identifying property, are also collected from the deceased's immediate family members. A day is fixed for all members of the extended lineage to gather. Each person will pick one item of choice from the collection, even if it is an oversized coat or only one from a pair of slippers. Through this process, each person who believes he or she has a claim on the deceased has the opportunity to assert it.[5]

Although we assumed (along with Robin Horton) that the practice of decorating the bed and walls with cloth was an old tradition, field interviews in 1988 revealed that this practice had probably begun somewhere around the turn of the twentieth century; this was confirmed in a 1988 conversation with Horton.[6] In one account, members of one family said that sons of a wealthy chief rebelled against the practice of burying family wealth with the chief, that family goods should be passed from generation to generation. In 1998 one man in his midfifties, proud of his interest in Kalabari history, told Eicher that before the migration from Elem-Ama to Buguma they dressed the corpse in so much cloth that you could not see the corpse:

The last time all things were buried with the chief was about 80 years ago. The chief was Ikpoye Ikiriko (from Harry compound). When he died the family decided to put everything—*kalali* (coral), all the cloth he had into the coffin and his first son, Chief Benibo Ikiriko, protested that some of these things should be kept for the younger ones to use, so he forced his way to the coffin and brought some of these things out. So the family said, "Oh, you must have wanted your father to die so you could inherit these," and they invaded him. So he ran to King Abbi [Amachree] and took refuge. Then after some time, King Abbi gave him some land to settle (at the other end of town) as he could not come back to his former compound. That was how the whole thing ended. (Eicher 1988)

He elaborated further:

This thing of dressing the wall started not more than 60 years ago in Buguma, or so, maybe 50 years ago. It was not so in Old Shipping. Chief Brown West, when he died, his uncle, Chief Kio Young Jack of Abonnema came for the burial. When he came for the burial, it was a stick building, not a real building, but old, almost falling down, a dirty building. It didn't look like where somebody can paint it. Before now, when a chief dies, what they do, they put down the bed, then exhibit his wealth by hanging *doni* on the wall, not with hanger, but knock some nail. Now this man said, if we hang these on the wall, expensive india and so on, they'll be dirty because house is so dirty, so why don't we use some cloth to seal the whole room before hanging the expensive cloth. So they asked women to bring less expensive cloth—*accraa* cloth and so on. So Chief Young Jack introduced it to the Kalabari. (Eicher 1988)

His account implies a date of 1930, paralleling that of an elderly woman who said that the Chief Fubara Brown-West main house erupted in a fire, which raged for ten days, destroying the property and owner. Subsequently, an unnamed man brought his own personal property to dress the chief's funeral bed: "Instead of looking at the corpse, they looked at walls and beds, and this showed the family was still wealthy" (Eicher 1988). This woman remembered that at the time of this fire, her son, born in 1928, was crawling, making the date approximately 1929–1930.

CONCLUSION

Before the 1980s, these arts of dressing the bodies of the mourners and the beds for the deceased had gone undocumented except for the brief passages mentioned by Talbot (1926). By the 1980s, however, the practice appeared so well established that lavish funerals were referred to as "traditional." What purpose does a flamboyant funeral serve? Obviously, the practice began with honoring the life of chiefs in Kalabari life, the men who had established themselves in the communities by providing the base that sustained their extended families. The fruits of their success, as shown through the imported artifacts they had accessed for themselves and their loved ones, were displayed to emphasize and underscore their importance and prestige. Sometime later, the possessions were no longer buried with the noted individual. Using these same items of accomplishment, the fanciful art of dressing the beds and walls developed, primarily practiced by women. This visible display announces to the community the success of the deceased and the high regard in which they are held by family members.

The intersection of male and female in Kalabari life became intertwined in the funeral event with the display of the family artifacts lovingly arranged by the women. In addition, the intersection of the living with the spirits, the ancestral dead, and the one who goes on to join them is of paramount concern. The display of family wealth in the funeral through an elaborate and gorgeous array of material artifacts of textiles and personal belongings from global trade provides the acknowledgment of how a particular family came to have prestige, power, and wealth, symbolizing at the same time the contribution of the water people (owuame) to a particular family.

In the twenty-first century, many Kalabari people are Christian; the Christian communities within each island town are vigorously healthy with large Sunday service attendance. However, an overlay of what is termed the "traditional" Kalabari belief system with the four categories of the self has influenced the funeral practices that continue today. Therefore, how people are treated after death takes on major importance as they are entering the world of the ancestors. If an individual was mean-spirited or happy in life on earth, he or she will continue to be so in the world of the ancestors (the duein). These ancestors must feel appreciated and well regarded by the family who honors their death: "They are seen as taking care of their living descendants even as they did before they died. They demand respect from their heirs" (Erekosima, Lawson, and MacJaja 1991).

Significant shifts occurred during the twentieth century in carrying out a fitting farewell. Through the pervasive embrace of Christian beliefs and practices, many ritual elements have been dropped or diluted. Their significance is largely forgotten, if not deliberately denied. The ceremonial component has become more prominent and underlines a shift of new economic and power alignments in the public sphere. The earlier emphasis on moral order and cultural reaffirmations recedes under the influence of a globally advancing secularization and greater focus on material well-being and display.

JOANNE B. EICHER, PhD, is Regents Professor Emerita in the Department of Design, Housing, and Apparel at the University of Minnesota. She is coeditor of *The Anthropology of Dress and Fashion: A Reader*; coeditor of *The Visible Self: Global Perspectives on Dress, Culture, and Society*, 4th ed.; and editor in chief of the *Encyclopedia of World Dress and Fashion*.

TONYE VICTOR EREKOSIMA (1940–2008), PhD, native-born Kalabari, lived in the Igbo towns of Owerri and Umuahia, because his father was an educator and secondary-school principal, until Erekosima's university years in the United States. He was steeped in Kalabari cultural tradition, however, thanks to his family's routine travel to Buguma, his parents' birthplace, for holidays and significant events like funerals. Following his PhD, he served as Director, General Studies, Rivers State College of Education, and Director, Instructional Resources Center, University of Port Harcourt. He coedited *A Hundred Years of Buguma History in Kalabari Culture* (1984) and *Buguma 1984 Centenary Symposia on Kalabari* (1991).

NOTES

Adapted from Eicher and Erekosima (2002).

1. Bloodline members designated to reach to the fourth generation.

2. Horsfall was a Buguma War-Canoe House leader who had rejected Christianity. Amachree was a pastor until ascending the Kalabari throne, then he became subject to upholding the culture's treasured rituals.

3. In these relationship-focused cultures, the capital offenses ranged from adultery as a chief's wife to the mere failure of one man to greet another that he passes on the road. Such suspicious show of unfriendliness was interpreted, in a society that put a premium on social solidarity within the community, as an intent of ill will toward the other. This could culminate in causing his death if not the infliction of lesser misfortunes if left unchecked. The loaded meaning of such omission could lead to an accusation of witchcraft by the offended party. And if not effectively disposed of locally through vigorous denial by a prescribed ritual response, the matter could end up for arbitration in the court of the Aro oracle.

4. Usually the family members who went on the journey to Aro Chukwu with the accused were shown the blood of goats sprinkled into a stream and told it belonged to their relative as a result of the deity's mangling when innocence was denied. The verdicts were generally accepted because they were frequently proved to be fair. Unbeknownst to most litigants, the Aro people who settled clusters of their community members in most of these societies used them as scouts to gather detailed intelligence on almost all cases and to pass the information dossier through their secret village-to-village link back to the oracle site.

5. This continuing practice was confirmed in an email from a Kalabari respondent with Eicher in January 2020.

6. Eicher conversation with R. Horton, 1988.

20

Centenary and Masquerade Rituals

Joanne B. Eicher

ALTHOUGH KALABARI FUNERAL rituals comprised a major part of our collaborative research, I observed two other ritual events in 1984 and 1991 with Erekosima and a research assistant. The first, the 1984 Buguma Centenary, celebrated the Kalabari migration to Buguma from their original Kalabari settlement on the island of Elem-Ama (also called "Old Shipping"). The second, the 1991 massive Owuarusun masquerade, a culmination of yearly masquerades held since the last Owuarusun in 1973, was organized by the Ekine Society. I directed a male videographer from the US who was allowed in the sacred area of the town square (Eicher 1994).

THE 1984 BUGUMA CENTENARY CELEBRATION

Buguma, the second largest city of River State, throbbed with excitement during a mélange of festivities marking its Centenary Celebration from December 14 to December 30, 1984, virtually eclipsing Christmas. Competing and overlapping activities, sometimes running from 6:00 a.m. until the next dawn, captured attention and exhausted participants and spectators during three weekends and each weekday. I arrived in time to attend organizing meetings about the preparations and went by boat to follow the re-creation of the 1884 migration.

Festivities began when the flag-bearing war canoes of the seven major compounds pushed off at daybreak from the island of Elem-Ama to Buguma. Several thousand residents and visitors cheered the *Amanyanabo*, His Royal Highness Obaye Abbiye-Suku Amachree X (CON), stepping ashore in Buguma at

Fig. 20.1. Miss Buguma, 1984, and Ella Prest, a former Miss Buguma.

Fig. 20.2. Buguma Ascendant Youth Group parading for Buguma Centenary, 1984.

the day's end after participating in the day's migration to and fro, amid shots from ancient cannons on the canoes.

A lavish opening ceremony the next day ended with the centenary ball and choosing Miss Buguma, shown in figure 20.1, a special centenary event. Chair of opening ceremonies, Chief G. K. J. Amachree, greeted the guest of honor, the state governor, Police Commissioner Fidelis Oyakhilome. The Amanyanabo poured a libation, gave a short address, and cut a seventeen-layer centenary cake. He, his council of chiefs, the honored guest, and the centenary committee sat under canopies in King Amachree Square to watch the first of many parades.

Schoolchildren in uniform were led by members of seventy-five men's and women's societies. Each group carried a banner and wore matching wrappers, as seen in figure 20.2, to identify them. The guest of honor released one hundred pigeons from a cage; apparently dazed by the hot sun, they half-heartedly fluttered to freedom. The high point was the two chiefs from Benin City, who represented their Oba, unveiling an imposing concrete statue in front of the

Fig. 20.3. Horsfall Chieftaincy boat for Buguma Centenary, 1984.

town hall. This statue was of King Abbi Amachree, Kalabari ruler from 1863 to 1900 and Bugama's 1884 founder.

A *poku doku*, a traditional boat regatta (usually held to mark a chief's death or visit of an important personality), provided a daylong event for the second Saturday. For each major compound, war canoes joined chieftaincy boats bedecked with flags, ceremonial cloth, and compound chiefs wearing traditional gowns, hats, jewelry, and accessories (see fig. 20.3), exhibiting their prowess by speeding to neighboring Kalabari islands of Abonnema and Degema and back. The accidental sinking of the Ombo lineage's chieftaincy boat early on caused a brief delay, but compound members hurried to refurbish it and rejoined the expedition. On the fleet's return to Buguma, cheering crowds thronged the waterside. The Amanyanabo and entourage disembarked first, followed by the warriors, all surging to the city square to pay homage to Owamekaso, the Kalabari goddess.

Each of the three Sundays featured religious services observing the centenary, climaxing on December 30 in an ecumenical event in the biggest of the cathedral churches, St. Saviour's African Church. On weekdays, the Ekine Society sponsored selected Owu masquerades, traditionally

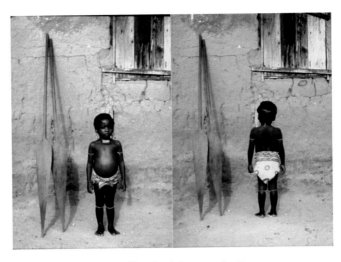

Fig. 20.4a and b. A small girl celebrating the Buguma
Centenary in 1984 wearing the first stage of traditional
dress (front and back view).

danced after New Year's Day. The masquerades delighted Buguma residents
and other Kalabari visitors, ending with a mini Owuarusun on the final Saturday. Owuarusun normally signals the formal ending of the twenty-five- to
thirty-year masquerade cycle. This Owuarusun included only masquerades
occurring since the 1973 Owuarusun, documented by the Kalabari scholar
C. W. Jenewari (1973).

The day before Christmas, several compounds held "Feasting of the Ancestors," ritually slaughtering and cooking goats for communal consumption.
These ceremonies aimed at winning the goodwill of the lineage deities (*duein*)
to protect and prosper their offspring. All churches held religious services on
Christmas Eve and Christmas Day, but the December 25 feasting of the chiefs
by the Amanyanabo in the city square was the peak event. Selected women's
societies provided dance entertainment. After the Amanyanabo left, the finale
was a traditional dance by members of the centenary coordinating committee.

On the day after Christmas, the Amanyanabo presided over the feasting
for King Amachree I, who founded the current Kalabari dynasty, invoking his
progenitor with libations and other sacrificial offerings to bring blessings on
Buguma and provide guidance for all Kalabari people. Later that week, he and
his chiefs conducted a formal outing (*igolomenji*), including a visit to an arts and

culture display at Saint Saviour's School showing traditional basketry, games, carving, and textile arts including *pelete bite.*

Traditions from the past (some dwindling in recent years, others still vibrant) were featured throughout the celebration. Using shells and fruit seeds, middle-aged and older adults demonstrated children's and women's games of cooperation and competition. Tiny girls (as in fig. 20.4), flowering teenagers, and older women preened and posed in numerous variations that displayed all stages of *iria.*

Kalabari distinctive patterns of dress, rituals and aesthetic achievements were salient throughout. Personal dress, masquerade dances, pageantry of the Amanyanabo, the chiefs, war canoes, and chieftaincy boats confirmed their global trading legacy. The art of dress, a notable feature each day, was especially highlighted by elaborate outfits of women and chiefs. The Kalabari brought out many fabrics—embroidered Indian velvet, handwoven *accraa* strip cloth, *Akwete,* English printed woolen flannel, antique madras, and pelete bite—from family trunks along with gold and coral jewelry. Women combined gorgeous and intricate lace and eyelet blouses with their wrappers, and many men displayed their prized *ajibulu* headwear.

The serious and intellectual side of the Kalabari emerged in the series of eight evening symposia focusing on contemporary life: Kalabari education, religion, funerals, language, women's roles, men's status, economic development, leadership, and unity. Each symposium featured a formal presentation and three discussants, all prominent Buguma sons and daughters. At each evening symposium, the chair, discussants, and audience (sometimes up to 150 people) dissected and debated the arguments.

Celebrating its hundredth year of settlement was a tribute to the organizing abilities of those who planned the centenary to honor their forebears. Sanctioned by the Amanyanabo and his council of chiefs and initiated and carried out by the central coordinating committee chaired by Sir (Chief) O. K. Isokariari, the event lauded the past, applauded the present, and beckoned the future, frequently referencing life in "2084." Ten subcommittees totaling 116 people began early in 1984 to allocate planning responsibilities.

The seventeen-day celebration pointed to Kalabari ingenuity and potential to cooperate on an identified common goal. The Kalabari recognize and quickly acknowledge current problems in education, land disputes, and serious community rivalry. This occasion, however, emphasized that committed citizens from different backgrounds and with different skills can tackle a complex organizational challenge and execute it successfully.

The self-help aspect of the project was admirable. No government money supported the several million naira spent. (Two million naira alone was pledged to the construction of King Amachree Hall to symbolize citizen pride and function as a city government building). The commitment to development projects in "Great Buguma" emerged with collective contributions to control erosion, create a waterside embankment, and repair the malfunctioning municipal water and electricity systems. Thus, entrepreneurial management was exhibited at both individual and community levels.

On New Year's Eve, Buguma settled back into its workaday world. Satisfaction and fatigue marked the faces of celebrants as some stayed behind and others embarked on boats to return to work in Port Harcourt, Lagos, and Kano and face the business of the New Year. The equivalent of an African extravaganza and an African community development plan had coalesced with Kalabari society being both traditional and modern. Kalabari made selections from their contemporary world, combining them with traditional practices in art, family life, and economic achievement, not only in 1984 but also in 1991 at the Owuarusun festival parade, as I discuss below.

THE 1991 OWUARUSUN MASQUERADE FESTIVAL

Owuarusun, the name of a massive masquerade festival, climaxes a long series in a cycle of yearly masquerades celebrating the water people, prior ones occurring in 1908, 1927, and 1973. Each year during the cycle leading up to an Owuarusun, either a major family in Buguma or the whole town sponsors one or two masquerades. When the Ekine Society declares that the cycle is completed, all masquerades since the last Owuarusun parade in a two-day finale in the town square, then return to the sea to begin another cycle.

The town square is divided in two with the main road as separation. The sacred area contains the drum house, the water people's shrines, the masquerader's resting house, and the sacred well. The public section features a statue of King Abbi Amachree IV, the first king of Buguma, placed in front of the town hall, with shops at two sides. Only men, the dancing *sekiapu* members of the Ekine Society, perform the masquerades. Women must not step from the public to the sacred ground or near the drum house at any time, either during a masquerade or on nonfestival days; they may only appear on the edges as dancers to support a family masquerade. Also during masquerades, women may not approach the sacred ground wearing a printed textile but must wear Indian madras or other acceptable cloth. If a woman breaks the taboo, Ekine Society members announce a special ritual to cleanse and purify the sacred area before the masquerade continues.

Specific families own masquerades, and their masked dancer wears a designated costume. Either pelete bite or a similar fabric covers his face to mask his identity, allowing him to breathe and see through it. Spectators crowding around the town square enjoying performances wear Kalabari dress showing their identity as Kalabari. The king and chiefs wearing ebu, doni, and celebratory headwear sit with important invitees under a festive canopy. When a masqueraded dancer appears, family support groups accompany him, males dancing in both sacred and public areas and females only in the public space. Male Ekine Society dancers wear an etibo ensemble, adding sashes of handwoven fabric and fish-eagle feathers in their hats or hair, as seen in figure 20.5. Adult female dancers may dress as iriabo or in *bite sara*. Teenagers and small girls dress up in *ikuta de, bite pakri iwain*, and *konju fina* outfits, iria stages of dress no longer practiced except for celebratory occasions.

In 1991, the traditional healer, the Mgbula masquerade, was brought to cleanse the town both morning and evening of the first day, and launched Owuarusun. On the second day from dawn to midafternoon, Ekine members, masked and unmasked, danced in the town square. Some spectator favorites were *Tari Okoko*, the rooster, and *Bekinarosibi*, the white man's ship, a miniature sailing vessel three feet in length that was placed on a dancer's head. When the dancer swayed, goodies of candy and cookies associated with the white man spilled from the ship's deck for the crowd to seize.

Near sundown, all masked and unmasked dancers lined up behind the Ekine leader. Dressed in an opulent green silk robe and an elaborate hat trimmed with colored feathers, tinsel, and shiny Christmas tree balls, he led the sekiapu dancers around the square perimeter. As dancers approached the square's exit to the road leading to the beach, the male line of dancers broke, racing down the road. When reaching the water, they jumped in for their ritual cleansing to appease the water people. Females were banned from approaching the beach, not allowed to view the dancers' ritual, only lingering behind the male spectators. As a special visitor, however, I was allowed to enter a small boat and watch the masked dancers remove their headdresses as companions carried the headdresses away. Emerging from the water, dancers returned home to dress, and townspeople meandered along the main road, sometimes through the night, gossiping about good dancers, good masks, and family arguments.

All participants wore significant textiles during the performances. Masked dancers wore costumes appropriate to their specific character, sometimes a person, sometimes an animal such as an elephant, monkey, pig, or crocodile. Each wore Indian madras on his body in either discrete or obvious display. For example, *Aki*, the crocodile, was held by a leash of twisted madras that

Fig. 20.5. Male Ekine Society dancers wear Indian madras wrappers and special shirts, sashes of handwoven fabric, and hats with African fish-eagle feathers, 1991.

restrained him from running amok into the crowd; other dancers wore madras wrappers. Priestesses of the goddess's shrine, the *Egbele Ereme*, wore Indian madras, as required. Spectators also dressed in Kalabari apparel, and chiefs wore ebu or attigra gowns.

Cultural authentication is integral to Kalabari masquerades. Foreign items of dress and foreign textiles combine in new ways, important when being seen as Kalabari is paramount. Kalabari identity is tied to the sacred masquerade cycle by what is worn while performing. Use of revered textiles and other artifacts of dress acquired by their ancestors marks a significant ethnic identity that highlights being Kalabari in pluralistic Nigeria.

The day after the festival, the master drummer and other Ekine Society members rolled the big drum from the drum house to the sacred well, signaling a moratorium before starting another cycle. Significantly, men wore their etibo outfits, marking the transition to everyday life for work, school, and other daily activities, whether on the islands or in Port Harcourt. The Owuarusun masquerade epitomized Kalabari use of culturally authenticated dress and textile artifacts by spectators and dancers, visibly demonstrating their involvement in a global world.

JOANNE B. EICHER, PhD, is Regents Professor Emerita in the Department of Design, Housing, and Apparel at the University of Minnesota. She is coeditor of *The Anthropology of Dress and Fashion: A Reader*; coeditor of *The Visible Self: Global Perspectives on Dress, Culture, and Society*, 4th ed.; and editor in chief of the *Encyclopedia of World Dress and Fashion*.

NOTES

Adapted from Eicher (1985, 1993).

21

Kalabari Rituals and Dress as Multisensory Experiences

Joanne B. Eicher

KALABARI RITUALS and their dress, amassed from global trade with elegance and fastidiousness, engage the five senses of sight, sound, touch, smell, and even taste (Eicher 1995; Roach and Eicher 1973) and one that can be added, related to balance (Geurts 2002). Some scholars, Shusterman (1996) and Drewal (2012), refer to focus on the body and senses as somaesthetics. At funerals, family members intend that proper dress and activities will guarantee the correct send-off with much pomp and ceremony for the deceased to become one of the ancestors. Similarly, participants at other rituals, such as the centenary event and masquerades, are keenly aware of the water people and ancestors as part of their heritage and intentionally reflect important sensory aspects of dress in their participation.

The visual includes delight in color and pattern, touch involves the textures in fabrics and accessories, and sound occurs from various accessories as individuals walk or dance. Kalabari enjoy the kinetic experience of dance in their ritual events. Celebrants display and wear vibrantly colored and sensuously textured textiles, also filling funeral compounds and the city square with music and drumming.

SENSORY ASPECTS VISUAL OVERVIEW: COLOR AND TEXTURE

After the many hours spent in deliberations, sometimes heated arguments and skillful negotiations, the formal ritual for a funeral begins when the corpse leaves the mortuary after being dressed by the chief mourner and adult kin

260

of the same sex as the deceased. Mourners choose specific dress to escort the corpse. Women's white eyelet blouses and indigo *pelete bite* wrappers and men's long white *etibo* and pelete bite wrappers provide stark color contrast. Sometimes the deceased's family gives mourners T-shirts printed with the loved one's name and portrait to wear instead of blouses and etibo shirts.

The textiles and coordinated coverings on the walls of funeral rooms and accessories on the bed provide both color and texture. For the corpse and beds, extended family members lend textiles and accessories, like coral and canes, from their own cloth boxes. Important accessories provide color and texture: the smooth, white ivory tusk, the coral-beaded hats, brown or black canes with gold trim or knobs, the flamboyant *ajibulu* headdress with colorful feathers, shiny baubles, and the target-shape *biaba* symbol. Textiles are sometimes purchased specifically, as in the case of embroidered white velvets for a funeral or the brown velvet attigra for Sir Isokariari's chieftaincy installation. The visual is evident in textile colors, designs, garments, and accessory shapes and forms worn by participants.

For funerals, the cloths displayed on walls and beds, from room to room, widely vary in texture and color. The combination of textiles chosen for the bed and the walls parallel the combinations for wrapper outfits: *injiri/Akwete, loko/india, loko/sinini*, and *accraa/blangidi*. (Eicher field notes 1983, 1984). Textures vary. Madras plaids are smooth; Akwete cloth is heavily textured with inlaid threads. Silk striped *loko* is also smooth, as is the unembroidered soft, short pile *sinini* velvet when compared to the heavy, plush, and metallic-embroidered velvet. Textures of mourners' ensembles also vary from smooth etibo and gabardine doni to the eyelet blouses, shadowy pelete bite; heavy, embroidered india; and smooth, shiny loko.

SOUND

Visual images only provide a partial sensory reconstruction of funerals, the centenary, or a masquerade. Other senses, like sound, intermingle. For example, when discussing installation of Kalabari funeral beds, Erekosima asked, "But what about the music? Music and dancing are integral parts of the experience." Thus, various sounds are integral to Kalabari rituals. The most obvious ones are not connected with dress itself but with the ambience provided for participants, both kin and community visitors. First, a series of cannon shots announce an impending funeral. Next, throughout the funeral celebration, almost continuous music and drumming throbs, sometimes live music with drummers, more often, recorded music blasting from loudspeakers at the dance arena edge. In addition, women contribute stylized wailing and praise singing, usually the wife or wives, sisters, or daughters. The praise singing consists of original compositions of the individual singer about the accomplishments of the deceased. The dancers' feet softly pad and thump, sounds not always clearly heard above the speakers or drum. Kalabari families organize their funeral celebrations according to age-grades, and simultaneously different groups choose different music. Younger family members supply contemporary music for dancing and entertainment. Older groups play more classic Kalabari songs. During Friday evenings for Christian families, a two-hour hymn-singing period provides contrasting musical ambience.

ODORS, FRAGRANCES, AND TASTE

An indigenous Kalabari funeral involves several types of odors. Camphor, prominent while the corpse is present, is placed on small pieces of cotton inserted in the nostrils of the corpse. In addition, textiles pulled from the extended families' storage in cloth boxes have odors of mothballs or tiny red peppers used as insecticides. In contrast, wrappers brought out to wear or to decorate the bed may have been aired in the sun, leaving an immediate scent of fresh air.

Other odors may be detected during the several days of a funeral, like those from the breath of mourners who have been drinking various alcoholic beverages of whiskey, gin, or palm wine. And the host family provides familiar aromas when preparing meals, like cooking stews in large pots over an open fire outside the family house.

The indigenous kola nut, offered to guests in many ethnic groups in Nigeria on arrival to one's compound and often at a funeral, has a bitter taste as well as an energizing effect after chewing. Other flavors and tastes may be found in refreshments that are offered throughout the celebration.

TEXTURE AND KINESIS

The kinetic experiences of dressing the body, parading, and dancing play key roles for males and females. Kalabari appreciation of a fulsome body for a mature woman involves wrappers that emphasize roundness and plumpness whether her wrapper be a celebratory knee-length or full-length. I watched a woman being dressed as chief mourner for the Saturday funeral parade honoring her mother. As is common, she did not dress herself, but as expected, other women dressed her. They first placed a series of madras underwrappers, covering her from her waist to her knees, before tying the top madras wrapper. They fussed with the textiles, twisting and turning them in the process so that she looked properly plump when they were finished. In another example, a woman told me those who dressed her placed many underwrappers to circle her slim body, so that she could be acceptably presented as her mother's chief mourner for the evening dance. In becoming dressed, an interactive process of kinetic and tactile qualities takes place among the women—for those doing the dressing and the one being dressed, who is touched and prodded during the process.

Men ordinarily dress themselves, but women carefully monitor them before they leave the compound, enforcing propriety in men's dress. They comment on whether the wrappers hang straight, meaning parallel to the ground, and whether garments are properly pressed, a mandatory condition. White garments, like shirts and blouses, must be spotless and sparkling. As discussed in chapter 13, Kalabari men frequently choose to wear white knickers under their wrappers, wanting the knickers' white eyelet trim to be seen briefly when striding along with the wrapper sides flaring open.

At the first burial I attended in 1980, I wanted to photograph two men standing together. One refused at first but then agreed to be photographed with a third man who walked up. Puzzled, I showed the photographs later to Erekosima, who was not initially present. Knowing Kalabari etiquette, he explained that for my initial request, the first man, nattily attired in fresh white etibo and immaculate madras wrapper, did not consider the second man, barefoot, wearing a rumpled, ordinary white shirt and wrinkled wrapper, as an equal. The third man, walking up in a freshly pressed etibo and madras wrapper, indicated social equality. Clean and smooth textiles, freshly laundered, provide a smart appearance with a different visual impression than soiled, shabby ones and a bedraggled appearance. The challenge of meeting the requirement for pressed and clean clothes additionally can be great when using a charcoal iron for pressing, the common practice during my fieldwork experience.

Different textiles have different textures. For example, lightweight madras, changed by the removal of threads to make pelete bite, becomes even lighter in weight, feeling airy when worn. Gowns of heavy, embroidered velvets provide a completely different experience, as Sir (Chief) O. K. Isokariari (2012) indicates with details of his chieftaincy installation outfit: "Indeed it was a big day. [I was] traditionally dressed for the occasion in India-cloth attire, gold studs, coral beads, plume-made hat [ajibulu] and with the woven fan and tusk in both hands" (215). He goes on to describe how he felt after the morning process, the installation, and the reception at his Ojuka compound with a photograph taken in his regalia:

By the time I retired home to rest, it was past 4 pm and I was sweating
profusely under the thick, air-tight India robe. It was even the second robe
I wore on the day, because I had to completely change attires [sic] and
the accessories from the plume-made hat to the footwear for the Sekobiri
presentation after my acceptance by the Buguma Council of Chiefs earlier
in the day. If I was not strong and healthy, I would have collapsed with the
length of time I had to put on the air-tight apparel . . . I really would advise
anyone that is elderly who is going into such a venture against using such
thick fabrics for a dress. (216)

In contrast, the roomy chieftain's gown, the *ebu*, is lightweight madras with a
different quality regarding its size and texture, as one of Ikiri John Bull's daughters, Madam Ekenta, recalled: "She and other little children would hide under
her father John Bull's flowing ebu (a chief's flowing dress) during hide and seek
plays known in Kalabari as *'oli nwaa, aboaro boe.'* He would open his legs and
the children would hide under the ebu. The 'seeker' in the game would ask him,
'Da, ntoanga buro?' ('Father, where did they pass?'), and he with his very small
and stammering voice would trick them *'mmangi paka te'* ('They have run to
the outside')" (JohnBull 2004, 90).

How charming to learn that Ikiri John Bull turned from chiefly duties by using his loosely hanging and lightweight madras gown to play with his children.
With twenty-two wives and numerous children (including foster children),
how many times might he have used his gown to have fun with them over the
years?

Other items of dress also have definite tactile qualities. For example, the
large men's headwear, the ajibulu, mentioned by Sir Isokariari as the "plume-
made hat," worn during his chieftaincy installation, means holding one's head
carefully to keep the complex headpiece upright. As anthropologist Kathryn
Geurts (2002) suggests, the importance of learning balance for one's body
comes into play, as illustrated by keeping the Kalabari hat on one's head when
dancing or walking. The turban tied on a chief male mourner's head on the
burial day is not common for men, as funerals are the only occasions during
which a man or boy wears a turban-style headdress. Women, although frequently wearing head ties, also must carefully avoid them falling off or becoming untied. The coral hats of women worn during iriabo when dancing and
parading involves the same challenge. Kalabari expectations for proper stance
and deportment include men standing straight and tall, never slumping, and
women also standing erect.

Another tactile aspect for women is that when they dress as iriabo and dance, they must dance barefoot so that their footsteps are seen. Shoes would not only spoil the ensemble's effect but also would not allow proper execution of dance steps. Barefooted, they are literally "grounded," that is, one with the red earth of the Kalabari islands.

Good dancing is important, which both onlookers and the dancers understand. One part of Kalabari dance involves bending forward at the waist, projecting and shaking their buttocks behind them. Onlookers praise good dancers by bestowing gifts of money and walking into the dance arena, placing currency bills on the forehead or shoulders of the dancer who does not stop to pick them up. Dancers leave that task to a support person who gathers up the bills as they fall and keeps them for the dancer. Dancing well and without embarrassment while engaging in vigorous movement means the dancers must keep their hats and headdresses in place. Similarly, the women's wrappers, fastened only by tucking in the ends of the cloth around the waist, must stay in place and not become undone.

Jewelry adds a tactile aspect to dress; heavy coral necklaces feel weighty around the wearers' necks. Also, glass bead or coral armlets and knee bands tied around women's upper arms and below their knees can feel tight, as they must be securely fastened to stay in place without slipping.

CONCLUSION

Dress is a system of nonverbal communication, and the Kalabari are proudly aware of the use and propriety of involving all the senses in dressing for significant occasions such as funerals and other celebrations. The Kalabari response to death is to launch the deceased into the next life through a proper funeral with all senses involved. The visual aspect of dress for self and mourners and dress for funeral rooms and beds is paramount, with texture, smell, and sound easy to recognize, but taste less obvious. Erekosima proposed that the Kalabari assume a construct of continuity. They organize a proper funeral in a pragmatic way, involving the senses, facing death by taking care that the deceased joins the ancestors, properly sent forth on the journey by those left behind who conduct themselves appropriately. The propriety of dress and setting relate intimately to their moral code for presentation of self to communicate effectively with community members and the deceased who is becoming an ancestor. Similarly, propriety of dress and setting applies to other life events and celebrations found in diaspora settings where the Kalabari continue to choose appropriately what they will wear.

JOANNE B. EICHER, PhD, is Regents Professor Emerita in the Department of Design, Housing, and Apparel at the University of Minnesota. She is coeditor of *The Anthropology of Dress and Fashion: A Reader*; coeditor of *The Visible Self: Global Perspectives on Dress, Culture, and Society*, 4th ed.; and editor in chief of the *Encyclopedia of World Dress and Fashion*.

IV

The Kalabari Diaspora

Chapter 22 concentrates on how the culturally authenticated dress and rituals from Kalabari heritage and life in Nigeria, stemming from their global trade history, continue as vital in the diaspora. Four examples I experienced in the United States from 1999 through 2018 document this persistent pride in being Kalabari. These examples typify the determination they and other diaspora groups continue to display with their customs, even when living away from their heritage birthplace.

22

The Kalabari Diaspora in the Twenty-First Century

Joanne B. Eicher

FOUR DIASPORA KALABARI events in which I participated after my 1991 fieldwork provide details about Kalabari enduring cultural practices in the United States.[1] In the diaspora, they continue to display their creativity and cultural authentication heritage while adapting items of global trade. These culturally authenticated artifacts and aesthetics distinguish them from other Nigerians and Africans.

I continued publishing with Erekosima and colleagues after 1991 and attended Kalabari events in 1999, 2004, 2008, and 2018. A 1999 *iriabo* celebration honored a mother's successful delivery of her child in Oakland, California. In 2004, in Los Angeles, California, a Kalabari National Association (KNA) reunion gala with dinner and dancing took place. Erekosima's funeral service occurred in 2008 near Baltimore, Maryland, as did the 2018 KNA event. News about these occasions came from Erekosima, until his death; his wife, Dinah; their sons, Dagogo and Onimi; and his extended family, including his brother, Telema, and cousin, Rose Barango. I briefly describe the iriabo celebration and Erekosima's funeral, and I elaborate on KNA in 2018, in which I participated more fully than in 2004. At each I observed how the Kalabari maintained their dress and ritual practices.

1999 IRIABO "COMING OUT"

The initial diaspora event was an iriabo party of buffet dinner and dance that Rose Barango (Buguma-born, but a resident of the San Francisco Bay area for many years) organized for her daughter, Otonye Amatoru (Lagos-born but

Bay area resident). Barango planned the event to follow as closely as possible as if practiced in Buguma (it was the second event she had held in the US for Amatoru's successful delivery of three daughters). The 1999 event was held in a rented church hall.

The evening began when a Kalabari woman, following custom, led Amorturo as iriabo with a procession behind her that included Amatoru's husband, their first daughter (two and a half years old), Barango, and other women. Amatoru dressed in *bite kpuluma*, a short beige madras wrapper with a madras length over her shoulder, and danced barefoot for observers to see her footsteps. Barango picked a green head tie, white blouse, and *bite sara* of a red and black *accraa* upper cloth and black-figured *blangidi* lower one. Amatoru's husband, Ipalibo, chose a black *doni* gown and black, decorated *ajibulu* hat. Amatoru later changed into a cream-colored, embroidered-velvet wrapper set and cream blouse. Kalabari men at the festive occasion wore *etibo* and doni ensembles, one with a white lace tunic and trousers. Women wore bite sara of varied textiles. Non-Kalabari guests selected contemporary fashions.

As in Buguma, the family attended church the next morning, choosing First Presbyterian Church of Oakland, California, to both give thanksgiving and baptize the baby daughter, Orusoso. Amatoru chose a red and green india bite sara with gold blouse and beaded hat (*sun*), a typical celebratory ensemble if held in Buguma. Her mother wore bite sara of white lace blouse, damask red wrappers, and a red head tie. Re-creating an iriabo event and thanksgiving demonstrated commitment to Kalabari cultural heritage by celebrating a successful birth, showing Amatoru off to her immediate community, and giving thanks at church. Culturally authenticated apparel displayed and reinforced Kalabari identity. Importantly, the textiles for Amatoru's wrapper sets came from her mother's trunk of gifts at her Kalabari marriage in Buguma.

2008 FUNERAL SERVICE

After Erekosima's death on August 1, 2008, I attended his funeral in his Hyattsville, Maryland, home church sanctuary, Church of the Living God. His family dressed his corpse in a white, india full-length men's doni gown with coral beads and uncovered head. His widow wore a white wrapper set. Kalabari male and female mourners dressed in Kalabari style with some women, family, and close friends, selecting matching wrappers (a common Nigerian practice for special events) for their bite sara ensembles, with white blouses.[2] Kalabari men primarily wore *woko* or etibo with trousers or wrappers (see chap. 13). Because Erekosima actively belonged to many community organizations involving international friends and acquaintances, several wore their cultural dress. Other guests dressed in Western fashions: suits, dresses, and pantsuits.

Following the ceremony, his body was transported to Nigeria for burial, with one service in Port Harcourt at his former church and another in Buguma at Seaview, his family home. Textiles from the cloth boxes of his extended family, as traditionally expected, decorated one large room. For these life celebrations, mourners dressed in Kalabari dress; his corpse again wearing the white velvet doni. Thus, in both the US and Nigeria, Kalabari dress customs prevailed.

THE 2018 KALABARI REUNION

Although I attended the Kalabari reunion in Los Angeles in 2004, I only observed the Saturday evening gala where Kalabari male and female attendees primarily wore Kalabari ensembles. In 2018, however, I participated in the complete weekend with Catherine Daly near Baltimore at the KNA Kalabari World Congress Inaugural (see program cover, fig. 22.1). Details follow with

Fig. 22.1. Program cover, Inaugural Kalabari World Congress and Heritage Celebration.

selected images. The weekend activities had 175 participants arriving from the US and Canada wearing Kalabari cultural dress. We arrived for the Friday reception and attended the Saturday business meetings and gala dinner (with program, dance, and masquerade), along with the Sunday morning second business meeting. Professor Anthony Saka, the event planner, and his wife (see fig. 22.2) hosted the Friday night reception with buffet dinner, featuring Kalabari food, at their home.

Daly and I saw out-of-town attendees arriving at the hotel on Friday for their reserved rooms. Women wore bite sara wrappers and blouses; men wore woko or etibo with trousers. They chose the same type of attire for the reception as they wore for travel. Women's wrapper textiles varied from Akwete to pelete bite. Orange had been designated as the featured Saturday gala color for women's blouses and head ties by "Ma" David, founder of the Kalabari Washington and Baltimore Kalabari Association or KASA (KASA is a local chapter of KNA, and the meaning of its acronym is inconsistent throughout the chapter). A head tie expert, a local Yoruba woman, was hired to meet women at the host's home. The women could choose to have the expert create their head ties from cloth they brought, stiff and opaque fabrics, taffeta-like, providing the body to hold imaginative shapes. The expert first placed a soft, resilient fabric on a woman's head; next, she folded the head tie cloth over it in pleats and twists, constructing an elegant headpiece, as shown in figure 22.3. On completion, she removed the head tie for the owner to take away to wear the next day, then began the process again for another woman.

Kalabari dress predominated for the Saturday morning business meeting; women wore bite sara, primarily Akwete wrappers with lace blouses and head ties of many styles and colors. Some women from the KASA club wore matching Akwete wrappers with "Kalabari Association of Washington/Baltimore Metroplex (KASA)" woven on them, paired with white blouses and red, silk-like head ties, as seen in figure 22.4. Simple jewelry ranged from coral to gold and silver necklaces and earrings, sometimes a pendant. Men generally dressed in a variety of etibo and doni upper garments worn with wrappers or trousers, but a couple of Kalabari chiefs (alapu) selected an ebu gown. Men primarily sported hats from top hats to straw boaters because Kalabari men wear hats both indoors and outside to complete a proper ensemble.

This reunion event moved beyond a social get-together. The business meeting indicated a commitment to people "at home" with an impressive formal agenda. The purpose included promoting community change and sponsoring medical missions. Their medical mission report listed an account of medical, dental, ophthalmic, and optical health services. Physicians, nurses, and others volunteered, paying for their own travel and expenses from North America to

Fig. 22.2.
Professor Anthony Saka, wearing a doni, Principal Event Planner and Moderator, Inaugural Kalabari World Congress and Heritage Celebration, 2018. His wife, Kienanga Saka, wears bite sara with orange blouse and head tie. Photo: Anthony Saka, 2018.

Fig. 22.3.
Hands of the head tie expert fold stiff orange fabric into pleats and twists on KASA's Commissioner for Culture, Mrs. Malinda Davies, 2018.

Fig. 22.4. Women wearing Kalabari Association of Wash-
ington/Baltimore wrappers and head ties. KWHC, 2018.

the designated Kalabari community. During the five-day mission, volunteers
saw 3,000 patients, performed 88 surgeries and 30 eye surgeries, distributed
1,000 pairs of eyeglasses, conducted 140 dental procedures, diagnosed 30 HIV
cases and 300 highly suspicious breast cancers, *and* helped with a difficult delivery of a pair of twins.

At the Saturday evening gala, attendees entered the dining room garbed
in elaborate, culturally authenticated dress. Women, encouraged to wear the
combined accraa (top) and blangidi (bottom) wrapper sets with orange head
ties and matching blouses, dominated the scene. Jewelry consisted of both
family heirloom necklaces and new fashions in coral. Because the Erekosima
family considers me a family member, Rose Barango dressed me in an orange
blouse, an accraa and blangidi wrapper set, and my own coral beads;[3] I chose
not to wear a head tie.[4] Men's outfits included etibos and wokos with wrappers

Right, Fig. 22.5. Two Kalabari women, Mrs. Lolo Agina-Obu (right) and
Mrs. Owanate Erekosima, at gala wearing family coral and "Ethnic Chic"
velvet, appliqué on velvet ground (madras showing at waist). KWHC, 2018.
Photo: M. Catherine Daly.

Top, Fig. 22.6. Shark masquerader at KNA/KWHC, 2018.

Left, Rose Barango in accraa (up wrapper) and blangidi (down) and orange
blouse. KNA/KWHC, 2018.

Fig. 22.8. Chief Diamond Tobin West (right) and Ibinabo
Erekosima (left) departing after KNA/KWHC, 2018.

or trousers; some wore the doni—one chief chose a top hat. Two chiefs wore
madras ebu gowns, one with a bowler and the other, a top hat. Men displayed
elegant silver and gold studs with their etibo and woko garments and coral
strands. Younger people chose some Kalabari ensembles and others, world
fashions—dresses, trousers, and shirts.

After dinner Daly and I showed a PowerPoint of our research, which was
well received. Medical mission donations were requested, and a shark masquerade was the finale and high point. As in Nigeria, the shark masquerader's
entourage consisted of men accompanying him. A disc jockey provided music
with a drummer alongside. Women also encircled him, some having changed
into iriabo short wrappers of madras or "ethnic chic" velvet with lace blouses
and family coral (see fig. 22.5); other audience members danced alongside in

their evening apparel. The masquerader in a madras wrapper had a folded piece of madras hanging over his protruding "tail," a Kalabari target symbol called *biaba* on his arm, and pelete bite covering his face, as shown in figure 22.6. Evening participants posed in their Kalabari apparel for formal portraits, like Barango (see fig. 22.7), with matching head tie and blouse and accraa and blangidi wrapper set.

A Sunday morning business meeting completed the weekend. Attendees, both in arriving and departing, comfortably wore Kalabari dress, just as Daly and I saw them both on the delta islands of Abonnema and Buguma and larger cities of Port Harcourt and Lagos, like the two men in figure 22.8. Kalabari dress throughout the weekend documented Kalabari involvement in global trade and cultural authentication wearing imported textiles in varied ensembles with coral jewelry and other accessories: a fitting culmination of our longitudinal research journey.

CONCLUSION

The Kalabari people in the diaspora treasure their cultural background and cherish their customs of dress and special celebrations arising from their trading history. Significantly, many North American residents for years, some educated in the United States and Canada, others in the United Kingdom and elsewhere, continually value being proudly Kalabari and maintaining their identity with material resources. Like other immigrants, they are American or Canadian citizens or have residency. They work in a wide variety of jobs and professions: academics, physicians (specialists like the first urogynecologist in North America), nurses, lawyers, entrepreneurs, academics, businesspeople, office and blue-collar workers, and students. They revel in their heritage. They stage cultural events, dress in Kalabari attire, eat Kalabari delicacies, and actively participate in Kalabari rituals and ceremonial practices.

Many cultural or ethnic groups like the Kalabari live in the United States in the twenty-first century and are committed to displaying their traditions.[5] Such ethnic groups share language and cultural heritage and practice foodways, dress, manners, etiquette, and decorum—sometimes daily, but especially for ceremonial and ritual events handed down through generations. Witnessing these four Kalabari diaspora events reinforced my data and fieldwork recollections from my research in the mangrove swamp islands. The 2018 Kalabari World Congress provided evidence of cultural authentication and global trade with artifacts incorporated into their lives from birth to death. Textiles accessed globally, from India and elsewhere; coral jewelry with Italian origins; and other items documented throughout this volume were prized, proudly worn, and displayed.

JOANNE B. EICHER, PhD, is Regents Professor Emerita in the Department of Design, Housing, and Apparel at the University of Minnesota. She is coeditor of *The Anthropology of Dress and Fashion: A Reader*; coeditor of *The Visible Self: Global Perspectives on Dress, Culture, and Society*, 4th ed.; and editor in chief of the *Encyclopedia of World Dress and Fashion*.

NOTES

1. Although I focus on dress in this chapter, the Kalabari diaspora carry food customs and many other cultural practices with them. Certain Kalabari dishes, such as the one made of mashed yams and plantain, called onunu, are frequently made for special meals in the US. In addition, Kalabari etiquette related to respect for elders continues to be taught, which I have seen practiced in the US. A younger person learns to carry parcels for someone older; for example, when Erekosima was in his fifties, I saw his cousin in his forties, a physician, on an occasion when we were in Washington, DC, grasp Erekosima's briefcase to carry it for him without request. Kalabari children and younger adults offered to carry parcels for me, even my purse. In Buguma, during fieldwork, Erekosima found himself in an awkward spot in 1984 as we left for a Buguma Centenary event. Because he was younger, and I was carrying a camera bag, he felt obligated to carry my bag. And as a male dressed in Kalabari garb, this was inappropriate. He solved the situation by calling for a "house boy" to accompany us for the evening to carry it.

2. This occurs for many life celebrations, whether weddings, birthdays, or funerals. The practice began with the Yoruba people of western Nigeria who call it aso ebi (meaning family cloth) and has become frequently used by others who called it a "uniform." See Nwafor (2011, 2013).

3. The Erekosima family listed me as a daughter in the funeral program of Chief I. D. Erekosima's sister, Elizabeth Ere J. T. Princewill (1900–2001) held on April 7, 2001, in Buguma. She was a wife of Amanyanabo Amachree VII, J. T. Princewill, who died February 1960. She resided for the rest of her life on the John-Bull compound where I stayed during my fieldwork.

4. Rose Barango also dressed me in bite sara for Erekosima's funeral, which she brought for me to wear.

5. Two examples in Minneapolis and St. Paul, Minnesota, are the Hmong and Somali peoples with whom colleagues and I conducted research. They continue distinctive food, dress, and other cultural practices in the twenty-first century. For Hmong, see Lynch, Detzner, and Eicher (1995, 1996) and Lynch (1995, 1999). For Somali, see Akou (2004, 2007, 2011).

Glossary

Abbi ikaki Fabric said to be from England with small diamond shapes.

Accraa Handwoven strips of fabric woven by Ewe men in Ghana on horizontal looms, so called because of the proximity to the capital of Ghana, Accra.

Adire A traditional Yoruba form of resist-dyeing art that involves applying a wax or cassava flour resist to a fabric and then coating the fabric with indigo dye. The resulting fabric is usually elaborately patterned and colored in rich shades of indigo.

Ajibulu Extravagantly decorated crescent-shaped hat worn by Kalabari men.

Aka Small, colored, inexpensive beads strung as bracelets and kneebands.

Akwete Strips of fabric handwoven by Igbo women from the Igbo town of Akwete, north of the Kalabari. Also called *akwa miri,* meaning "cloth of the water."

Alabo (plural, alapu) A Kalabari chief.

Amanyanabo Kalabari king.

Amasiri A motif meaning "tiger's paws," and a type of tightly woven cloth of indigo and white plaid used to create pelete bite.

Angra Miniature Christmas balls.

Ari i lekiri Personal cloth box for storing wrappers and other accessories.

Asa-ti A demeanor of nonchalant leisureliness or "dashing, sporty living."

Attigra Men's gown, usually of embroidered velvet, but early types were handwoven strip cloths.

Awu Red; also red camwood dye.

Buloo Blue.

Beri suai Earrings.

Bibi fe Literally "buying the mouth of the wife-to-be"—when the fiancé brings food to the intended bride's family.

Biokiri Family room (second room dressed for a funeral).

Bite igbe Family cloth box.

Bite kpuluma Short wrappers worn from waist to knee.

Bite pakri iwain Iria stage for girl wearing cloth when she starts her menses. Meaning "half the length of a piece of cloth."

Bite sara Wrapper worn from waist to ankle with a blouse.

Blangidi Heavy flannel fabric, said to be from the UK. Also called amatiye.

Buba Yoruba term for blouse; may be used instead of kappa.

Buo po Kneebands.

Buruma Indigo patterns painted on the body.

Corallium The genus of the deep-water precious coral, in contrast to reef and other corals. *C. rubrum*, a Mediterranean red coral, called Sardegna in Italy.

Doni Men's hip-length top garment, with buttonholes for studs, often of gabardine.

Duein The dead or ancestors.

Duein fubara Literally "the forehead of the dead." Screens with typically three wooden sculptures representing ancestors, found in the wari meeting house.

Ebre A common form of tying a woman's waist-to-ankle wrapper set from right over left, tucking the right side of the fabric in at the left side of the waist.

Ebu Men's full-length gown made of madras with square-shaped rear style of collar, worn with a matching madras wrapper underneath.

Ededapu Women who dress the Kalabari funeral beds.

Egwa (Igwa) A form of marriage arrangement involving a small bridewealth payment. Wife remains with her kin group, and children are considered hers. Contrasted to Iya marriage.

Etibo Men's hip-length top garment, similar to a shirt, usually of white cotton and one buttonhole for a stud.

Feni bene "Big" market day or every eighth day.

Fimate bite Cut-thread cloth, with only some weft threads removed.

Gom Striped cloth of undocumented origin, possibly England or India.

Hayes A stiff, silklike fabric imported from the UK for Nigerian women's headwraps.

Igodoye moru A somber indigo, red, and white cloth of narrow stripes used to create pelete bite patterns that are often asymmetrical.

Ikaki Tortoise.

Ikaki mgbe An indigo and white checked cloth used to create pelete bite patterns that are often geometrical and symmetrical.

Ikuta Beads.

Ikuta de Iria stage when wearing beads.

India Originally, heavy velvet embroidered with metallic thread, gold, or silver, imported from India; later, commercially produced, machine-embroidered velvets.

Injiri Kalabari name for imported plaid or checked Indian textile, called madras in US and "George" by Igbo people.

Iria The transitional stages of womanhood related to dress, involving sequential periods of female physical maturation.

Iriabo (plural, iriapu) A woman wearing a special ensemble, celebrating the birth of a child.

Iya The highest form of Kalabari marriage. Husband pays high bridewealth, wife moves to his compound, and children are considered his.

Iyi-iria Seclusion after the birth of a child. Mother and infant cared for and dressed in madras.

Jackreece bead Imported glass bead worn by Jackreece family members.

Kalabio Personal bedroom (first room decorated for a funeral).

Kappa Kalabari term for clothing, sometimes specifically referring to a blouse.

Kieni A warp-striped fabric named for the merchant who commonly imported it into Kalabariland.

Kilali Coral (see Corallium).

Konju Fina Iria stage when a young woman ties a waist cloth that indicates she is maturing.

Konju sua ye Put something on the waist.

Krukru (also kurukuru) Dark or black. Krukrubite means dark injiri cloth.

Loko (loko bite) A brightly colored striped silk fabric, often used in wrappers and to decorate funeral rooms.

Nunuma Bracelet; can mean wristwatch.

Okuru Raffia cloth made by the *Ndoki* people of southeastern Nigeria.

Onunga Strips of fabric handwoven by Yoruba from the western part of Nigeria.

Owamekaso A Kalabari female deity, said to have introduced trade and performed miracles with the aid of magic cloth.

Owuarusun Extravagant masquerade festival held after several yearly masquerades.

Pelete bite Cut-thread cloth, with both warp and weft threads removed to make a pattern.

Pina pina White.

Polo Wari's geographic location.

Rumal A one-yard-square cloth with borders and a central field filled with printed, woven, or embroidered motifs. Used by Muslim men to cover the head during prayer and to wipe the hands and face after washing in preparation for prayer. Madras Handkerchiefs and Ventapollam Handkerchiefs originated as a blend of the checked weave of Guinea Stuffs and the bordered format of rumals.

Sangolo Fish gill.

Sengi Hand-gathering, pleating, and rolling folds of a wrapper, means "wavelike."

Sibi dalaye Hair comb.

Sibifina bite Head tie cloth, usually worn by Kalabari women wearing bite sara.

Sibi suka ai Miniature Christmas balls.

Sinini Soft, lightweight commercial velvet.

Sun General term for a hat, varied elliptical shapes for men and women.

Wari or War Canoe House A lineage denoting social, economic, and defense unit supporting a main chief.

Wariku Formal parlor (third room decorated for a funeral).

Woko A top garment worn by Kalabari gentlemen. It is made of simply cut sturdy fabrics in neutral colors and hangs from the shoulders of the wearer, with a front placket and no collar. The woko is frequently worn with an injiri wrapper but can also be worn with trousers.

Wrapper One or two lengths of cloth wrapped horizontally from waist to ankles. Called *pagne* in French West Africa. Men wear one. Women wear two, a "down" wrapper first, with "up" wrapper placed on top of it.

Bibliography

Adams, Captain John. 1823. *Remarks on the Country Extending from Cape Palmas to the River Congo*. London: Routledge.

Akobo Data Ine. 1985. *Oral Traditions of Buguma: Iria Ceremony, a Case Study*. Ibadan, Nigeria: University of Ibadan.

Akou, Heather M. 2004. "Nationalism Without a Nation: Understanding the Dress of Somali Women in Minnesota." In *Fashioning Africa: Power and the Politics of Dress*, edited by Jean Allman, 50–63. Bloomington: Indiana University Press.

Akou, Heather M. 2007. "Building a New 'World Fashion': Islamic Dress in the Twenty-First Century." *Fashion Theory: The Journal of Dress, Body & Culture* 11 (4): 403–422.

Akou, Heather M. 2011. *The Politics of Dress in Somali Culture*. Bloomington: Indiana University Press.

Alagoa, Ebiegberi Joe. 1965. "The Settlement of the Niger Delta: Kuo Oral Traditions." Unpublished PhD diss., University of Wisconsin, Madison.

Alagoa, Ebiegberi Joe. 1966. "Ijo Origins and Migrations I." *Nigeria Magazine* 91:279–288.

Alagoa, Ebiegberi Joe. 1967a. "Ijo Origins and Migrations II." *Nigeria Magazine* 92:47–55.

Alagoa, Ebiegberi Joe. 1967b. "Delta Masquerades." *Nigeria Magazine* 93:144–165.

Alagoa, Ebiegberi Joe. 1970a. "Long Distance Trade and States in the Niger Delta." *Journal of African History* 2 (3): 405–419.

Alagoa, Ebiegberi Joe. 1970b. "Delta Masquerades." *Nigeria Magazine* 90:168–183.

Alagoa, Ebiegberi Joe. 1972. *A History of the Niger Delta: An Historical Interpretation of Ijo Oral Tradition*. Ibadan, Nigeria: Ibadan University Press.

Alagoa, Ebiegberi Joe. n.d. "God Is Mother: An Introduction to the Role of Women in Niger Delta History." Unpublished manuscript.

Allen, Jamey. 2006. Personal communication to Joanne B. Eicher via email.

Amalsad, D. M. 1926. "The Development of the Madras Handkerchief and Lungi or Kaily Industry in the Madras Presidency." Department of Industries Bulletin 22.

Appadurai, Arjun, ed. 1986. *The Social Life of Things: Commodities in Cultural Perspective.* Cambridge: Cambridge University Press.

Aronson, Lisa. 1980a. "History of Cloth Trade in the Niger Delta: A Study of Diffusion." *Journal of Textiles History* 2:89–107.

Aronson, Lisa. 1980b. "Patronage and Akwete Weaving." *African Arts* 13 (3): 62–66, 91.

Aronson, Lisa. 1982. "Popo Weaving in Southeastern Nigeria." *African Arts* 15 (3): 43–57, 90–91.

Aronson, Lisa. 1989. "Akwete Weaving: Tradition and Change." In *Man Does Not Go Naked: Textilien und handwerk aus Afrikanischen und andren landern,* vol. 29, edited by Renee Boser-Sarivaxevanis (Festschrift), Beate Englebrecht, and Bernhard Gardi, 197–207. Basel, Switzerland: Basler Beitrage zur Ethnologie.

Aronson, Lisa. 2001. "'We Weave It:' Akwete Weavers, Their Patrons, and Innovation in a Global Economy." In *Cloth Is the Center of the World: Nigerian Textiles, Global Perspectives,* edited by Susan Torntore, 17–28. St. Paul: Goldstein Gallery, University of Minnesota.

Asante, Molefi Kete. 1993. "Location Theory and African Aesthetics." In *The African Aesthetic: Keeper of Tradition,* edited by Kariamu Welsh-Asante. Westport, CN: Greenwood.

Ascione, Mauro. 2000. Interview by Susan Torntore, May.

Atkinson, Jane M. 1982. "Review: Anthropology." *Signs* 8, no. 2 (Winter): 236–258.

Balletta, Francesco, and Caterina Ascione. 1992. "I Gioielli del Mare: Coralli e Cammeri a Torre del Greco." In *Napoli, and Assessorato all' Artigianato, Torre del Greco,* edited by Dick Peerson. Napoli: Villa Campolieto.

Barbot, John. 1746a. "An Abstract of the Voyage to New Calabar River, or Rio Real, in the Year 1699." London: Printed by assignment from Messrs. Churchill for Henry Lintot and John Osborn.

Barbot, John. 1746b. "A Description of the Coasts of North and South Guinea." In *A Collection of Voyages and Travel,* 3rd ed., edited by Awnsham and John Churchill. London: Henry Lintot & John Osborne.

Barley, Nigel. 1987. "Kalabari Ancestral Screens as Pop Art." *Art History* 10, no. 3 (September): 369–380.

Barley, Nigel. 1988. *Foreheads of the Dead.* Washington, DC: Smithsonian Institute of African Art.

Bean, Susan. 1989. "Ghandi and Khadi, the Fabric of Indian Independence." In *Cloth and Human Organization*, edited by Jane Schneider and Annette Weiner. Washington, DC: Smithsonian Institution.

Belk, Russell W., and Melanie Wallendorf. 1997. "Of Mice and Men: Gender, Identity, and Collecting." In *The Material Culture of Gender: The Gender of Material Culture*, edited by Kenneth Ames and Katherine Martinez. Ann Arbor: University of Michigan Press.

Ben-Amos, Paula Girshick. 1980. *The Art of Benin*. London: Thames & Hudson.

Bhushan, Jamila Brij. 1958. *The Costumes and Textiles of India*. London: F. Lewis.

Bhushan, Jamila Brij. 1990. *Indian Embroidery*. New Delhi: Publications Division, Ministry of Information and Broadcasting.

Bickford, Kathleen E. 1995. "Knowing the Value of Pagne: Factory-Printed Textiles in Côte d'Ivoire." Unpublished PhD diss., Indiana University.

Biebuyck, Daniel P., and Nelly Van den Abbeele. 1984. *The Power of Headdresses: A Cross-Cultural Study of Forms and Functions*. Brussels, Belgium: Tendi, SA.

Blake, John W., ed. 1942. *Europeans in West Africa, 1450–1560*. London: Hakluyt Society.

Boahen, A. Adu. 1971. *The Horizon History of Africa*. New York: American Heritage.

Bourdieu, Pierre. 1977. *Outline of a Theory of Practice*. London: Cambridge University Press.

Bronfenbrenner, Urie. 1979. *The Ecology of Human Development*. Cambridge, MA: Harvard Press University.

Bronfenbrenner, Urie. 1989. "Ecological Systems Theory." *Annals of Child Development* 6:187–249.

Brunnschweiler, A. O. 1957. "History of the Madras Handkerchief Trade." Unpublished notes from Dakshinachitra, Madras.

Campbell, Andrew C. 1976. *The Coral Seas*. New York: Putnam.

Chaudhuri, K. N. 1978. *The Trading World of Asia and the English East India Company 1660–1760*. Cambridge, MA: Cambridge University Press.

Chib, Sukhdev Singh. 1978. *The Beautiful India: Uttar Pradesh*. Delhi: Light and Life.

Curtin, Phillip D. 1984. *Cross-Cultural Trade in World History*. Cambridge, MA: Cambridge University Press.

Dalrymple, William. 2019. *The Anarchy: The East India Company, Corporate Violence, and the Pillage of an Empire*. New York: Bloomsbury.

Daly, M. Catherine. 1982. Unpublished field notes.

Daly, M. Catherine. 1983a. "Dressing for Respect: Communicating Wealth, Status, and Prestige at Kalabari Funerals." Paper presented at Sixth Triennial Symposium of African Art, Norman, University of Oklahoma, April 7.

Daly, M. Catherine. 1983b. "The Kalabari Tradition of Iria: Examples of Cloth Use and the Female Life Cycle." Textile Council of the Minneapolis Institute of Arts Newsletter, September.

Daly, M. Catherine. 1983c. "Coming Out: The Process of an Appearance among the Kalabari." Paper presented at the 47th Annual Meeting of the Mid-American Art Association, St. Louis, MO, October 7–11.

Daly, M. Catherine. 1983d. "Abonnema's Centenary: An Occasion for All That Is Kalabari." Paper presented at the Annual Meeting of the African Studies Association, Boston, MA, December 7–10.

Daly, M. Catherine. 1984a. "Kalabari Female Appearance and the Tradition of Iria." PhD diss., University of Minnesota.

Daly, M. Catherine. 1984b. "Ah, a Real Kalabari Woman!: Toward a Reflexive Approach to the Study of Appearance." Paper presented at the Annual Meeting of the Society for Cross-Cultural Research, Boulder, CO, February 17–19.

Daly, M. Catherine. 1987. "Iriabo Appearance at Kalabari Funerals." *African Arts* 21, no. 1 (November): 58–61, 86.

Daly, M. Catherine, Joanne B. Eicher, and Tonye V. Erekosima. 1984. "Art and Decorum in Kalabari Dress." Paper presented at the African Studies Association Annual Meeting, Los Angeles, CA, October 25–28.

Daly, M. Catherine, Joanne B. Eicher, and Tonye V. Erekosima. 1986. "Male and Female Artistry in Kalabari Dress." *African Arts* 19, no. 3 (May): 48–51, 83.

Danforth, Loring. 1982. *The Funeral Rites of Rural Greece*. Princeton, NJ: Princeton University Press.

Dapper, Olfert. 1686. *Description de L'Afrique*. Amsterdam: Wolfgang, Waesberge, Boom, and van Someren.

Darish, Patricia. 1989. "Dressing for the Next Life: Raffia Textile Production and Use among the Kuba of Zaire." In *Cloth and Human Experience*, edited by Annette Weiner and Jane Schneider. Washington, DC: Smithsonian Institution Press.

Davidson, Basil. 1966. *Africa: History of a Continent*. London: Weidenfeld & Nicolson.

Davis, Ralph. 1954. "English Foreign Trade, 1660–1700." *Economic History Review* 7 (2): 150–166.

de Cardi, Le Comte C. N. 1899. "A Short Description of the Natives of the Niger Coast Protectorate with Some Account of Their Customs, Religion, Trade, Etc." In *West African Studies*, appendix I, edited by Mary Kingsley, 442–511. London: Macmillan.

Dhamija, Jasleen. 1989. "Indian Velvets." In *Handwoven Fabrics of India*, edited by Jasleen Dhamija and J. Jain. Ahmedabad: Mapin.

Dhamija, Jasleen. 1993. "Tilia Ruma, Asia Rumal, Real Madras Handkerchief: A Footnote to Global Textile Trade." Unpublished paper for Cloth and Economy Conference at Dartmouth College, Hanover, NH, April.

Dhamija, Jasleen. 1994. "The Geography of Indian Textiles: A Study of the Movement of Telia Rumal, Real Madras Handkerchief, George Cloth & Guinea Cloth." Paper presented at the Seminar on Real Madras Handkerchief: A Cross Cultural World Trade Perspective, Madras, India, February 5–7.

Dhamija, Jasleen. 2005. Personal communication to Sandra Lee Evenson.

Dike, Kenneth Onwuka. 1956. *Trade and Politics in the Niger Delta: 1830-1885: An Introduction to the Economics and Political History of Nigeria.* 1st ed. London: Oxford University Press.

Dike, Kenneth Onwuka. 1962. *Trade and Politics in the Niger Delta: 1830–1885: An Introduction to the Economics and Political History of Nigeria.* 2nd ed. London: Oxford University Press.

Dodwell, Henry. 1920. *Calendar of the Madras Despatches, 1744–1755.* Madras: Madras Government Press.

Douglas, Mary. 1982. *Natural Symbols: Explorations in Cosmology.* New York: Pantheon.

Douglas, Mary Tew, and Baron Isherwood. 1979. *The World of Goods.* New York: Basic Books.

Douglas Camp, Sokari. 2019. "Robin Horton Obituary." Guardian. https://www.theguardian.com/science/2019/dec/31/robin-horton-obituary. December 31, 2019.

Drewal, Henry John. 2012. "African Art and the Senses." *Sensory Studies.* (Originally published in *African Arts,* Summer 2005.) http://www.sensorystudies.org/sensorial-investigations/african-art-and-the-senses/.

Eicher, Joanne B. 1976. *Nigerian Handcrafted Textiles.* Ile-Ife, Nigeria: University of Ife Press.

Eicher, Joanne B. 1980a. "Design Components of West African Textile Production." In *The Nigerian Textile Industry: Resource Potentials,* edited by Samuel C. O. Ugbolue and P. O. Adegbile, 52–67. Kaduna, Nigeria: Textile Institute.

Eicher, Joanne B. 1980b. Unpublished field notes. March 12.

Eicher, Joanne B. 1980c. *African Wax Prints.* Public presentation at Corvallis, Oregon State University, May 18.

Eicher, Joanne B. 1981. "The Power of Dress." Lecture at University of Minnesota, St. Paul, November 12.

Eicher, Joanne B. 1981a. "Review: Textiles of Africa by Dale Idiens and K. G. Ponting." *African Arts* 15 (1): 17.

Eicher, Joanne B. 1981b. "Review: The Fabrics of Culture: The Anthropology of Clothing and Adornment by Justine M. Cordwell, Ronald A. Schwarz." *African Arts* 15 (1): 19–21.

Eicher, Joanne B. 1982a. *Identity as Symbolized by West African and Imported Textiles.* New York: Wenner Gren Foundation.

Eicher, Joanne B. 1982b. "Analyzing Dress of Other Cultures: The Concept of Cultural Authentication." Paper presented to Textile Educators Association of NSW, Sydney Australia, August 28.

Eicher, Joanne B. 1982c. "Influence of Changing Resources on Clothing, Textiles, and the Quality of Life: Dressing for Reality, Fun, and Fantasy." Paper presented at Association of College Professors of Textiles and Clothing, Central Region, St. Louis, MO, October 28–30.

Eicher, Joanne B. 1982d. "Future Dress and the Self." Paper presented at Textiles and Clothing Seminar, Iowa State University, Ames, November 19.

Eicher, Joanne B. 1983. Unpublished field notes.

Eicher, Joanne B. 1985. "A Kalabari Celebration (Buguma Centenary)." In *West Africa* (March 11): 463, 465.

Eicher, Joanne B. 1988a. Unpublished field notes.

Eicher, Joanne B. 1988b. "A Hierarchy of Cloth: A Kalabari Case Study." Paper presented at International Federation of Home Economics, University of Minnesota, Minneapolis, July 27.

Eicher, Joanne B. 1989. "Dress as Symbol of Identity of Kalabari Chief O.K. Isokariari." Paper presented at African Studies Association Meeting, Atlanta, GA, November 1–4.

Eicher, Joanne B. 1990. Unpublished field notes.

Eicher, Joanne B. 1992. "World Fashion and Its Impact on Ethnic and National Dress." Paper presented to Korean Society of Clothing and Textiles, Seoul, Korea, October.

Eicher, Joanne B. 1993. "Textile Trade and Masquerade Among the Kalabari of Nigeria." *Research and Exploration* 9 (2): 253–255.

Eicher, Joanne B. 1994. Textile Trade and Masquerade Among the Kalabari of Nigeria, Part I and II. DVD. Directed and produced by Joanne B. Eicher. Saint Paul, MN: University of Minnesota.

Eicher, Joanne B. 1995. "Cosmopolitan and International Dress." In *Dress and Identity*, edited by Mary Ellen Roach-Higgins, Joanne B. Eicher, and Kim K. P. Johnson, 461–462. New York: Fairchild.

Eicher, Joanne B. 1996. "Usi delle Perle in una Societa' Africana: i Kalabari della Nigeria [The Use of Beads in an African Society: The Kalabari of Nigeria]." *La Ricerca Folklorica* 34:35–42.

Eicher, Joanne B. 1997. "Social Change and Dress Among the Kalabari of Nigeria." In *Changing Rural Social Systems: Adaptation and Survival*, edited by N. Johnson and C. L. Wang, 223–244. East Lansing: Michigan State University Press.

Eicher, Joanne B. 1998. "Beaded and Bedecked Kalabari of Nigeria." In *Beads and Beadmakers: Gender, Material Culture and Meaning*, edited by Lidia Sciama and Joanne B. Eicher, 95–116. London: Berg.

Eicher, Joanne B. 2000. Interview by Elisha Renne. December 6.

Eicher, Joanne B. 2001a. "Dress, Gender, and the Public Display of Skin." In *Body Dressing*, edited by Joanne Entwistle and Elizabeth Wilson. Oxford, London: Berg.

Eicher, Joanne B. 2001b. "Preface: Cloth as the Center of My World." In *Cloth Is the Center of the World*, edited by Susan Torntore, 7–8. St. Paul: Goldstein Gallery, University of Minnesota.

Eicher, Joanne B. 2004a. "Kalabari Dress and Textiles in Two Rites of Passage." In *Life Passages: Women, Dress, and Culture*, editor unknown. Manhattan: Kansas State University, 19–27.

Eicher, Joanne B. 2004b. "Kalabari Splendor: Indian Gold-embroidery Velvets in Nigeria." In *Asian Embroidery*, edited by Jasleen Dhamija, 234–248. New Delhi, India: Abhinav.

Eicher, Joanne B. 2005. "Finishing Life with a Flourish: Kalabari Funerals in Nigeria as a Multi-Sensory Experience." Prepared Keynote [not presented] for Dress in Southern Africa, University of KwaZulu-Natal Pietermaritzburg, South Africa, August 5–7.

Eicher, Joanne B. 2006. "Kalabari Identity and Indian Textiles in the Niger Delta." In *Textiles from India*, edited by Rosemary Crill, 153–171. New Delhi: Seagull Books.

Eicher, Joanne B. 2009. "Kalabari Dress of Nigeria as an Example of Cultural Authentication." Paper presented at the Goldstein Museum of Design, University of Minnesota, Minneapolis, April 2.

Eicher, Joanne B. 2010. "Snapshot: Kalabari Peoples of Nigeria." In *Encyclopedia of World Dress and Fashion*, vol. 1: Africa, edited by Joanne B. Eicher and Doran Ross, 329–330. New York: Oxford University Press.

Eicher, Joanne B. 2014a. "India to Africa: Indian Madras and Kalabari Creativity." In *Global Textile Encounters, Ancient Textiles Series*, vol. 20, edited by Marie-Louise Nosch, Feng Zhao, and Lotika Varadarajan, 295–302. Oxford and Philadelphia: Oxbow Books.

Eicher, Joanne B. 2014b. "The Sacred Use of Indian Textiles by the Kalabari of Nigeria." In *Sacred Textiles*, edited by Jasleen Dhamija, 77–86, 94–105. New Delhi, India: Marg.

Eicher, Joanne B. 2015a. "Subtle and Spectacular: Dressing in Kalabari Style." In *Extravagences: Habits of Being 4*, edited by Paula Rabinowitz and Christina Giorcelli, 227–240. Minneapolis: University of Minnesota Press.

Eicher, Joanne B. 2015b. "Dress, the Senses, and the Public, Private, and Secret Selves." Paper presented at the Fashion and the Senses Symposium, London, London College of Fashion, March 27.

Eicher, Joanne B., M. Catherine Daly, and Tonye V. Erekosima. 1985. "The Art of Celebration in a Kalabari Centenary." Paper presented at the Annual Meeting of the African Studies Association, New Orleans, LA, November.

Eicher, Joanne B., and Tonye V. Erekosima. 1980. "Distinguishing Non-Western
    Dress from Western Dress: The Concept of Cultural Authentication." Paper
    presented to the Association of College Professors of Textiles and Clothing,
    Washington, DC.
Eicher, Joanne B., and Tonye V. Erekosima. 1981. "The Simple Tools and Complex
    Designs of Kalabari Textile Artists." Paper presented at the 24th Annual Meet-
    ing of the African Studies Association, Bloomington, IN, October 21–24.
Eicher, Joanne B., and Tonye V. Erekosima. 1983. "The Art and Socio-Economic
    Significance of Kalabari Funerals." Paper presented at the Sixth Triennial
    Symposium on African Art, University of Oklahoma, Norman, April 7.
Eicher, Joanne B., and Tonye V. Erekosima. 1987. "Kalabari Funerals: Celebration
    and Display." *African Arts* 21, no. 1 (November): 38–45, 87.
Eicher, Joanne B., and Tonye V. Erekosima. 1988. "Kalabari Headdresses
    of Power." Paper presented at African Studies Association, Chicago, IL,
    October 28.
Eicher, Joanne B., and Tonye V. Erekosima. 1989. "Kalabari Funeral Rooms as
    Handicraft and Ephemeral Art." In *Man Does Not Go Naked: Textilien und
    handwerk aus Afrikanischen und andren landern*, vol. 29, edited by Renee Boser-
    Sarivaxevanis (Festschrift), Beate Englebrecht, and Bernhard Gardi, 197–207.
    Basel, Switzerland: Basler Beitrage zur Ethnologie.
Eicher, Joanne B., and Tonye V. Erekosima. 1993. "Taste and 19th Century Pat-
    terns of Textile Use among the Kalabari of Nigeria." Paper presented at Cloth,
    the World Economy, and the Artisan: Textile Manufacturing and Marketing in
    South Asia and Africa, 1780–1950, Dartmouth College, Hanover, NH.
Eicher, Joanne B., and Tonye V. Erekosima. 1995. "Why Do They Call It Kalabari?
    Cultural Authentication and the Demarcation of Ethnic Identity." In *Dress and
    Ethnicity*, edited by Joanne B. Eicher, 139–164. Oxford/Washington, DC: Berg.
Eicher, Joanne B., and Tonye V. Erekosima. 1996. "Indian Textiles in Kalabari
    Funerals." *Asian Art and Culture* 9:68–79.
Eicher, Joanne B., and Tonye V. Erekosima. 1997. "Bronfenbrenner's Ecological
    Systems Model and the Use of Imported Madras Cloth Among the Kalabari."
    Family and Consumer Sciences Research Journal 25 (4): 413–432.
Eicher, Joanne B., and Tonye V. Erekosima. 2002. "Fitting Farewells: The Fine
    Art of Kalabari Funerals." In *Ways of the Rivers: Arts of the Niger Delta*, edited
    by Martha Anderson and Philip Peek. Los Angeles, CA: Fowler Museum of
    Cultural History, UCLA, 2002.
Eicher, Joanne B., Tonye V. Erekosima, and Carl Liedholm. 1982. "Cut and
    Drawn: Textile Work from Nigeria." *Craft International* 2 (Summer): 16–20.
Eicher, Joanne B., and Tonye V. Erekosima, with Otto C. Thieme. 1982. "Pelete
    Bite: Kalabari Cut-Thread Cloth." Exhibit Catalog. Goldstein Gallery, Univer-
    sity of Minnesota, May.

Eicher, Joanne B., and Sandra L. Evenson. 2008. *The Visible Self: Global Perspectives on Dress, Culture, and Society.* 3rd ed. New York: Fairchild.

Eicher, Joanne B., and Sandra L. Evenson. 2014. *The Visible Self: Global Perspectives on Dress, Culture, and Society.* 4th ed. New York: Fairchild.

Eicher, Joanne B., and Kim A. Miller. 1994. "Dress and the Public, Private, and Secret Self: Revisiting the Model." International Textiles and Apparel Association Annual Meeting: Proceedings, 145. Minneapolis, MN, October.

Eicher, Joanne B., and Mary Ellen Roach-Higgins. 1992. "Describing Dress: A System for Classifying and Defining." In *Dress and Gender: Making and Meaning,* edited by Ruth Barnes and Joanne B. Eicher. Oxford: Berg.

Eicher, Joanne B., and Barbara Sumberg. 1995. "World Fashion, Ethnic, and National Dress." In *Dress and Ethnicity,* edited by Joanne B. Eicher, 295–306. Oxford/Washington, DC: Berg.

Eicher, Joanne B., Sandra L. Evenson, and Hazel A. Lutz, H.A. 2000. *The Visible Self: Global Perspectives on Dress, Culture and Society.* 2nd ed. New York: Fairchild.

Ejituwu, Nkparom Claude. 1971. *Christian Mission in Kalabari: 1875–1885.* Madison: University of Wisconsin–Madison.

Emery, Irene. 1966. *Primary Structures of Fabrics: An Illustrated Classification.* Washington, DC: Textile Museum, 1966, 247–248.

Enabulele, Arlene Bette. 1985. "The Role of Women's Associations in Nigeria's Development: Social Welfare Perspective." In *Women in Nigeria Today,* edited by Women in Nigeria. Bath, England: Bath Press.

Ereks (Erekosima), Tonye V. 1973. "Kalabari Categories of the Self: A Philosophical Extrapolation in Cultural Dynamism." *Oduma* 1, no. 1 (October): 21–27.

Erekosima, Tonye V. 1979. "The 'Tartans' of Buguma Women: Cultural Authentication." Paper presented at African Studies Association Conference, Los Angeles, CA, October 31.

Erekosima, Tonye V. 1982. *The Use of Apparel and Accessories for Expressing Status in Nigerian Societies: The Kalabari Case Studied as an Education Technology.* Port Harcourt, Nigeria: Instructional Resources Centre, University of Port Harcourt.

Erekosima, Tonye V. 1984. *A Hundred Years of Buguma History in Kalabari Culture.* Port Harcourt, Nigeria: Haig-Betanova.

Erekosima, Tonye V. 1988. "Reply to Nigel Barley." Unpublished message.

Erekosima, Tonye V. 1989. "Analysis of Learning Resource for Political Integration Applicable to Nigerian Secondary School Social Studies: The Case of Kalabari Men's Traditional Dress." PhD diss., Catholic University of America.

Erekosima, Tonye V. 1991. "The Changing Patterns of Status among Kalabari Men." Paper presented at a symposium marking the 1984 Centenary Anniversary of the founding of Buguma City.

Erekosima, Tonye V. n.d. "The Color White." Unpublished paper.

Erekosima, Tonye V., and Joanne B. Eicher. 1980. "Kalabari Men's Dress: A Sophisticated Response to Cultural Contact." Paper read at the African Studies Association, Philadelphia, PA, October 15.

Erekosima, Tonye V., and Joanne B. Eicher. 1981. "Kalabari Cut Thread Cloth: An Example of Cultural Authentication." *African Arts* 14, no. 2 (February): 48–51, 87.

Erekosima, Tonye V., and Joanne B. Eicher. 1994. "The Aesthetics of Men's Dress of the Kalabari of Nigeria." In *Aesthetics of Textiles and Clothing: Advancing Multi-Disciplinary Perspectives*, edited by Marilyn DeLong and Ann Marie Fiore. Monument, CO: ITAA.

Erekosima, Tonye V., W. H. Kio Lawson, and Obeleye MacJaja, eds. 1991. *Buguma 1984 Centenary Symposia on Kalabari (Under the auspices of the Buguma Centenary Committee 1984)*. Lagos: Sibon.

Evenson, Sandra L. 1991. "The Manufacture of Madras in South India and Its Export to West Africa: A Case Study." Master's thesis, University of Minnesota.

Evenson, Sandra L. 1994. "A History of Indian Madras Manufacture and Trade: Shifting Patterns of Exchange." PhD diss., University of Minnesota.

Evenson, Sandra L. 2007. "Indian Madras Plaids as Real India." In *Dress Sense: Emotional and Sensory Experiences of the Body and Clothes*, edited by Donald Clay Johnson and Helen Bradley Foster, 96–108. London: Berg.

Francis, Peter, Jr. 1994. *Beads of the World: A Collector's Guide with Price Reference*. Atglen, PA: Schiffer.

Frölich, D. B. 1993. Unpublished notes, held at Dakshinachitra, Madras.

Frölich, N. 1981. *The Story of the Firm Frölich, Brunnschweiler & Cie*. Manchester: A. Brunnschweiler & Cie.

Fubara-Manuel, Alaye. 1977. *The Period of King Amachree in Kalabari History*. Port Harcourt, Nigeria: Labomie.

Fubara-Manuel, Alaye. n.d. "A History of Kalabari Part I: Kalabari in ObuAmafa from about 1370–1400 AD." Unpublished paper. Port Harcourt, Nigeria.

Geary, Sir William M. N. 1927. Nigeria Under British Rule. London: Routledge.

Gell, Alfred. 1986. "Newcomers to the World of Goods: Consumption among the Muria Gonds." In *The Social Life of Things: Commodities in Cultural Perspective*, edited by Arjun Appadurai, 110–138. Cambridge: Cambridge University.

Geurts, Kathryn. 2002. *Culture and the Senses: Bodily Ways of Knowing in an African Community*. Berkeley: University of California Press.

Gupta, Charu Smita. 1996. *Zardozi: Glittering Gold Embroidery*. New Delhi, India: Abhinav.

Guyer, Jane. 1995. "Wealth in People, Wealth in Things—Introduction." *The Journal of African History* 36: 83–90.

Hamilton, Jean A., and James W. Hamilton. 1989. "Dress as a Reflection and Sustainer of Social Reality: A Cross-Cultural Perspective." *Clothing and Textile Research Journal* 7 (2): 16–22.

Hannerz, Ulf. 1998. "Transnational Research." In *Handbook of Methods in Cultural Anthropology*, edited by H. Russell Bernard, 235–256. Walnut Creek, CA: Sage.

Hansen, Karen Tranberg. 2017. "From Grandmother's Dress to the Fashion Runway: Chitenge Styles in Zambia." In *African-Print Fashion Now! A Story of Taste, Globalization, and Style*, edited by Suzanne Gott, Kristyne Loughran, Betsy D. Quick, and Leslie Rabine, 160–162. Los Angeles: Fowler Museum, UCLA.

Hansen, Karen Tranberg. 2019. "Not African Enough? Global Dynamics and Local Contestations over Dress Practice and Fashion Design in Zambia." *ZoneModa Journal* 9 (2): 1–15.

Hardin, Kris. 1993. *The Aesthetics of Action*. Washington, DC: Smithsonian Institution.

Haynes, Douglas. 1986. "The Dynamics of Continuity in Indian Domestic Industry: Jari Manufacture in Surat, 1900–1947." *Indian Economic and Social History Review* 23 (2): 127–149.

Higgins, J. P. P. 1993. *Cloth of Gold: A History of Metalized Textiles*. London: Lurex.

Hill, Samuel. 1927. *Catalogue of the Home Miscellaneous Series of the India Office Records* 6:1631–1664. London: His Majesty's Stationery Office.

Horton, Robin. 1960a. "The Gods as Guests: An Aspect of Kalabari Religious Life." *Nigeria Magazine*, special publication.

Horton, Robin. 1960b. "New Year in the Delta." *Nigeria Magazine* 67:256–297.

Horton, Robin. 1962. "The Kalabari World-View." *Africa* 32:197–220.

Horton, Robin. 1963. "The Kalabari Ekine Society: A Borderland of Religion and Art." *Africa* 33:94–114.

Horton, Robin. 1965. "Kalabari Sculpture." Apapa, Nigeria: Department of Antiquities, Federal Republic of Nigeria.

Horton, Robin. 1967. "The Tortoise Masquerade." *Nigeria Magazine* 94:226–239.

Horton, Robin. 1969a. "Types of Spirit Possession in Kalabari Religion." In *Spirit Mediumship and Society in Africa*, edited by John Beattie and John Middleton, 14–49. New York: Africana.

Horton Robin. 1969b. "From Fishing Village to City State." In *Man in Africa*, edited by Mary Douglas and Phyllis M. Kaberry. London: Tavistock.

Horton, Robin. 1969c. "Ikpataka Dogi: A Kalabari Funeral Rite." *African Notes* 5 (3): 57–72.

Horton, Robin. 1970. "Kalabari Culture and History." *African Notes* 2:5–7.

Horton, Robin. 1971. "A Hundred Years of Change in Kalabari Religion." In *Black Africa*, edited by John Middleton. New York: MacMillan.

Horton, Robin. 1975. "Ekineba: A Forgotten Myth." *Oduma* 2:33–36.

Hutchinson, Thomas Joseph. 1858. *Impressions of West Africa*. London: Longman, Brown, Green Longman, and Roberts.

Iacobelli, Paolo. 2000. Interview by Susan Torntore. April.

Ingold, Tim, David Riches, and James Woodburn. 1991. *Hunters and Gatherers, Volume II: Property, Power, and Ideology*. London: Berg.

Irwin, John. 1955. "Indian Textile Trade in the Seventeenth Century: Western India." *Journal of Indian Textile History* 1:4–33.

Irwin, John. 1956. "Indian Textile Trade in the Seventeenth Century: Coromandel Coast." *Journal of Indian Textile History* 2:24–42.

Irwin, John, and Margaret Hall. 1973. *Indian Embroideries*. Ahmedabad: S. R. Bastikar.

Irwin, John, and P. R. Schwartz. 1966. *Studies in Indo-European Textile History*. Ahmedabad: Calico Museum of Textiles.

Isokariari, Sir (Chief) Okoma Kio. 2012. *My Mission: Autobiography*. London: 1st Byte.

Isokariari, Tubonimi J. 1983. "The Legacy of Madam Orupumbu Tariah of Buguma: A Biographical Essay." BA diss., University of Port Harcourt, Nigeria.

Iyalla, B. S. 1968. "Womanhood in the Kalabari." *Nigeria Magazine* 98:216–224.

Jackreece, Telemate. 2006. Personal communication with Joanne B. Eicher via email.

Jalees, Farida. 1989. *Glittering Threads: A Socio-Economic Study of Women Zari Workers*. Ahmedabad: Sewa Bharat.

Jarmon, Charles. 1988. *Nigeria: Reorganization and Development Since Mid-20th Century*. New York: E. J. Brill.

Jenewari, Charles E. W. 1973. "Owu Aru Sun: Kalabari's Most Colourful Ceremony." *Oduma* 1, no. 1 (October): 27–31.

Jenewari, Charles E. W. 1976. "The Identification of Ethnolinguistic Units in Early European Records: The Case of Kalabari." *Journal of Niger Delta Studies* 1:9–18.

JohnBull, Enefaa W. 2004. *Ikiri JohnBull of Kalabari (1810–1893) in the Niger Delta*. Port Harcourt, Nigeria: Sonite.

JohnBull, Enefaa W. 2005. *Omekwe Horsfall of Kalabari (1817–1895) in the Niger Delta*. Port Harcourt, Nigeria: Sonite.

JohnBull, Enefaa W. 2012. *Owu Aru Suun Alali: The Kalabari Masquerade Festival*. Port Harcourt, Nigeria: Sonite.

Jones, Gwilliam Iwan. 1963. *The Trading States of the Oil Rivers: A Study of Political Development in Eastern Nigeria*. London: Oxford University Press.

Jones, Gwilliam Iwan. 1965. "Time and Oral Tradition with Special Reference to Eastern Nigeria." *Journal of African History* 6:153–160.

Kingsley, Mary Henrietta. 1899. *West African Studies*. London: Macmillan.

Kingsley, Mary Henrietta. 1964. *West African Studies*. 3rd ed. London: Taylor & Francis.

Kobayashi, Kazuo. 2019. *Indian Cotton Textiles in West Africa: African Agency, Consumer Demand and the Making of the Global Economy, 1750–1850*. London: Palgrave Macmillan.

Laan, H. Laurens van der. 1983. "A Swiss Family Firm in West Africa: A. Brunnschweiler & Co., 1929–1959." *African Economic History* 12:287–97. https://doi.org/10.2307/3601329.

Lamb, Venice. 1975. *West African Weaving*. London: Duckworth.

Lawson, Philip. 1993. *The East India Company: A History*. London: Longman.

Leis, N. 1974. "Women in Groups: Ijaw Women's Associations." In *Woman, Culture, and Society*, edited by Michelle Zimbalist Rosaldo and Louise Lamphere, 223–242. Stanford, CA: Stanford University Press.

Leis, Philip. 2002. "Preface." In *Ways of the Rivers: Arts of the Niger Delta*, edited by Martha Anderson and Philip Peek. Los Angeles: Fowler Museum of Cultural History, University of California, Los Angeles.

Leung, Terence. 2000. Personal communication with Susan Torntore.

Lewin, Kurt. 1935. *A Dynamic Theory of Personality*. New York: McGraw-Hill.

Liu, Robert K. 1995. *Collectible Beads: A Universal Aesthetic*. Vista, CA: Ornament.

Liverino, Basilio. 1989a. "Red Coral: Jewel of the Sea." In *Industrial History* series, edited by Edizioni Analisi, translated by J. H. Johnson. Bologna, Italy: Analisi.

Liverino, Basilio. 1989b. *Il Corallo: Esperienze e Ricordi di un Corallaro*. Napoli, Italy: Analisi.

Liverino, Basilio. 1998. *Il Corallo: Dalle Origini ai Nostri Giorni*. Napoli, Italy: Arte Tipographia Editrice.

Liverino, Basilio. 2000. Interview by Susan Torntore. April.

Lutz, Hazel. 1993. "The Continuing Tradition of Indian Ornate Velvets." Unpublished master's thesis. University of Minnesota, St. Paul.

Lutz, Hazel. 2001. "Designed for Wrapping: Design Changes in Indian Zari-Embroidered Velvets Produced for West Africa." Wrapped and Draped: Alternative Fashion Symposium, St. Paul, MN.

Lutz, Hazel. 2003. "Design and Tradition in an India-West Africa Trade Textile: Zari-Embroidered Velvets." Unpublished PhD diss., University of Minnesota.

Lutz, Hazel. 2006. "Changing Twentieth-Century Textile Design and Industry Structure in the India-West Africa Embroidery Trade." In *Textiles from India: The Global Trade*, edited by Rosemary Crill, 173–194. Oxford: Seagull.

Lutz, Hazel, and Joanne B. Eicher. 1996. "Gold Embroidered Velvets: From the Indian Embroiderer's Frame to the West African Dressed Body." Paper presented at the 25th Annual Conference on South Asia, Madison, WI, October.

Lynch, Annette. 1995. "Hmong American New Year's Dress: The Display of Ethnicity." In *Dress and Ethnicity*, edited by Joanne B. Eicher. Oxford: Berg.

Lynch, Annette. 1999. *Dress, Gender, and Cultural Change: Asian American and African American Rites of Passage.* Oxford and New York: Berg.

Lynch, Annette, Daniel Detzner, and Joanne B. Eicher. 1995. "Hmong American New Year Rituals: Generational Bonds Through Dress." *Clothing and Textiles Research Journal* 13 (2): 111–120.

Lynch, Annette, Daniel Detzner, and Joanne B. Eicher. 1996. "Hmong American New Year Rituals: Transmission and Reconstruction of Gender Through Dress." *Clothing and Textiles Research Journal* 14 (4): 257–266.

Maclean, C. D., ed. 1982. *Glossary of the Madras Presidency: Containing a Classification of Terminology, a Gazetteer, and Economic Dictionary of the Province and Other Information, the Whole Arranged Alphabetically and Indexed.* Reprinted by Asian Educational Services, New Delhi, 372.

Madume, Victor Solomon. 1976. "Owu Tradition: An Embodiment of Kalabari Mythology, Ritualism and Aesthetics." BA thesis, University of Nigeria: Nsukka.

March, Kathryn S., and Rachelle L. Taqqu. 1986. *Women's Informal Associations in Developing Countries: Catalysts for Change?* Boulder, CO: Westview.

Mazza, Grazia. 2000. Interview by Susan Torntore. Torre del Greco, Italy, May 11.

McNaughton, Patrick R. 1982. "The Shirts That Mande Hunters Wear." *African Arts* 15, no. 3 (May): 54–58, 91.

Mehta, R. N. 1956. "The Historical Evidence of Two Jain Velvets from the First Quarter of the 18th Century." *Journal of Indian Textile History* 2.

Mehta, Rustam J. 1968. *The Handicrafts and Industrial Arts of India.* Bombay: D. B. Taraporevala Sons.

Michelman, Susan O. 1987. "Kalabari Female and Male Aesthetics: A Comparative Visual Analysis." Unpublished master's thesis. University of Minnesota, St. Paul.

Michelman, Susan O. 1990. "Forum." *Clothing and Textiles Research Journal* 8 (1): 203–209.

Michelman, Susan O. 1992. "Dress in Kalabari Women's Organizations." PhD diss., University of Minnesota.

Michelman, Susan O., and Joanne B. Eicher. 1995. "Dress and Gender in Kalabari Women's Societies." *Clothing and Textiles Research Journal* 13 (2): 121–130.

Michelman, Susan O., and Tonye V. Erekosima. 1992. "Kalabari Dress: Visual Analysis and Gender Implications." In *Dress and Gender: Making and Meaning in Cultural Context*, edited by Ruth Barnes and Joanne B. Eicher. Oxford: Berg.

Nielsen, Ruth. 1980. *African Wax-Prints.* Corvallis: Oregon State University and Horner Museum.

Nilson, Per. 2000. Interview by Susan Torntore at International Bead Expo, Miami, FL, May 26.

Nissim, J. (1900) 1976. "A Monograph on Wire and Tinsel in the Bombay Presidency." In *Art in Industry through the Ages: Monograph Series on Bombay Presidency.* New Delhi: Navrang, 287–299, front piece, plates 1–18.

Nwafor, Okechukwu. 2011. "The Spectacle of Aso Ebi in Lagos, 1990–2008." *Postcolonial Studies* 14 (1): 45–62.

Nwafor, Okechukwu. 2013. "The Fabric of Friendship: Aso Ebi and the Moral Economy of Amity in Nigeria." *African Studies* 72 (1): 1–18.

Ogbonnaya, Obioma. 2020. "Robin Horton, A Quintessential Professor Takes Final Exit." This Day Live. January 17, 2020. https://www.thisdaylive.com /index.php/2020/01/17/robin-horton-a-quintessential-professor-takes-final -exit/.

Ogilby, John. 1970. *Africa, Being an Accurate Description.* London: Translation of Dapper.

Ortner, Sherry B. 1974. "Is Female to Male as Nature Is to Culture?" In *Woman, Culture, and Society,* edited by Michelle Zimbalist Rosaldo and Louise Lamphere. Stanford, CA: Stanford University Press.

Perani, Judith. 1992. "The Cloth Connection: Patrons and Producers of Hausa and Nupe Prestige Strip-Weave." In *History, Design, and Craft in West African Strip-Woven Cloth: Papers presented at the Symposium Organized by the National Museum of African Art, Smithsonian Institution, February 18, 1988.* Washington, DC: National Museum of African Art, 95–112.

Pereia, Duarte Pacheco. 1937. *Esmeraldo de situ orbis.* Translated and edited by George Herbert Tinley Kimble. London: Hakluyt Society.

Petgrave, Manuella Daba [Manuella Daba BobManuel-Meyer Petgrave]. 1992. "Indian Madras in Kalabari Culture." Master's thesis, University of Minnesota.

Piaget, Jean, and Bàrbel Inhelder. (1948) 1967. *The Child's Conception of Space.* Translated by F. J. Langdon and J. L. Lunzer. New York: Norton.

Piaget, Jean, and Bàrbel Inhelder. 1969. *The Psychology of the Child.* New York: Basic Books.

Picton, John. 1992. "Tradition, Technology, and Lurex: Some Comments on Textile History and Design in West Africa." In *History, Design, and Craft in West African Strip-Woven Cloth: Papers Presented at the Symposium Organized by the National Museum of African Art, Smithsonian Institution, February 18, 1988.* Washington, DC: National Museum of African Art, 13–52.

Plankensteiner, Barbara, and Nath Mayo Adediran, eds. 2010. *African Lace: A History of Trade, Creativity and Fashion in Nigeria.* Ghent, Netherlands: Snoek.

Pokornowski, Ila Pelkey. 1974. "Social Significance of African Beads: Case Studies of the Yoruba and Bini Peoples." Master's thesis, Michigan State University.

Renne, Elisha. 1985. "Pelete Bite: Motifs and Meaning." Master's thesis, University of Minnesota.

Renne, Elisha. 2001. "'Our Great Mother . . . Tied This Cloth': Pelete-Bite Cloth, Women, and Kalabari Identity." In *Cloth Is the Center of the World*, edited by Susan Torntore, 29–41. St. Paul: Goldstein Gallery, University of Minnesota.

Renne, Elisha, and Joanne B. Eicher. 1994. "The Transformation of Men into Masquerades and Indian Madras into Masquerade Cloth in Buguma, Nigeria." In *Contact, Crossover, Continuity: Proceedings of the Fourth Biennial Symposium of the Textile Society of America*, 45–62. Los Angeles: UCLA Fowler Museum of Cultural History.

Ricci, Franco Maria. *FMR: The magazine of Franco Maria Ricci*, all editions and formats. New York: Franco Maria Ricci International, Milan, 1984–2009.

Ricci, Franco Maria. 1985. *FMR: The magazine of Franco Maria Ricci* 4, no. 7 (Christmas).

Roach, Mary Ellen, and Joanne B. Eicher. 1973. *The Visible Self: Global Perspectives on Dress, Culture, and Society*. Englewood Cliffs, NJ: Prentice Hall.

Ryder, Alan Frederick Charles. 1969a. "Dutch Trade on the Nigerian Coast During the 17th Century." *Journal of the Historical Society of Nigeria* 3:195–210.

Ryder, Alan Frederick Charles. 1969b. *Benin and the Europeans, 1485–1897*. New York: Humanities.

Salter, Eric. 2000. Interview by Susan Torntore at International Bead Expo, Miami, FL, May 27.

Schneider, Jane, and Annette B. Weiner. 1986. "Cloth and the Organization of Human Experience." *Current Anthropology* 27 (2): 178–184.

Schwartzberg, J. E., ed. 1992. *A Historical Atlas of South Asia: Second Impression*. New York: Oxford University Press.

Shusterman, Richard. 1996. *Practicing Philosophy: Pragmatism and the Philosophical Life*. 1st ed. London: Routledge.

Shusterman, Richard. 2012. *Thinking Through the Body: Essays in Somaesthetics*. Cambridge: Cambridge University Press.

Sieber, Roy. 1972. *African Textiles and Decorative Arts*. New York: Museum of Modern Art.

Silverberg, Robert. 1965. *The World of Coral*. New York: Duell, Sloan, and Pearce.

Smart, Ellen S., and Dale C. Gluckman. 1989. "Cloth of Luxury: Velvet in Mughal India." In *Quest of Themes and Skills—Asian Textiles*. Bombay: Marg.

Smith, Fred T., and Joanne B. Eicher. 1982. "The Systematic Study of African Dress and Textiles." *African Arts* 15 (3): 28.

Spencer, Anne M. 2001. "Of Polominats and Alphabets: The Eicher Collection of Wax Printed Cloths." In *Cloth Is the Center of the World: Nigerian Textiles, Global Perspectives*, edited by Susan J. Torntore. St. Paul: Goldstein Gallery, University of Minnesota.

Stazione Esperimentale del Vetro. 1998. Report to Joanne B. Eicher. Venice, Italy, December 18.

Steiner, Christopher B. 1994. *African Art in Transit*. Cambridge: Cambridge University Press.

Stewart, Susan. 1984. *On Longing: Narratives of the Miniature, the Gigantic, the Souvenir, the Collection*. Baltimore: Johns Hopkins University Press.

Subrahmanyam, Sanjay. 1993. *The Portuguese Empire in Asia 1500–1700*. London: Longman.

Sumberg, Barbara. 2010. *Textiles: Collection of the Museum of International Folk Art*. Layton, UT: Gibbs Smith.

Sumberg, Barbara, ed. 2011. *Young Brides, Old Treasures: Macedonian Embroidered Dress*. Santa Fe, NM: Museum of International Folk Art.

Sumberg, Barbara, and Joanne B. Eicher. 1995. "India and West Africa: Transformation of Velvets." In *The Woven Silks of India*, edited by Jasleen Dhamija, 141–154. Bombay, India: Marg.

Sundstrom, Lars. 1974. *The Exchange Economy of Pre-Colonial Tropical Africa*. New York: St. Martin's.

Swarup, Shanti. 1968. *5000 Years of Arts and Crafts in India and Pakistani*. Bombay: D. B. Taraporevala Sons.

Talbot, Percy Amaury. 1926. *The Peoples of Southern Nigeria*. London: Oxford University Press.

Talbot, Percy Amaury. 1967. *Tribes of the Niger Delta: Their Religions and Customs*, 2nd ed. New York: Barnes and Noble.

Tamuno, Tekena N. 1980. "King Amachree I of Kalabari." In *Eminent Nigerians of the Rivers State*, edited by Tekena N. Tamuno and Ebiegberi Joe Alagoa. Ibadan, Nigeria: Heinemann Educational Books.

Tariah, D. A. 1976. "Kalabari Material Culture." BA thesis, Ahmadu Bello University.

Tariah, Danate A. 1982. "The Masquerades of Kalabari Ekine Society." In *The Masquerade in Nigerian History and Culture: Workshop Proceedings*, edited by Nwanna Nzewunwa, 295–316. Port Harcourt, Nigeria: School of Humanities, University of Port Harcourt.

Tarlo, Emma. 1996. *Clothing Matters: Dress and Identity in India*. Chicago: University of Chicago Press.

Tepowa, Adebiye. 1907. "A Short History of Brass and Its People." *Journal of the African Society* 7 (15): 32–88.

Thieme, Otto Charles. 1982. "Technical Analysis." In "Pelete Bite: Kalabari Cut-Thread Cloth." Joanne B. Eicher, Tonye V. Erekosima, and Otto C. Thieme. Minneapolis: University of Minnesota Press.

Torntore, Susan J. 1999. "The Italian Coral Horn as an Object of Intimate Cultural Expression and Meaning." Master's thesis, University of Minnesota.

Torntore, Susan J. 2001. *Cloth Is the Center of the World: Nigerian Textiles, Global Perspectives*. St. Paul: Goldstein Gallery, University of Minnesota.

Torntore, Susan J. 2002. "Italian Coral Beads: Characterizing Their Value and Role in Global Trade and Cross-Cultural Exchange." PhD diss., University of Minnesota.

Uwechue, Raph, ed. 1991. *Makers of Modern Africa: Profiles in History*, 2nd ed. London: Africa Books.

Van der Lann, H. Laurens. 1983. "A Swiss Family in West Africa: A. Brunnschweiler & Co., 1929–1959." *African Economic History* 12:287–297.

Vogt, John. 1975. "Notes on the Portuguese Cloth Trade in West Africa, 1480–1540." *International Journal of African Historical Studies* 8 (4): 623–651.

Waddell, Hope. 1863. *Twenty-Nine Years in the West Indies and Central Africa*. London: Nelson.

Wass, Betty. 1975. "Yoruba Dress: A Systematic Case Study of Five Generations of a Lagos Family." Unpublished PhD diss., Michigan State University.

Watson, John Forbes. 1866. *The Textile Fabrics of India: Series I*. London: India Office.

Watson, John Forbes. 1873. *The Textile Manufactures of India: Collection of Specimens and Illustrations of the Textile Manufactures of India: Series II*. London: India Museum.

Weiner, Annette. 1986. *Women of Value, Men of Renown*. Austin: University of Texas.

Williams, Gloria M. 1984. "The Esthetics of Everyday Life." In *Home Economics Teacher Education: Knowledge, Technology, and Family Change*, in Yearbook IV: Teacher Education Section, A.H.E.A., edited by Patricia J. Thompson, 215–236. Bloomington, IN: Bennett & McKnight.

Wilson, Kax. 1979. *The History of Textiles*. Boulder, CO: Westview.

Wolf, Eric R. 1982. *Europe and the People Without History*. Berkeley: University of California Press.

Wolff, Norma H. 2001. "Leave Velvet Alone: The Adire Tradition of the Yoruba." In *Cloth Is the Center of the World: Nigerian Textiles, Global Perspectives*, edited by Susan J. Torntore, 51–65. St. Paul: Goldstein Gallery, University of Minnesota.

Index

Page numbers in italics refer to illustrations.